THE PRICE OF CITIZENSHIP

INSIDE THE NATIONAL TAX SYSTEM

BY

SREEKESH PUTHUVASSERY

PUBLISHER

APC BOOKS

The Price of Citizenship : Inside The National Tax System

Published by: APC BOOKS
ISBN: 978-93-343-0233-2
Cover and Interior Design: Designed by the Author
Paperback Edition

Printed in USA
First Edition (2025)

For inquiries, permissions, or rights:
Email: books.apc@gmail.com

Dedication

To every ordinary citizen who works hard, dreams big,
and silently bears the weight of the system
designed to take more than it gives.

This book for those who dare to question,
who seek to understand, and who belives awareness
is the first step to true freedom.

About the Author

Sreekesh Puthuvassery is an independent author, researcher, and analyst dedicated to uncovering the hidden frameworks of control that shape human lives. His work dives deep into the intersections of governance, history, and ancient philosophies, presenting readers with thought-provoking insights on how unseen systems silently dictate everyday realities.

Known for his bold and analytical writing, Sreekesh's books dissect complex topics with clarity and depth. His exploration of how taxation, identity, and societal structures are used as tools of subtle exploitation has resonated with readers seeking to understand the true cost of modern civilization.

Apart from "The Price of Citizenship: Inside the National Tax System," he is also the author of:

"Golden Cage: Trapped in a Life You Didn't Choose" — a powerful exposé on how societal systems control individuals from birth to death.

"The Depth of Ultimate Nothingness" — a philosophical work delving into the hidden truths of existence, blending esoteric wisdom with modern consciousness.

Sreekesh's unique approach connects ancient spiritual traditions with contemporary socio-political analysis, offering a rare lens through which readers can examine the world. His writing is not just informative but also an invitation to question, reflect, and awaken.

Based in Kerala, India, Sreekesh continues his independent research, working outside institutional boundaries to preserve the integrity of his findings. His mission is to empower individuals with knowledge that challenges official narratives and promotes true awareness.

For more information:
Contact: books.apc@gmail.com

Acknowledgements

This book was not written in isolation — it is the result of years of quiet observation, relentless questioning, and the encouragement of those who dared to think differently.

To the silent majority — the workers, the thinkers, the taxpayers — whose struggles and sacrifices inspired these pages, I owe the deepest gratitude. You are the reason this book had to be written.

I thank the independent researchers, whistle-blowers, and alternative historians who continue to expose uncomfortable truths, often without recognition or support. Your courage echoes through every chapter.

To my readers, especially those who have followed my earlier works — "Golden Cage: Trapped in a Life You Didn't Choose" and "The Depth of Ultimate Nothingness" — thank you for your trust and intellectual curiosity. You fuel my resolve to keep writing what others are afraid to say.

A heartfelt thanks to the small circle of friends and supporters who offered honest feedback, motivation, and critical insight throughout the writing process. You know who you are.

Finally, I acknowledge the unseen — the forces within and beyond that guided the research, protected the truth, and made this book possible.

This work is dedicated to awakening. If it stirs questions, discomfort, or clarity within you, then it has served its purpose.

— Sreekesh Puthuvassery

Contents

Dedication 3
About the Author 4
Acknowledgements 5
Preface. 8

Chapter 1

The Indian Tax System – An Overview 20

Chapter 2

Income Tax - Attacking the middle class 44

Chapter 3

GST – The Everyday Tax Trap. 63

Chapter 4

Hidden and Everyday Taxes. 87

Chapter 5

Poor Pay the Most – The Silent Victims 112

Chapter 6

Fear, Confusion, and Forced Compliance 136

Chapter 7

Where Does the Money Go? 157

Chapter 8

A System Built to Trap You 179

Chapter 9

What Other Countries Do Right 202

Chapter 10

The Way Ahead – Reform or Break Down. 219
Glossary 235
Bibliography 238

Preface

Citizenship is often celebrated as a symbol of identity, belonging, and rights—a badge of pride linking individuals to a nation's story. Yet, beneath this idealized image lies a less visible reality: citizenship is, fundamentally, a lifelong financial contract. The Price of Citizenship: Inside the National Tax System invites readers to look beyond patriotic rhetoric and confront the true cost of belonging to a modern nation-state.

From birth, a person enters an economic ledger—registered, tracked, and poised to become a taxpayer. The seemingly simple act of issuing a birth certificate or identification number is the first step in a vast system of economic monitoring. These administrative steps do more than confirm identity; they mark the individual's future as a contributor to state coffers. Taxation is widely praised as the price of civilization. The roads we travel, schools we attend, hospitals we rely on, and defences that protect us are cited as returns on our financial contribution. But the reality on the ground is often starkly different. Visible public goods represent only a portion of where tax money goes. A significant share disappears into the gears of bureaucracy, inefficiency, and vested interests far removed from the taxpayer's welfare. This disparity begs the question: Is the citizen truly a stakeholder in governance, or just a resource to be harvested?

Tax systems are not simply born of necessity; they reflect power structures, historical inequalities, and economic agendas aimed at maintaining the status quo. Taxation—whether direct or indirect, overt or concealed—is a subtle yet pervasive force shaping how people think, act, and dream. Every financial decision becomes measured against compliance, costs, and penalties. The citizen is trained to see the world through a fiscal lens, often sacrificing desire for what is economically permissible.

Historically, taxation has been a flashpoint of both empire-building and rebellion. From ancient levies enforced by kings to the colonial taxes that sparked revolutions, revenue collection has always been contested. In modern democracies, taxation is cloaked in legality and procedural norms, masking its coercive essence. The idea that paying taxes is voluntary persists, even though refusal or evasion can lead to harsh consequences that upend lives.

India's tax system exemplifies this complexity—a hybrid shaped by colonial legacies, socialist ideals, and capitalist realities. It is an intricate web of laws, exemptions, and loopholes that affect social groups unevenly. Wealthy corporations and elites often navigate the system with professional help and influence, while the average citizen struggles alone with confusing regulations. This imbalance shifts the heaviest burden onto those least able to bear it.

This book peels back these layers not through abstract economics but by centering the lived experiences of ordinary citizens—the silent victims of systemic extraction. The goal is not to demonize taxation but to expose its opaque mechanisms and wide-ranging impacts. Armed with this understanding, readers can question, critique, and push for a fairer system of civic contribution. Stripped of sentiment, citizenship emerges as an ongoing negotiation between the individual and the state. But this negotiation is rarely equal. The state wields legislative power and administrative machinery, setting terms with little input from citizens. Most navigate these terms without full awareness or choice. This fundamental imbalance is the heart of our inquiry.

As you read on, you will encounter stories that challenge accepted narratives, data revealing hidden truths, and analysis connecting policy decisions to everyday hardship. This is not merely an academic exercise but a call to rethink the systems we inhabit and the roles we unknowingly accept within them. Ultimately, this book seeks to reclaim the conversation on taxation from technocrats and politicians. It reminds us that the price of citizenship is not a static figure but a shifting relationship between governance, accountability, and civic engagement. Recognizing this opens the door to transforming taxation from an imposed burden into a shared, participatory act of building the nation.

Citizenship is often celebrated as a bundle of rights — the right to vote, to free speech, to justice. Yet beneath this ideal lies an unspoken contract, silently binding every individual from birth: the obligation to pay taxes and comply with a system designed to extract fiscal value at every stage of life. This contract isn't signed or spoken aloud; it is embedded deep within state mechanisms and governs the citizen's entire existence, shaping choices, opportunities, and freedoms in subtle yet profound ways.

The moment a birth is registered, a seemingly simple document—the birth certificate—ushers a new-born into the vast and complex tax ecosystem. This document is more than just proof of identity; it is the first formal link between an individual and the state's financial machinery. From here onward, the child's identity is connected to multiple numerical identifiers—PAN, Aadhaar, voter ID—each expanding the surveillance net and the reach of fiscal accountability. Though the child is unaware, they have now become an economic unit, their potential income and consumption earmarked for future taxation.

Education, often hailed as a great equalizer, is deeply entangled with taxation and economic burden. Whether schooling is public or private, every fee paid, every scholarship sought, is part of a broader economic transaction influenced by tax policies. Far from being a universally accessible right, education has become commodified, with the state providing minimal support while shifting the financial burden onto families. Parents, eager to give their children a better future, navigate a maze of tax deductions and hidden charges, underscoring how deeply fiscal responsibility is woven into this essential phase of life.

Adulthood brings the citizen into full tax compliance. Employment transforms individuals into active contributors, with salaries dissected and taxed through various direct mechanisms. Income tax, provident fund deductions, and professional taxes reduce take-home pay, often without full clarity on how these funds are utilized. The narrative that taxes fuel national development is omnipresent, yet for many, the disconnect between payment and benefit breeds frustration and skepticism.

Consumption expands the scope of taxation even further. Goods and services, from daily groceries to luxury items, are laden with indirect taxes such as GST, excise duties, and import levies. These taxes are embedded invisibly in prices, making every purchase a subtle act of fiscal contribution. Indirect taxes are often regressive, disproportionately impacting lower-income groups who spend a larger share of their income on taxed essentials. Despite this inherent inequality, such impacts rarely surface in mainstream tax debates or policy discussions.

Property ownership introduces additional layers of fiscal responsibility. The dream of owning land or a home is frequently shadowed by recurring charges—stamp duties, registration fees, property taxes—that continuously funnel revenue to the state. For many, property becomes less a symbol of security and more a financial liability, as ownership translates into ongoing tax obligations. This dynamic starkly contrasts with the notion of land and shelter as fundamental rights, exposing the state's prioritization of revenue over individual stability. Even personal milestones are not exempt. Marriage registrations, ceremonial expenses, and gift taxes convert intimate cultural practices into sources of fiscal revenue. The state's reach penetrates the private and sacred, reinforcing the message that no aspect of life escapes economic scrutiny or obligation.

Entrepreneurship, often hailed as a key to economic progress, presents its own fiscal challenges. Small business owners face a labyrinth of licenses, registrations, GST compliance, and audits. While large corporations can employ resources to manage these complexities, smaller entrepreneurs often find themselves overwhelmed by bureaucracy that drains their time, money, and enthusiasm. Rather than fostering enterprise, the tax system frequently acts as a deterrent, particularly for those lacking expert guidance.

Retirement offers no true reprieve from taxation. Pension income, senior savings, and health-related expenses are all subject to tax rules that erode the financial security meant to reward decades of contribution. Far from being a peaceful phase, retirement becomes another phase of financial vigilance and continued extraction. Even death does not release one from the tax net. Inheritance taxes, estate duties, and succession regulations ensure that the state claims a portion of the deceased's legacy. Families mourning their loss must grapple with complex procedures to retain what is rightfully theirs, a final reminder that citizenship's cost extends beyond a single lifetime.

Through this continuous cycle—from birth to death—the citizen's role as taxpayer defines their life narrative. The discourse of rights and freedoms coexists uneasily with the ever-present demands of fiscal compliance. This juxtaposition prompts fundamental questions: Is the citizen truly a partner in the nation's progress, or merely a resource to be harvested?

This book does not romanticize tax rebellion or rejection. Instead, it seeks to shed light on the stark realities of a system that often prioritizes revenue extraction over citizen empowerment. By unveiling the myriad ways taxation permeates daily life, it urges readers to reflect critically on their place within this system. Awareness, after all, is the first step toward reclaiming agency.

The unseen contract of taxation binds us all, dictating terms that shape life's possibilities and limits. Understanding this contract is essential not only for personal clarity but also for envisioning a fairer, more transparent relationship between the individual and the state. Only through such recognition can citizenship move beyond burden and become a truly participatory act of shared responsibility and mutual respect. The modern tax system is often introduced as a logical necessity — a structured method to fund public welfare, infrastructure, and national development. On the surface, this argument appears irrefutable. However, beneath this veneer of civic duty lies a web of intricate policies, deliberate complexities, and subtle mechanisms of control that far exceed simple revenue collection. Taxation, when entwined with governance, evolves into a powerful tool of compliance and behavioural engineering.

Today, taxation is no longer a straightforward transaction between citizen and state. It has transformed into a multi-layered framework that influences the economy, personal choices, and societal trends. Direct taxes like income, corporate, and wealth taxes are merely the visible peaks. Beneath them lies a sprawling network of indirect taxes, cess, surcharges, duties, and levies designed to tap into every conceivable economic activity. From earning, spending, saving, investing, inheriting, to even gifting, every financial gesture is monitored, assessed, and taxed.

Indirect taxation is one of the most effective tools in this control matrix. Unlike direct taxes, indirect taxes are embedded within the price of goods and services, making them invisible to the average consumer. India's Goods and Services Tax (GST), promoted as a unifying and simplifying measure, has in practice added compliance burdens on businesses while silently shifting the tax load onto consumers. The beauty of indirect taxes lies in their stealth — people comply without conscious resistance, making them an ideal mechanism for mass-scale revenue collection. Beyond formal taxes, regulatory compliances act as indirect revenue streams. Every business license, vehicle registration, environmental clearance, or professional certification involves fees and renewals, ensuring continuous state income while extending bureaucratic oversight. Though not officially classified as taxes, these charges function identically, creating a landscape riddled with hidden financial drains. For small entrepreneurs and professionals, these compliance costs often surpass direct tax liabilities, deepening economic strain.

The sheer complexity of this compliance ecosystem becomes a formidable barrier, especially for the economically marginalized. Filing returns, managing audit trails, reconciling GST credits, and navigating shifting regulations demand specialized knowledge. This necessity gives rise to a secondary industry of intermediaries — chartered accountants, tax consultants, and legal advisors — whose services further burden the taxpayer. What should be a straightforward civic duty thus becomes a convoluted, costly ordeal. Importantly, this complexity is not accidental. A deliberately intricate tax system benefits the state in multiple ways. Firstly, it overwhelms citizens, keeping their focus trapped in procedural mechanics rather than questioning the fairness of the taxes themselves. Secondly, it enables selective enforcement. With regulations open to interpretation, authorities wield discretionary power, rewarding allies and penalizing dissenters under the guise of law.

An insidious by-product of this tax labyrinth is the normalization of financial surveillance. Tax filings, bank account linkages, Aadhaar integration, and transaction monitoring construct comprehensive data profiles of every citizen's economic life. While justified in the name of transparency and anti-corruption, these measures expand state control, diminishing financial autonomy. Every significant transaction now passes through layers of scrutiny, making individual economic freedom increasingly theoretical.

Behavioural engineering through tax incentives and penalties further tightens this control. Investment patterns, insurance purchases, and spending habits are subtly directed by rebates, deductions, and exemptions. Citizens are nudged towards government-favoured financial products, not always for their intrinsic merit but for tax benefits. Thus, the state's fiscal agenda reshapes personal financial landscapes through calculated reward-punishment mechanisms. Adding to this is the rigid penal structure of tax laws. Non-compliance — whether deliberate or due to ignorance — invites severe penalties, including fines, property seizures, and legal action. For the average citizen, often unaware of nuanced regulations, this fosters a climate of fear-driven compliance. Tax violations are frequently treated with uncompromising severity, irrespective of intent or capacity, unlike civil disputes where context matters.

However, this harsh reality applies unevenly. For corporations and the affluent, the same tax system offers pathways to minimize liabilities. Armed with resources and legal expertise, they exploit loopholes, exemptions, and aggressive tax planning strategies. Corporate tax holidays, Special Economic Zones (SEZs), and sector-specific incentives legally reduce their tax burdens. Consequently, those least capable of paying contribute proportionally more, while the wealthy navigate through systemic gaps with precision.

Taxation's political dimension further complicates the picture. Policies are often shaped by electoral strategies, lobbying pressures, and populist narratives rather than pure economic logic. Promises of tax cuts and relief packages during elections are frequently offset by increased levies in politically convenient periods. This cyclical manipulation prioritizes short-term political gains over long-term economic equity, using taxation as a strategic electoral tool.

Amid these dynamics, the original narrative of taxation as a collective investment in national progress becomes increasingly diluted. The citizen's role reduces to that of a perpetual payer, ensnared in a system that demands more than it delivers. The psychological toll of continuous extraction fosters widespread disillusionment, eroding trust in governance and breeding a culture of passive compliance mixed with quiet resentment. Ultimately, taxation has transcended its fiscal role to become a potent instrument of societal control, behavioural manipulation, and economic stratification. Recognizing this reality is essential for fostering meaningful discussions on civil rights, governance accountability, and economic justice.

The national tax system is often projected as a fair and necessary mechanism where every citizen contributes based on their capacity and, in return, benefits from collective progress. Yet, beneath this rhetoric lies a profound asymmetry in how the tax burden and its benefits are distributed. While the poor and middle classes bear the brunt of financial obligations, the wealthy and powerful adeptly manoeuvre through legal avenues to minimize their contributions. This section examines the uneven impact of taxation and the paradox it creates in the pursuit of fiscal justice.

Understanding who truly bears the tax burden requires differentiating between direct and indirect taxes. Direct taxes—such as income tax and corporate tax—are intended to be progressive, ensuring that higher earners contribute a larger share of their income. Indirect taxes, however, are embedded in the prices of everyday goods and services. Unlike direct taxes, these are regressive by nature, impacting lower-income groups disproportionately because essentials consume a larger share of their income.

For the average citizen, daily expenses on food, fuel, transport, and utilities are taxed through mechanisms like the Goods and Services Tax (GST). Since these essentials are non-negotiable, indirect taxes quietly drain the incomes of the poor and middle classes. In contrast, the wealthy, whose consumption patterns favour savings, investments, and tax-sheltered instruments, experience a comparatively lighter tax impact. This quiet perpetuation of inequality under a universal tax structure is often overlooked in mainstream narratives. Further compounding this inequity is the restricted access to tax exemptions and benefits for economically vulnerable groups. Relief measures often cater to formal sector employees or asset owners, side-lining informal workers, small traders, and rural populations. These sections, despite contributing heavily through indirect taxes, are excluded from many fiscal benefits, resulting in a scenario where those least able to pay end up shouldering a heavier relative burden.

Property taxation adds another layer to this asymmetry. While homeownership symbolizes economic stability, high stamp duties and recurring property taxes disproportionately strain middle-income households. On the other hand, large landowners and real estate developers benefit from policy incentives, abatements, and legal loopholes, further skewing the tax advantage towards the affluent.

Corporate taxation, though a major revenue source, suffers from systemic loopholes that allow large corporations to legally minimize their liabilities. Techniques like transfer pricing, profit shifting, and the use of offshore tax havens enable multinationals to reduce effective tax rates significantly. Domestic conglomerates similarly exploit exemptions and incentives. Consequently, the erosion of the corporate tax base shifts the fiscal load onto individual taxpayers, particularly salaried employees and small businesses, who face tighter compliance and fewer relief options.

The concept of "tax incidence" reveals that even when corporations pay taxes, the costs are often passed down to consumers through price hikes or to employees via wage suppression. Thus, the burden ultimately trickles down to ordinary citizens, further distorting perceptions of fairness.

Government spending, financed by tax revenues, also reflects a lopsided benefit distribution. Essential public services like healthcare, education, and social security, crucial for empowering disadvantaged groups, remain underfunded or poorly managed. Conversely, infrastructure projects, subsidies, and fiscal incentives disproportionately favour urban elites and industrial interests. The social contract—where taxes are meant to fund public welfare—thus appears increasingly hollow for the majority. This systemic imbalance breeds disillusionment. Citizens observe a governance model where tax compliance is strictly enforced on the poor and middle classes, while elite evasion continues unchecked. This fosters a psychological environment of mistrust and resentment, pushing many towards tax avoidance mindsets and civic disengagement. When fiscal systems are perceived as unjust, they erode the very legitimacy of state authority.

Tax policies also shape social mobility and economic opportunity. High indirect taxes on essential goods curtail consumption choices for lower-income families, limiting access to better nutrition, education, and healthcare. Meanwhile, tax incentives favouring investments in real estate, equities, and luxury spending widen the wealth gap, making upward mobility increasingly difficult. Over time, these disparities cement social stratification, restricting economic advancement for those at the bottom.

The administrative complexity of tax compliance further burdens small businesses and informal workers. Navigating through intricate regulations, maintaining documentation, and hiring consultants impose additional costs. For many, these barriers result in non-compliance or exclusion from formal financial systems, which in turn blocks access to credit, insurance, and government schemes. Thus, the very backbone of the economy is left vulnerable and marginalized.

Despite these stark realities, public discourse on taxation often remains detached from the lived experiences of ordinary citizens. Discussions tend to revolve around macroeconomic indicators and revenue targets, ignoring how policies tangibly affect daily lives. This disconnect exacerbates public apathy and fosters a growing divide between policy intent and societal impact. At its core, taxation is built on a paradox: those who pay the most in relation to their income receive the least benefits, while those who contribute the least in relative terms enjoy the largest share of advantages. This inversion of fiscal justice challenges fundamental notions of governance, equity, and citizenship. Addressing such deep-rooted inequities requires not just policy tweaks but a reimagining of the social contract between citizens and the state.

Recognizing the uneven distribution of the tax burden and benefits is essential for fostering an informed and equitable discourse. Until this acknowledgment translates into tangible reforms, the promise of taxation as a tool for collective welfare remains unfulfilled, leaving ordinary citizens trapped in a cycle of disproportionate sacrifice with minimal returns. The national tax system, often seen as a mechanism for revenue generation, is equally a tool of governance and control. Yet, within its complexities and imbalances lies the potential for reform. Reimagining taxation as a transparent, accountable, and equitable instrument can transform it from a burdensome obligation into a catalyst for societal progress.

The first cornerstone of such transformation is transparency. A major failing of many taxation systems is the opacity surrounding tax collection, allocation, and expenditure. Most citizens remain unaware of how their taxes are used, fostering suspicion and disengagement. True transparency demands that governments provide clear, accessible information on revenue generation and its deployment. Public disclosures should not be limited to technical data but must link taxes paid to visible outcomes — improved healthcare, education, infrastructure, and social welfare. Moreover, the tax code itself must be transparent. Overly complex and convoluted tax laws alienate the common taxpayer while creating opportunities for manipulation by the affluent. Simplifying tax structures, eliminating contradictory clauses, and providing unambiguous guidelines reduce both confusion and administrative costs. A straightforward, comprehensible tax system encourages voluntary compliance, rooted in understanding rather than fear.

Hand in hand with transparency is accountability. Accountability must operate on multiple fronts — from citizens fulfilling their tax obligations to government institutions justifying their fiscal decisions. Efficient audit mechanisms, independent oversight bodies, and citizen participation in budgetary processes are essential for a robust fiscal ecosystem. When people can track spending, raise concerns, and demand answers for mismanagement, the credibility of the tax system is strengthened.

Tools like participatory budgeting, independent fiscal watchdogs, and accessible digital grievance platforms enable a two-way dialogue. Citizens evolve from passive payers into active stakeholders. Governments, in turn, must ensure that enforcement focuses on genuine evasion rather than harassing honest taxpayers. A balanced approach, combining strict measures against defaulters with empathetic treatment of compliant citizens, is crucial. The principle of equity lies at the heart of fair taxation. A truly progressive tax system should ensure that those with greater capacity contribute proportionally more. While nominal tax rates often appear progressive, systemic loopholes and evasive practices allow the affluent to significantly reduce their effective tax burdens. Closing these loopholes is imperative to prevent undue pressure on middle and lower-income groups.

Equity also requires addressing the regressive nature of indirect taxes. Since such taxes consume a larger share of income from the poor, compensatory measures like reduced rates on essential goods, targeted subsidies, and direct benefit transfers must be implemented. Aligning tax policies with broader social objectives — inclusive growth, environmental sustainability, and welfare enhancement — can transform taxation into a tool for societal upliftment rather than a source of disparity.

Technology plays a pivotal role in this transformation. The digitalization of tax administration streamlines compliance, curbs corruption, and enables data-driven policy decisions. Online portals for filing returns, transparent tracking of government spending, and real-time grievance redressal systems enhance both transparency and accountability. However, technology must be leveraged inclusively, ensuring that marginalized populations are not excluded due to digital illiteracy or infrastructural gaps. Accessibility and data privacy should remain central to technological interventions. Reforming the tax system is not merely a technical exercise — it is a political and cultural shift. Citizens must reclaim their rightful place as equal partners in fiscal governance. This requires fostering widespread financial literacy and public education on taxation. An informed populace is better equipped to scrutinize policies, demand accountability, and resist exploitative practices.

Civil society, academia, media, and grassroots movements are vital in this endeavour. These actors bridge the gap between complex policy frameworks and public understanding, mobilizing collective action and advocating for reform. A vigilant, engaged citizenry remains the strongest bulwark against fiscal misgovernance. The challenge of taxation extends beyond national borders. In an era of globalized economies, international cooperation is essential to address cross-border tax evasion, profit shifting, and harmful tax competition. Coordinated efforts are needed to ensure multinational corporations contribute their fair share, safeguarding national tax bases from erosion and preventing a race to the bottom in tax policies.

This book has sought to unravel the hidden intricacies of the national tax system — exposing its inequities, control mechanisms, and socio-economic impacts. Recognizing these realities is the first step towards meaningful reform. The aim is not to vilify taxation itself, but to question its current structures and envision a more just and inclusive system.

The path to reform is fraught with challenges, but it is indispensable. A tax system founded on transparency, accountability, and equity is the bedrock of a just society. Such a system restores public trust, reduces inequalities, and fosters sustainable development. When citizens see their contributions translating into tangible societal benefits, taxation ceases to be a burdensome duty and becomes a shared commitment to collective progress.

Reimagining taxation in this light is not an idealistic aspiration but a democratic necessity. It is an opportunity to recalibrate the relationship between the citizen and the state, ensuring that governance serves the many, not the privileged few. The promise of a fair tax system is, ultimately, the promise of a fairer society.

Chapter 1
The Indian Tax System – An Overview

India's tax system is a vast and intricate web that touches the life of every citizen, whether they recognize it or not. From the money you earn to the goods you buy, from the property you own to the services you use, taxation is deeply embedded in the daily routine of living in this nation. Yet, despite its overwhelming presence, few truly understand how it functions, why it exists in its current form, or who it ultimately serves. This chapter lays the foundation for unpacking the Indian tax structure—exploring its history, categorization, power dynamics between Centre and State, institutional mechanisms, and global comparisons. By exposing the underlying principles and the many contradictions within, we begin to see taxation not just as a financial obligation, but as a mirror reflecting the priorities, inequalities, and operational failures of the Indian state.

1.1 What is Tax and Why It Exists

Tax is one of those words that every citizen hears often but rarely understands deeply. On the surface, it seems like a simple transaction: the government takes a portion of what you earn, spend, or inherit. But behind that transaction lies a system that touches every corner of our lives, whether we realize it or not. In the most basic sense, tax is a financial charge imposed by the government on individuals, businesses, and transactions, supposedly to fund public services and infrastructure. But in a deeper sense, tax is a symbol of our participation in the larger machinery of the state—a non-negotiable contract that binds us to the nation's survival and growth, whether we consent to the terms or not.

The official justification for tax is quite logical. A government cannot run without money. Roads, schools, hospitals, public transport, defence, judiciary, welfare schemes—all require funding. Since the government does not produce goods or services like a private business, it must collect money from those who do. In theory, citizens give up a part of their earnings to ensure that the state functions smoothly and can return value in the form of public goods and services. This sounds fair on paper. However, the reality of taxation is much more complicated, especially in a country like India, where the gap between taxpayer expectations and state delivery is embarrassingly wide.

Historically, taxation has existed in nearly every form of organized society. From the ancient kingdoms that demanded grain and gold from their subjects, to modern democracies that draft annual budgets in parliament, the principle is the same: citizens pay, rulers spend. In India, taxation goes back to the times of the Mauryas, where Kautilya's Arthashastra laid out detailed instructions on how a king should collect taxes without destroying the prosperity of his subjects. The text warned against excess, advised fairness, and emphasized the importance of using the tax for public welfare. Ironically, despite having such enlightened origins, the modern Indian tax system often feels exploitative, inefficient, and unjust.

The fundamental problem lies in the imbalance between taxation and representation. In democratic theory, taxes are the price we pay for civilization. But in practice, many taxpayers feel they are financing a system that neither listens to them nor delivers to them. The sense of participation is missing. Most Indians have no real say in how taxes are structured, who pays how much, and where the collected funds are allocated. Once the money leaves your wallet, it disappears into a black hole of government bureaucracy, often resurfacing in news reports about scams, wasteful spending, or political freebie schemes. The idea that you are paying for your own oppression is not an exaggeration for many.

Moreover, the modern justification of tax—that it helps reduce inequality—is also full of cracks. In reality, the rich often find ways to minimize their tax burden through legal loopholes, offshore investments, or policy lobbying. The poor may not pay income tax, but they suffer heavily from indirect taxes like GST, which apply equally to everyone regardless of income. The middle class, caught between the two, ends up being the most consistent contributor and the least rewarded. This has created a dangerous perception: that taxation is not a tool of nation-building, but a system of legalized looting targeted at those who follow the rules.

The psychological burden of tax is another under-discussed dimension. When a citizen earns money and then sees a third of it vanish even before they touch it, the emotional impact is real. Unlike other payments where value is visible—such as rent for a home, or price for a product—tax feels like a blind surrender. And in a country where government services often fail to meet even basic standards, the resentment grows deeper. People don't mind paying if they see roads without potholes, schools without bribes, or hospitals without corruption. But when none of that exists, the very idea of tax feels like a punishment for being honest.

The principle of compulsory contribution is not necessarily wrong. After all, no society can function without shared responsibility. But the manner in which taxation is designed and executed in India turns a civic duty into a burden. Transparency is minimal. Simplification is rare. Accountability is negligible. Citizens are expected to trust a system that offers them no trust in return. And while the government uses patriotic language to justify tax collection, it seldom shows the same nationalism in how that money is spent.

Another factor to consider is the erosion of voluntary contribution. In ancient times and even during India's freedom struggle, citizens voluntarily gave their wealth and services to collective causes. Today, the tax system relies not on willing participation, but on coercion backed by legal threats, penalties, and audits. This shift has made taxation a source of fear rather than pride. It turns the taxpayer into a suspect by default—guilty until proven innocent.

To conclude, taxation should ideally be a noble contribution to the nation, a demonstration of collective strength and mutual support. But in India, it often feels like a toll gate to a broken system that demands loyalty but offers no service. Until tax is aligned with transparency, representation, and real public benefit, it will continue to be seen not as the price of nationhood, but the cost of being trapped in it.

1.2 Direct vs Indirect Taxes – Who Really Pays?

The Indian tax system is broadly divided into two major categories: direct taxes and indirect taxes. On paper, this division is meant to create a balanced framework—where direct taxes like income tax are levied on individuals and entities based on their ability to pay, while indirect taxes like GST are collected on the consumption of goods and services. However, beyond the textbook definitions lies a far more skewed and troubling reality. The deeper you go, the more you begin to see that while this division might seem logical, in practice, it creates layers of hidden inequality and a burden that disproportionately affects those who can least afford it.

Direct taxes are taxes paid directly to the government by individuals or organizations. These include income tax, corporate tax, and capital gains tax. These taxes are supposed to be "progressive," meaning the more you earn, the more you pay. In theory, this makes sense—those with greater financial capacity contribute more toward national development. But the reality is murkier. A very small fraction of India's population actually pays income tax—around 6 to 7 percent. And even among them, the tax burden is not equitably distributed. Salaried employees—especially the middle class—end up bearing a huge share of the burden simply because their income is transparent, traceable, and regularly deducted at the source through TDS. The wealthy, on the other hand, often escape through clever accounting, offshore investments, or by routing income through tax shelters.

Corporate tax, another form of direct taxation, also reveals serious loopholes. While large corporations are expected to contribute significantly to the exchequer, many manage to reduce their tax liability through exemptions, deductions, and policy manipulations. The government, eager to attract investment, often lowers corporate tax rates and offers holidays to big businesses—effectively reducing their contribution. Meanwhile, the burden silently shifts onto consumers and common citizens through indirect taxation.

This brings us to the more sinister half of the equation: indirect taxes. These are taxes not on your income, but on your expenditure. GST, customs duties, excise, service tax (before it was absorbed into GST), and even cesses on fuel—all fall under this category. Indirect taxes are considered "regressive" because they apply uniformly, irrespective of the payer's income. Whether you earn Rs. 5,000 or Rs. 5,00,000 per month, the tax you pay on a biscuit packet or a mobile recharge is the same. The government might argue that luxury goods are taxed higher, and essentials lower—but the line between luxury and necessity is often arbitrarily drawn. For the poor, even taxed essentials become unaffordable.

The most alarming part about indirect taxes is that they are hidden in plain sight. When you buy a product, you rarely stop to calculate how much of the price goes to the government. It's baked into the cost—silently extracted without any emotional or mental engagement. Unlike income tax, where the act of deduction is visible and the annual filing process is a reminder of one's contribution, indirect taxes drain your wallet invisibly and continuously. This stealth mode of taxation makes it highly efficient for the state, but brutally unfair to the citizen.

Let's take a common example: petrol. Fuel prices in India are among the highest in the world, not because of global oil rates, but because of heavy taxation. The central and state governments both levy cesses and duties on petrol and diesel, which constitute more than 50 percent of the pump price. This is a pure form of indirect taxation, and it hits everyone equally—whether you drive a luxury SUV or a humble two-wheeler. Worse, it has a cascading effect, making transport costlier and thereby raising prices of vegetables, milk, and other essentials. Here again, the poor suffer disproportionately.

The cumulative effect of indirect taxes means that even those who technically fall below the income tax slab end up contributing heavily to the state's revenue. They pay tax on food, transport, electricity, mobile data, and more. This turns the "tax net" into a silent trap where people who think they are tax-exempt are, in fact, bleeding financially every single day. The dignity of being poor is further eroded by a system that extracts from them without even acknowledging them as formal contributors.

From a policy standpoint, this skew has long-term consequences. When a state relies more on indirect taxes than direct ones, it signals a regressive approach to public finance. It suggests that the government finds it easier to squeeze money out of consumption than to enforce accountability among the wealthy. It also creates a disincentive to formalize the economy—because those in the informal sector fear that entering the tax net will only bring more scrutiny and burden, not benefits. What's more, the burden of indirect taxes often overlaps with poor public service delivery. You're not just paying taxes on the food you eat or the fuel you buy—you're paying those taxes and still living with power cuts, water shortages, broken roads, and poor healthcare. The indignity multiplies when the government uses tax revenues not for structural improvements but for populist schemes and political optics. Citizens, instead of feeling empowered by their contributions, feel cheated.

In the end, the real question is not just about who pays more tax in numeric terms, but who suffers more because of taxation. A millionaire paying 30% income tax on crores can still live comfortably, travel abroad, and save. But a daily wage labourer paying 18% GST on a gas cylinder or 5% on a sanitary pad feels the pinch in their stomach and dignity. In the game of direct vs indirect taxes, the lines of fairness blur quickly, and the system reveals its true colours—not as a tool for equity, but as a cleverly disguised mechanism of control.

1.3 How Taxes Changed Since Independence

The story of India's tax system since independence is not just a tale of economic reforms—it's a reflection of shifting priorities, ideological experiments, and the state's increasing hunger for revenue. When India became independent in 1947, the country inherited a colonial tax framework built to serve the British Empire, not the Indian people. The system was designed to extract wealth from subjects, not empower citizens. Unfortunately, instead of a revolutionary overhaul, the post-independence tax system began as a mere extension of colonial principles, with cosmetic adjustments. Over time, it evolved into a complex structure riddled with contradictions, loopholes, and inequalities, driven less by vision and more by crisis management and political compulsions.

In the early years, India adopted a socialist economic model, with the state controlling major sectors. To fund its welfare and development ambitions, the government relied heavily on direct taxation, especially income tax and corporate tax. Income tax slabs in the 1950s and '60s were incredibly steep. In fact, at one point in the 1970s, the highest income tax rate, including surcharges, exceeded 90 percent. The logic was simple: soak the rich to fund the poor. But the result was predictable. Tax evasion skyrocketed, black money flourished, and a parallel economy started growing silently, outside the government's control. The tax base remained narrow, with only a tiny percentage of Indians actually filing returns, and even fewer paying anything substantial.

The 1980s marked the beginning of cautious reforms. Under pressure from mounting deficits and fiscal mismanagement, the government began to reduce marginal tax rates and rationalize the structure. This was intended to encourage compliance and expand the base. But the real shift came in 1991, when India faced a balance of payments crisis. This economic emergency forced the country to liberalize its economy. Along with de-licensing and opening up markets, tax reform became a critical part of the structural adjustment. The idea was to make taxation more broad-based, transparent, and growth-oriented.

Post-liberalization, both direct and indirect taxes saw major changes. Income tax slabs were rationalized, corporate tax rates were lowered, and efforts were made to simplify procedures. But while the rates came down, the number of tax payers remained shockingly low for a country of over a billion people. The problem wasn't just non-compliance—it was the lack of formal income for most citizens. A huge portion of India's workforce remained outside the purview of income tax because they earned less than the taxable threshold or operated in the informal sector.

Meanwhile, indirect taxation started becoming the government's favourite tool. Excise duties, customs, service tax, and value-added tax (VAT) emerged as major revenue generators. Indirect taxes were easy to collect and hard to evade, making them attractive despite their regressive nature. States were also allowed to levy sales tax, entertainment tax, entry tax, and a host of other levies, which made the system messy and unpredictable for businesses and consumers alike. Every purchase involved hidden layers of tax, and the same product could be taxed differently in different states.

The next major turning point came with the introduction of the Goods and Services Tax (GST) in 2017. Billed as the biggest tax reform since independence, GST was meant to unify India's fragmented tax landscape into a single, streamlined system. It subsumed a variety of state and central taxes, creating a supposedly "one nation, one tax" structure. But the implementation was hasty, flawed, and politically contested. Multiple tax slabs were introduced instead of a single rate, keeping the system complex. Essential items were taxed, refund mechanisms became bureaucratic nightmares, and small businesses suffered the most due to compliance burdens. Though GST increased indirect tax collections, it also exposed the fragile infrastructure of the Indian tax administration.

Another critical shift in tax policy since independence is the growing reliance on cesses and surcharges. These are special levies added on top of existing taxes, and often not shared with state governments. Cesses on education, healthcare, fuel, and infrastructure have been quietly stacked over time, allowing the central government to collect vast amounts without needing parliamentary approval for their usage. This trend has made taxation less democratic, as citizens are kept in the dark about how and where their money is being used.

In recent years, there's been a push toward digitization of tax processes. Online filing, faceless assessments, and data-driven enforcement are becoming the norm. While this has improved transparency and reduced corruption in some areas, it has also made compliance more difficult for those who are not tech-savvy—especially the elderly, rural citizens, and small traders. The tax system has become more data-hungry but not necessarily more humane or just.

Throughout these decades, one thing has remained constant: the lack of a fair social contract between the citizen and the state. While tax rates have been revised, processes digitized, and terminologies modernized, the core issue persists—people do not feel they are getting value in return for their taxes. Public services remain poor, corruption eats into funds, and honest taxpayers feel penalized while tax evaders roam free. The evolution of India's tax system has been reactive, not visionary. Policies have shifted in response to crises, elections, or IMF dictates, but never as part of a long-term roadmap to empower citizens.

Today, despite seventy-five years of independence, India still struggles with a tax regime that is uneven, mistrusted, and weighed down by complexity. The wealthy find ways to minimize their liability. The poor contribute unknowingly through indirect taxes. And the middle class, as always, carries the burden in full view—facing deductions, scrutiny, and the silent expectation to keep the nation afloat. The Indian tax system has indeed changed since independence, but the question that remains is: changed for whom?

1.4 Who Has the Power to Tax – Center vs State

Understanding who holds the power to tax in India requires looking at the very foundation of the Constitution. The Indian tax system is not arbitrary; it's structured through a detailed framework laid out in the Seventh Schedule of the Constitution, which divides the powers of taxation between the Centre and the States. This division is meant to maintain a balance in India's federal setup, where both central and state governments function as autonomous entities within their respective domains. However, over time, the balance has tilted drastically in favour of the Centre, creating a deep fiscal dependency of states on central allocations. This power imbalance has far-reaching implications—not just on governance and administration but also on the daily life of every Indian taxpayer.

The Constitution distributes the power to levy taxes through three lists: the Union List, the State List, and the Concurrent List. Taxes in the Union List, such as income tax (excluding agricultural income), customs duties, central excise, and corporate tax, are exclusively under the Central Government's control. States, on the other hand, can levy taxes like land revenue, stamp duty, state excise (on alcohol), and taxes on vehicles and entertainment, among others. The Concurrent List, interestingly, has no taxation powers—meaning that both the Centre and the States cannot simultaneously tax the same base unless explicitly authorized by constitutional amendments.

This neat division looks functional on paper, but reality tells another story. For decades, the Centre has maintained a strong grip on the most lucrative sources of revenue. It enjoys the lion's share of taxation powers, especially through income tax and corporate tax, which generate massive collections annually. States, in contrast, rely heavily on relatively narrow and unstable sources such as VAT on petroleum and alcohol, property registration fees, and road tax. Even when states do manage to raise revenue, a large portion of it is subject to rules, grants, and restrictions dictated by the Centre.

To manage this imbalance, the Constitution provided for the Finance Commission, a constitutional body that recommends how the Centre should distribute a portion of its revenues among states. Every five years, a new Finance Commission suggests devolution formulas to ensure states get their fair share. But these recommendations are not binding, and political motives often affect how funds are actually disbursed. Richer or larger states feel penalized, while poorer states feel neglected. This creates a race for political appeasement, where states must align with central policies to ensure a better financial package.

The introduction of the Goods and Services Tax (GST) in 2017 further centralized taxation. Earlier, states had significant autonomy in levying sales tax and service tax. GST unified many of these taxes into a single system, with both Centre and States having a role. The GST Council was formed to enable cooperative federalism, where both parties make joint decisions on rates, exemptions, and structure. However, in practice, the Centre dominates the proceedings. Most key decisions are influenced by central interests, and the one-vote-one-state mechanism does not always translate into fair representation for financially vulnerable states.

Another dimension of central dominance is the increasing use of cesses and surcharges by the Union Government. These are special levies collected on top of existing taxes, supposedly for specific purposes like education or infrastructure. The problem? These collections are not shared with states. Over time, the portion of Union tax revenue collected through cesses and surcharges has ballooned—accounting for almost 20% of gross tax revenue. This means a significant chunk of taxpayer money bypasses state treasuries entirely, leaving them further crippled and dependent on central mercy for fund releases.

This power dynamic doesn't just affect policy—it trickles down into everyday governance. States have limited flexibility to fund welfare schemes, invest in infrastructure, or respond to emergencies like floods, pandemics, or farmer distress. Their budget planning becomes hostage to central fund transfers, which may arrive late or with conditions attached. The idea of cooperative federalism often collapses under the weight of fiscal centralization, leaving states scrambling to meet basic development goals with limited financial autonomy.

Some states have tried to resist or innovate. For example, Kerala has explored new models of state-specific levies and social impact taxes. Tamil Nadu has consistently demanded a fair share of GST revenues and protested delays. Punjab and Maharashtra have spoken out against excessive central control over finances. Yet, despite these protests, states find themselves constitutionally handcuffed. The power to tax is deeply linked to the power to govern, and without adequate taxation authority, states remain junior partners in a supposed federal democracy.

One of the lesser-discussed casualties of this imbalance is local governance. Urban and rural local bodies, like municipalities and Panchayats, are supposed to collect property tax, user fees, and local levies. But their financial autonomy is severely limited by both state and central policies. As a result, basic civic services like garbage collection, water supply, and road maintenance suffer due to lack of funds. This creates a vicious cycle—people lose trust in governance, resist paying taxes, and the system decays from the bottom up.

The growing centralization of tax power is not just a policy issue—it is a democratic concern. When financial control is concentrated in the hands of a single authority, it undermines the principle of decentralization, accountability, and local relevance. Taxpayers in a distant village of Odisha or a tribal area in Jharkhand end up funding mega projects in Delhi without seeing any benefit in return. This disconnect breeds disillusionment and weakens the citizen-state contract. Instead of taxation being a tool for empowerment, it becomes a mechanism of control.

In essence, the power to tax in India has evolved into a complex game of control and dependency. While the Constitution imagined a fair division of power between Centre and States, today the reality reflects a strong Centre calling the shots and states left juggling limited resources with unlimited responsibilities. Until this equation is recalibrated in both spirit and structure, the Indian taxpayer—whether urban or rural—will continue to pay the price of nationhood without a voice in how that price is decided or spent.

1.5 Why We Have So Many Different Taxes

The Indian taxation system is a maze, packed with a bewildering variety of taxes levied at every stage of economic activity. From income and property to fuel, food, services, and even digital transactions, the common Indian ends up paying taxes in some form almost every day. But why does a single country need so many different taxes? The answer lies buried in a mix of historical legacy, federal complexity, revenue desperation, bureaucratic control, and political compulsions that have shaped India's tax landscape into a patchwork of levies that often defy logic and fairness.

To begin with, India's tax system is a product of its colonial past. The British introduced several taxes not just for revenue generation, but as tools of control and punishment. Land revenue, salt tax, excise duties on liquor, and stamp duties were all designed to squeeze money from the local population while maintaining administrative dominance. After independence, while India gained sovereignty, the structure of taxation remained layered and fragmented. Successive governments added new taxes to fund expanding welfare commitments, but rarely abolished the old ones. The result: an accumulation of taxes rather than rationalization.

Another reason for the multiplicity of taxes is India's federal structure. The Constitution divides taxing powers between the Centre and the States. To avoid overlap, specific taxes were earmarked for each level of government. The Centre levies income tax, customs duties, central excise, and corporate tax, while States impose taxes on property, alcohol, vehicles, and professions. In theory, this division ensures clarity and autonomy. In practice, it has created a cluttered system where different authorities collect different taxes from the same citizen, often on the same transaction. For example, buying a car involves GST (Centre and State), road tax (State), and registration fees (Local Authority), leading to layered taxation with little coordination.

Then comes the problem of fiscal hunger. Both the Centre and the States are perpetually short of funds to meet the rising cost of governance, infrastructure, subsidies, and social programs. Instead of streamlining the tax system, they often resort to creating new taxes, surcharges, cesses, and user charges. These instruments are easy to introduce and politically convenient because they often escape public scrutiny. For instance, the Swachh Bharat Cess, Krishi Kalyan Cess, and Education Cess were imposed on top of existing service taxes and GST, silently increasing the burden without formally raising tax rates. The fuel tax is another classic case. Though crude oil prices fluctuate globally, state and central governments rarely reduce fuel taxes, since it's one of the easiest sources of revenue with no direct taxpayer resistance.

A fourth layer of complexity arises from bureaucratic inertia and institutional turf wars. Various tax departments—Income Tax, Customs, Central GST, State GST, Municipal Revenue—operate in silos with their own rules, documentation, compliance requirements, and reporting formats. There is little incentive for them to harmonize or eliminate overlapping taxes because each department guards its revenue turf. The more complex the tax system, the more justification for manpower, surveillance, audits, and enforcement mechanisms. Simplification would mean giving up control—something the Indian bureaucracy is inherently reluctant to do.

Political compulsions also play a huge role in sustaining multiple taxes. Governments often use taxes as a populist or punitive tool. Alcohol, cigarettes, luxury goods, and fuel are heavily taxed under the pretext of public health or environmental concerns, but the real motive is high revenue with minimal resistance. Similarly, subsidies and exemptions are selectively given to voter blocs, favoured industries, or politically sensitive regions. These benefits are funded through indirect taxes on the broader population. Instead of introducing a progressive and transparent tax regime, politicians prefer a fragmented model that allows for tactical manipulation and vote-bank engineering.

This fragmentation affects the citizens in very tangible ways. For example, consider the purchase of a home. The buyer pays GST on construction, stamp duty on registration, property tax annually, and income tax on notional rent if the property is not self-occupied. That's four different taxes on a single asset. Add to that the charges for water connection, sewage, garbage disposal, and electricity—all of which include hidden taxes or surcharges. The lack of a unified tax view means taxpayers are constantly bombarded with levies without realizing the total burden they carry.

Another disturbing consequence is the regressive nature of this tax structure. Because indirect taxes form the bulk of India's tax collection, the poor and middle class end up paying proportionally more than the rich. A labourer buying a packet of biscuits pays the same GST rate as a millionaire. Yet the richer sections have access to exemptions, deductions, and financial advisors to legally minimize direct taxes. In contrast, the average person struggles to keep up with tax filings, compliance, and digital procedures, often ending up overpaying due to ignorance or fear of penalties.

Despite the implementation of the Goods and Services Tax (GST), which was meant to unify many of these indirect taxes, the system remains complicated. States still charge VAT on alcohol and petroleum. Municipalities have local levies. Some services and products are under composite schemes with unique tax treatments. Businesses need to manage multiple returns, invoices, and reconciliations just to remain compliant. For ordinary citizens, understanding what they pay and why becomes a herculean task, turning tax awareness into a domain of professionals.

In an ideal scenario, India could shift towards a simpler, more transparent system with fewer but broader taxes. A rationalized structure where a single transaction attracts one tax, and where essential goods are exempt or taxed minimally, would ease the burden on the common man. But achieving this requires political courage, bureaucratic reform, and above all, a shift in mindset—from extracting revenue at every step to respecting the taxpayer as a partner in nation-building.

Ultimately, the reason India has so many different taxes is because the system was never designed with the citizen's ease in mind. It was designed for control, convenience, and opportunistic revenue. Unless this philosophy changes, every Indian will continue to pay small amounts at many stages, without ever realizing the total price extracted in the name of duty, compliance, and nationalism.

1.6 Tax Departments and How They Work

India's tax system is not just about rates and rules; it's about the machinery that runs it—the vast network of departments, officers, portals, forms, assessments, and audits that together create the experience every taxpayer faces. Most citizens only interact with this system when they file income tax returns or receive a GST invoice. But behind that surface lies a complex bureaucratic web that is often intimidating, confusing, and heavily tilted in favour of the enforcers rather than the contributors. Understanding how tax departments work helps reveal why so many Indians feel taxed, watched, and cornered.

At the top of the hierarchy sits the Central Board of Direct Taxes (CBDT), which governs the administration of direct taxes like income tax, corporate tax, and capital gains. It functions under the Department of Revenue, Ministry of Finance. Its counterpart for indirect taxes is the Central Board of Indirect Taxes and Customs (CBIC), which handles GST, excise, and customs duties. Both boards act as policy-making bodies, and their directives filter down to regional and local offices where the actual interaction with the public happens. The Income Tax Department, for example, is divided into zones, circles, and wards. Each taxpayer is assigned a jurisdiction based on location and category (individual, corporate, etc.). Within this setup, you'll find Assessing Officers, Tax Recovery Officers, Commissioners, and Inspectors. Each role is tasked with specific responsibilities—some deal with processing returns, others handle scrutiny, surveys, or enforcement. While the structure appears logical, it often creates confusion for the common citizen because most don't know whom to approach for which issue, and offices don't coordinate efficiently across functions.

On the indirect tax side, GST is jointly administered by both the Centre and States. This means that depending on your business turnover or the nature of supply, you may have to deal with either Central GST authorities or State GST authorities—or both. This dual control leads to jurisdictional disputes, duplication of efforts, and frequent notice issuances. In essence, while GST was intended as a "one nation, one tax" reform, its administration still reflects the fragmented mindset of old tax regimes.

The major transformation in recent years has been the push towards digitization. The Income Tax Department now relies heavily on portals like the incometax.gov.in site, where taxpayers are expected to file returns, verify them, respond to notices, and track refunds. Similarly, the GSTN (Goods and Services Tax Network) handles registration, filing, invoice matching, and compliance through its online system. These digital platforms, while progressive in theory, pose a major challenge for the average Indian who may not be tech-savvy, English-proficient, or financially literate. As a result, an entire secondary industry has emerged—tax consultants, chartered accountants, and agents—who act as intermediaries between the citizen and the department. People have to spend extra money just to ensure that they are following rules correctly, even if they have nothing complex to report. This raises a basic question: if the system were truly simple and citizen-friendly, why would ordinary people need professional help to pay taxes?

Another concern is the power imbalance between the taxpayer and tax officials. Officers have the authority to conduct surveys, issue notices, freeze accounts, and impose penalties—even if the issue is later resolved in favour of the citizen. The threat of scrutiny or reassessment is often enough to silence any resistance, and many taxpayers comply out of fear rather than obligation. In certain high-pressure months like March (the end of the financial year), tax departments are known to issue mass notices or aggressively chase targets to meet collection goals. The system treats taxpayers as potential evaders first, contributors second.

Internal working of tax departments is also plagued by a target-oriented culture. Officers often have annual collection goals and audit quotas, which puts them in a position of conflict. Instead of facilitating honest compliance, they are incentivized to discover discrepancies—however small—and extract dues under pressure. This model rewards aggression and punishes genuine errors. It also leads to harassment and legal overreach, with taxpayers being stuck in appeals, tribunals, and legal battles for years.

The dispute resolution system within the tax departments is equally problematic. Even if a taxpayer disagrees with an assessment or penalty, they must first pay part of the demand before appealing. The first level of appeal usually lies with a higher officer within the same department, leading to inherent bias. Only after exhausting multiple stages can one approach independent tribunals or courts—a process that is long, expensive, and emotionally draining.

One might expect that such a powerful system would at least be transparent and accountable, but that's rarely the case. Officers are protected under various immunity clauses and have minimal personal liability for wrong assessments or delays. Refunds are delayed for months without explanation. Rectification requests sit pending in bureaucratic queues. Even when portals crash or generate errors, citizens are asked to comply without delay while departments rarely acknowledge technical faults.

What further complicates the working of tax departments is the lack of taxpayer education. There is no structured effort by the government to educate citizens about their tax rights, responsibilities, or grievance mechanisms. Public outreach is minimal, and most campaigns focus on threats (e.g., prosecution, penalty) rather than service. The tax department is still seen as a punitive institution rather than a public service body, which discourages voluntary compliance and breeds mistrust. In summary, tax departments in India operate like rigid institutions built to collect, control, and command rather than assist, educate, and empower. The bureaucratic culture, digital divide, and opaque grievance mechanisms make it extremely difficult for ordinary citizens to navigate the system. Instead of being treated as stakeholders, taxpayers are treated as suspects. Unless the philosophy and functioning of these departments change, tax compliance in India will remain a fear-based ritual rather than a proud civic duty.

1.6 Tax Departments and How They Work

India's tax system is not just about rates and rules; it's about the machinery that runs it—the vast network of departments, officers, portals, forms, assessments, and audits that together create the experience every taxpayer faces. Most citizens only interact with this system when they file income tax returns or receive a GST invoice. But behind that surface lies a complex bureaucratic web that is often intimidating, confusing, and heavily tilted in favour of the enforcers rather than the contributors. Understanding how tax departments work helps reveal why so many Indians feel taxed, watched, and cornered.

At the top of the hierarchy sits the Central Board of Direct Taxes (CBDT), which governs the administration of direct taxes like income tax, corporate tax, and capital gains. It functions under the Department of Revenue, Ministry of Finance. Its counterpart for indirect taxes is the Central Board of Indirect Taxes and Customs (CBIC), which handles GST, excise, and customs duties. Both boards act as policy-making bodies, and their directives filter down to regional and local offices where the actual interaction with the public happens.

The Income Tax Department, for example, is divided into zones, circles, and wards. Each taxpayer is assigned a jurisdiction based on location and category (individual, corporate, etc.). Within this setup, you'll find Assessing Officers, Tax Recovery Officers, Commissioners, and Inspectors. Each role is tasked with specific responsibilities—some deal with processing returns, others handle scrutiny, surveys, or enforcement. While the structure appears logical, it often creates confusion for the common citizen because most don't know whom to approach for which issue, and offices don't coordinate efficiently across functions.

On the indirect tax side, GST is jointly administered by both the Centre and States. This means that depending on your business turnover or the nature of supply, you may have to deal with either Central GST authorities or State GST authorities—or both. This dual control leads to jurisdictional disputes, duplication of efforts, and frequent notice issuances. In essence, while GST was intended as a "one nation, one tax" reform, its administration still reflects the fragmented mindset of old tax regimes.

The major transformation in recent years has been the push towards digitization. The Income Tax Department now relies heavily on portals like the incometax.gov.in site, where taxpayers are expected to file returns, verify them, respond to notices, and track refunds. Similarly, the GSTN (Goods and Services Tax Network) handles registration, filing, invoice matching, and compliance through its online system. These digital platforms, while progressive in theory, pose a major challenge for the average Indian who may not be tech-savvy, English-proficient, or financially literate. As a result, an entire secondary industry has emerged—tax consultants, chartered accountants, and agents—who act as intermediaries between the citizen and the department. People have to spend extra money just to ensure that they are following rules correctly, even if they have nothing complex to report. This raises a basic question: if the system were truly simple and citizen-friendly, why would ordinary people need professional help to pay taxes?

Another concern is the power imbalance between the taxpayer and tax officials. Officers have the authority to conduct surveys, issue notices, freeze accounts, and impose penalties—even if the issue is later resolved in favour of the citizen. The threat of scrutiny or reassessment is often enough to silence any resistance, and many taxpayers comply out of fear rather than obligation. In certain high-pressure months like March (the end of the financial year), tax departments are known to issue mass notices or aggressively chase targets to meet collection goals. The system treats taxpayers as potential evaders first, contributors second.

Internal working of tax departments is also plagued by a target-oriented culture. Officers often have annual collection goals and audit quotas, which puts them in a position of conflict. Instead of facilitating honest compliance, they are incentivized to discover discrepancies—however small—and extract dues under pressure. This model rewards aggression and punishes genuine errors. It also leads to harassment and legal overreach, with taxpayers being stuck in appeals, tribunals, and legal battles for years.

The dispute resolution system within the tax departments is equally problematic. Even if a taxpayer disagrees with an assessment or penalty, they must first pay part of the demand before appealing. The first level of appeal usually lies with a higher officer within the same department, leading to inherent bias. Only after exhausting multiple stages can one approach independent tribunals or courts—a process that is long, expensive, and emotionally draining.

One might expect that such a powerful system would at least be transparent and accountable, but that's rarely the case. Officers are protected under various immunity clauses and have minimal personal liability for wrong assessments or delays. Refunds are delayed for months without explanation. Rectification requests sit pending in bureaucratic queues. Even when portals crash or generate errors, citizens are asked to comply without delay while departments rarely acknowledge technical faults.

What further complicates the working of tax departments is the lack of taxpayer education. There is no structured effort by the government to educate citizens about their tax rights, responsibilities, or grievance mechanisms. Public outreach is minimal, and most campaigns focus on threats (e.g., prosecution, penalty) rather than service. The tax department is still seen as a punitive institution rather than a public service body, which discourages voluntary compliance and breeds mistrust. The tax departments in India operate like rigid institutions built to collect, control, and command rather than assist, educate, and empower. The bureaucratic culture, digital divide, and opaque grievance mechanisms make it extremely difficult for ordinary citizens to navigate the system. Instead of being treated as stakeholders, taxpayers are treated as suspects. Unless the philosophy and functioning of these departments change, tax compliance in India will remain a fear-based ritual rather than a proud civic duty.

1.7 India's Tax Collection Compared to GDP

The true health of a nation's tax system can be judged not just by how many people pay taxes, but by how much tax is collected as a proportion of the country's Gross Domestic Product (GDP). This ratio, known as the tax-to-GDP ratio, serves as a mirror reflecting the state's capacity to extract resources from its economy to fund public services, infrastructure, and welfare. In India's case, this reflection has long shown a picture of underperformance, inequality, and systemic inefficiency. For a country aspiring to be a $5 trillion economy, India's tax-to-GDP ratio remains embarrassingly low, hovering around 10–12%, far below the ideal threshold of 20% seen in developed economies.

To put this in perspective, let's look at the numbers. Developed nations like France and Sweden maintain a tax-to-GDP ratio above 30%, with even emerging economies like Brazil, South Africa, and Russia staying between 20–25%. These countries use their tax revenues to deliver robust public services—universal healthcare, free education, unemployment benefits, and efficient transport systems. India, despite being home to over 1.4 billion people and boasting a high-growth economy, has consistently struggled to cross even the 12% mark. This is not due to a lack of economic activity but because of structural issues in tax collection, evasion, exemptions, and narrow base of contributors.

A key reason behind the low tax-to-GDP ratio is the limited tax base. Out of the entire Indian population, less than 6% file income tax returns, and only about 1.5% actually pay income tax after deductions. This creates a dangerous imbalance—where a small group of honest taxpayers bears the burden of the whole system. Salaried middle-class individuals, who have little room for tax avoidance due to automatic deductions like TDS, contribute a disproportionately large share to the tax pool, while high-income professionals and businesses find loopholes, engage in underreporting, or route money through tax havens. The result is a system where collection is low not because India lacks wealth, but because the machinery fails to tap into it equitably.

The problem worsens when one looks at indirect taxes like GST. The government often claims an increase in GST collection as a sign of progress, but these taxes fall heavily on the common man. Even someone earning Rs. 500 a day pays GST on soap, clothes, bus tickets, and food items. These collections inflate the tax-to-GDP ratio on paper but don't reflect fairness. When indirect taxes form the bulk of tax revenues, it indicates a regressive system—where the poor and middle class pay more proportionately than the rich. This deeply contradicts the principle of progressive taxation, where higher earners should contribute more.

A low tax-to-GDP ratio also limits the government's ability to invest in public goods. India's spending on healthcare is just around 2% of GDP, and on education, it hovers near 3%, both figures being among the lowest for a major economy. Infrastructure, welfare schemes, rural development, and defence are all under constant budgetary stress. And when the government lacks funds from tax revenues, it resorts to borrowing. This increases the fiscal deficit, leads to higher debt servicing, and eventually reduces money available for actual development. In essence, a weak tax collection framework ends up becoming a direct obstacle to national progress.

Corruption and leakage further compound the problem. Even when taxes are collected, not all of it translates into public service. Funds are misallocated, siphoned off, or locked in unproductive schemes. The lack of transparency and accountability in how taxpayer money is used creates a trust deficit, discouraging people from willingly contributing more. When citizens see luxury for ministers and suffering for workers, it's natural for the average Indian to question—why should I pay more tax?

Another dimension of the tax-to-GDP crisis lies in unaccounted black money. A large portion of India's economy, especially in real estate, agriculture, small trade, and cash-intensive businesses, operates in the informal sector. Transactions often go unrecorded, incomes are underreported, and taxes are entirely evaded. The government's inability to formalize these sectors or bring them into the tax net keeps the official tax base small, despite trillions circulating informally. Measures like demonetization or GST were partly aimed at solving this—but their impact remains questionable and uneven. Additionally, frequent changes in tax laws, retrospective amendments, and aggressive tax demands also disincentivize compliance. Foreign investors get spooked, businesses lose confidence, and individuals resort to tax avoidance out of fear rather than greed. A stable, predictable, and fair tax regime could attract more voluntary compliance, ultimately improving the tax-to-GDP ratio. But in the current state, unpredictability breeds resistance.

There is also the issue of over-reliance on corporate tax breaks and exemptions. The government often reduces corporate tax rates or offers sector-specific sops to incentivize investment and job creation. But these benefits rarely trickle down. Instead, large corporations enjoy tax arbitrage while smaller businesses struggle under heavy compliance. As a result, even with growing corporate profits, the contribution of corporate tax to GDP has not kept pace.

It's important to understand that a low tax-to-GDP ratio is not merely an economic statistic—it is a social justice indicator. It shows how much a nation cares about equity, governance, and shared responsibility. If India wants to uplift its poorest, strengthen its infrastructure, and ensure dignity for all citizens, it must find a way to raise its tax collection—not by squeezing the already burdened, but by expanding the net, closing loopholes, and ensuring the rich pay their fair share.

Until that happens, the Indian taxpayer will continue to feel overworked, underpaid, and unsupported—while the nation's full potential remains trapped beneath a failing system. The government may chant slogans of progress, but unless the tax-to-GDP ratio reflects true participation and fairness, such progress will remain an illusion painted on the backs of a few who carry the burden for all.

1.8 How Other Countries Handle Taxes

The tax system of any nation is a reflection of its values—how it views its citizens, how it allocates responsibility, and how it ensures fairness in sharing the burden of development. When we examine how other countries handle taxes, we encounter a sharp contrast to India's complex, opaque, and often unfair mechanisms. In countries with well-designed tax systems, there is a simple principle: those who earn more contribute more, and in return, they receive services that uphold their dignity and basic rights. India, despite being a large democracy and a rising economy, still lags far behind in this approach. By comparing India with global tax practices, it becomes evident that the Indian taxpayer suffers not only from high tax burdens but also from a broken promise of public service delivery.

Let's begin with the Scandinavian countries—Sweden, Norway, Denmark, and Finland—often cited as models of balanced taxation. These nations have some of the highest tax-to-GDP ratios in the world, often exceeding 30–35%. At first glance, these high taxes may appear excessive, but citizens rarely complain. Why? Because in return, they receive world-class public healthcare, free education from kindergarten to university, monthly child support, unemployment benefits, pensions, and efficient public transportation. Tax filing is simple, digital, and almost effortless. In Sweden, for example, the tax authority pre-fills your income tax return; you simply confirm it via SMS. The clarity of rules, coupled with the tangible services people receive, makes tax compliance a social responsibility rather than a burden.

On the other side, we have countries like the United Arab Emirates, Qatar, Kuwait, and Bahrain, which follow a different model altogether. They are tax-free economies for individuals, funded primarily through oil revenues. Despite having zero personal income tax, these nations provide their citizens with free healthcare, education, and subsidized housing. While this model isn't replicable everywhere due to differences in natural resources, it shows that taxation is not the only way to fund welfare. What's important is that citizens feel supported and protected without being constantly harassed for payments and compliance.

Singapore offers another compelling case. With a low personal income tax rate capped at around 22%, and corporate tax at a flat 17%, it manages to maintain one of the cleanest, most efficient public systems in Asia. Singapore's tax administration is highly digitized, transparent, and customer-friendly. More importantly, tax money is visibly reinvested into society—through affordable housing, top-tier infrastructure, universal healthcare access, and pro-citizen schemes. Even their indirect taxes like GST are capped at 9%, with essentials excluded. Compare that with India, where GST on many everyday goods and services hits 18% or even 28%, leaving even basic survival taxed.

New Zealand and Australia operate on the principle of progressive taxation, ensuring that higher earners contribute more. Income tax slabs are simple and fewer in number. In Australia, healthcare is essentially free under the public system, and education loans are linked to income levels, ensuring people are not crushed under debt. Their tax departments communicate clearly, offer dispute resolution mechanisms, and avoid treating every taxpayer as a potential criminal—something that Indian citizens unfortunately face on a regular basis.

In Canada, personal income tax is high, but it's accompanied by a strong safety net—free public healthcare, subsidized education, unemployment insurance, child benefits, and elderly support. People see the value of what they pay. Their system prioritizes equity and transparency, offering digital access, multilingual assistance, and user-friendly filing. Taxpayers don't feel like prey being hunted by the government, but stakeholders in nation-building. Canada also levies indirect taxes like GST (5% federal), but the rates are low, and refunds are timely.

In contrast, India's system appears designed to confuse and extract, rather than serve and support. The number of tax types—income tax, GST, customs duty, excise, road tolls, stamp duties, property tax, cess, surcharge—makes compliance a nightmare. Filing requires either immense effort or paid professionals. Refunds are delayed. Notices are issued without clarity. Tax laws change yearly without taxpayer participation. While citizens in other nations feel pride in contributing to their nation, Indian taxpayers often feel trapped, tricked, and tormented.

Another striking difference is how other countries treat tax evasion. In India, large-scale tax evaders often go untouched due to their connections, while small errors by honest individuals invite harassment. In Germany and Japan, tax audits are surgical and professional, not predatory. There's no culture of intimidation. The message is clear: pay your fair share, and you will be respected. In India, the fear of being penalized even after paying taxes is very real, leading to low morale and mistrust.

Even in developing countries like Vietnam or Thailand, governments are actively simplifying tax codes, cutting red tape, and encouraging compliance through trust-building and visible improvements in public services. In India, despite a massive digital push like the Income Tax portal and GSTN network, glitches, lack of accessibility, language barriers, and poor grievance resolution have left common taxpayers frustrated and excluded.

Finally, public participation in tax policy is another major difference. In many Western democracies, tax changes are debated openly, with citizen input taken seriously. India's tax changes are often sudden, poorly explained, and rarely discussed publicly in meaningful ways. This breeds a culture of alienation, where taxpayers feel like outsiders in a system that affects their every rupee.

The tax system, in its current form, is a labyrinth that fails to serve its true purpose: fostering a prosperous society where every citizen feels the collective effort in nation-building. Instead of transparency and fairness, it breeds confusion, inequality, and fear. While other nations have built systems that ensure the wealth of the nation is used for the welfare of all, India's approach continues to leave its citizens burdened and disconnected. As long as the tax system remains as complex, punitive, and inequitable as it is today, the fundamental trust between the government and its people will remain fractured. Only when these systemic flaws are addressed—when simplicity, fairness, and accountability replace the current status quo—will India truly create a tax system that works for its citizens and contributes to the well-being of all.

Chapter 2
Income Tax - Attacking the middle class

When most Indians hear the word "income tax," a sense of burden instantly follows—especially for the middle class. It is not just a legal obligation but a recurring mental toll that affects every salaried individual, entrepreneur, and small business owner who dares to earn in a country where honest work is often punished more than rewarded. While the rich find ways to escape through loopholes and the poor are mostly untouched due to low income, the middle class becomes the primary and most consistent target of India's income tax system. What was meant to be a balanced contribution toward nation-building has turned into an unequal system that drains the pockets of those who are too responsible to default and too ordinary to escape. This chapter dives deep into how income tax laws, procedures, and practices disproportionately affect the middle class—emotionally, financially, and systemically.

2.1 Complex Rules That Confuse Everyone

The Indian Income Tax Act, 1961, has been amended so many times that its original structure is nearly unrecognizable. Over the decades, a continuous layering of rules, sub-rules, provisos, exceptions, and circulars has made the law incredibly difficult for ordinary citizens to understand. What should ideally be a straightforward explanation of how one pays tax on their income has turned into a legal jungle. Even tax professionals admit that the sheer volume of changes each year makes it challenging to keep up, let alone the average middle-class taxpayer trying to navigate his annual return. The language used in official documents is not citizen-friendly—it is legalistic, vague, and packed with jargon that requires interpretation. The difference between exemptions, deductions, rebates, and reliefs alone is enough to throw even a diligent person off track. This complexity is not accidental—it is the very structure that fuels dependency on tax consultants, chartered accountants, and lawyers. The system does not empower the citizen; instead, it confuses him into submission.

Consider the Income Tax Slabs—an average salaried person must choose between the "old regime" and the "new regime," each with its own benefits and limitations. On the surface, the new regime seems simplified with lower rates, but it removes deductions. For someone without adequate financial awareness, choosing the right regime becomes a gamble. The government introduces frequent changes in Section 80C deductions, home loan benefits, education loans, and medical expenses coverage—all of which require constant monitoring. Each budget season becomes a stressful event where taxpayers must decode cryptic clauses to see how their finances are affected. This kind of mental taxation creates fear, anxiety, and confusion. Instead of promoting voluntary compliance, it fuels distrust and disengagement.

The problem deepens with inconsistency between state and central regulations. For example, a professional earning in multiple states must be aware of state-specific surcharges or local taxation rules that may further complicate his filings. Those who freelance, switch jobs, or earn through multiple sources like investments or rentals are pulled into a whirlpool of declarations, advance taxes, estimated income, and form complexities. The individual ends up not just earning money but also devoting significant time and energy to figuring out how to report it. Many end up making innocent mistakes, and even small errors can lead to notices, penalties, and audits. Ironically, even those who wish to be honest and compliant often find themselves unintentionally non-compliant because the system is not designed to assist but to punish.

This complexity also fosters inequality. High-income individuals and corporations have dedicated advisors who know every loophole, every exemption route, and every way to minimize tax liability legally. Meanwhile, middle-class and lower-income earners struggle to decode Form 16 and reconcile it with Form 26AS. The introduction of new compliance tools like AIS (Annual Information Statement) or pre-filled forms was supposed to simplify the process, but in reality, they have added another layer of verification that few understand. These tools often come with mismatches or require manual corrections, again pushing citizens to pay professionals for something that should have been automated, intuitive, and accessible.

What is even more ironic is that most people do not even know why they are paying the tax they are paying. They simply follow what their employer deducts or what their accountant recommends. There is no clear communication from the authorities about how taxes are calculated and what benefits the citizen gets in return. There are hundreds of sections, subsections, and conditions that determine taxability. How is a school teacher or a small trader supposed to know about Section 44ADA, Section 24(b), or HRA exemptions under Section 10(13A) unless they invest time and energy they do not have?

The truth is, a system that should make taxpayers feel respected and informed instead makes them feel powerless and confused. Most citizens comply not out of understanding, but out of fear—fear of notices, raids, or legal action. The complexity has become a weapon of psychological control, ensuring that only the elite truly understand how to navigate the system while the rest are trapped in a cycle of confusion, dependency, and quiet submission. In such an environment, tax becomes less of a civic duty and more of an imposed burden.

2.2 Salaried People Always Pay the Price

The salaried middle class in India has long been the silent backbone of the tax system—obedient, consistent, and always under pressure. Despite earning a fixed income with no real room for manipulation or evasion, they continue to bear the brunt of the Indian tax burden. Their income is recorded, traced, and taxed at the source through the system of Tax Deducted at Source (TDS), making avoidance nearly impossible. While others—especially those in business or agriculture—may under-report income or use exemptions skillfully, the salaried individual remains the most visible, traceable, and taxable citizen. This consistent visibility has made the salaried class the easiest group to target and exploit through policies, often without their consent or consultation.

The average Indian employee wakes up each month to a payslip already reduced by a sizeable chunk in the name of income tax. This deduction happens before the person even touches the money, leaving them with a "net salary" that doesn't reflect their actual effort or worth. What adds to the injustice is the lack of significant deductions or rebates that could offer relief. The working professional is expected to manage household expenses, EMIs, health, education, transport, and often the needs of ageing parents, all from a reduced income. While inflation rises and cost of living soars, the tax slabs for salaried people often remain outdated and misaligned with economic realities. There is little recognition for inflation-linked salary hikes; instead, such hikes often push people into higher tax brackets, leading to a classic case of bracket creep—where more money earned doesn't translate to more money retained.

This problem is amplified by the limited and rigid nature of tax-saving options available to salaried people. The most popular section—80C—offers deductions up to ₹1.5 lakhs, but that limit has remained stagnant for years. Considering inflation and rising education or housing costs, this amount is grossly inadequate. Moreover, to avail of these deductions, the taxpayer must invest in specific government-approved instruments like PF, ELSS, or life insurance policies, which are often long-term, illiquid, and offer average returns. It's not about real freedom of choice—it's about steering middle-class earnings into government-approved channels. The result is a salaried class trapped between high deductions and poor investment flexibility.

Adding insult to injury is the contrasting treatment of other sectors. Agricultural income, no matter how high, remains tax-exempt. Businesspersons have more flexibility in income declaration and deductions—they can offset expenses, claim depreciation, or shift profit across different fiscal strategies. Corporate houses enjoy incentives, subsidies, tax holidays, and deferred tax liabilities. But the salaried person, with no control over tax planning, becomes a victim of a rigid system. He or she cannot deduct fuel costs, professional clothing, or work-from-home infrastructure. The tax department assumes that all personal spending is separate and unrelated to the profession, which is a flawed approach in the digital age where work and life have blurred boundaries.

Another bitter truth is the lack of representation. Policies affecting tax slabs, deductions, or reforms are discussed in elite circles or drafted by bureaucrats and politicians who have little understanding of a salaried person's daily financial grind. There is no consultation with middle-class groups or forums before imposing new compliance burdens. Every year, salaried individuals await the Union Budget hoping for some relief, only to be disappointed or handed cosmetic changes. The lack of meaningful reform for this group, year after year, reflects either apathy or a deliberate strategy to retain a docile revenue base while appeasing louder, more powerful constituencies.

Salaried professionals also suffer from a complete lack of job security in many sectors, yet are expected to pay taxes as if their income is stable and guaranteed.

Layoffs, medical emergencies, career gaps, and economic downturns are never considered in the tax narrative. The system assumes regular income and regular deductions, leaving no room for personal crises. If someone becomes unemployed, there's no refund or cushioning from the government for previously paid taxes. Compare this with nations where taxpayers receive unemployment benefits, tax credits, or medical relief during hard times—in India, the salaried person pays without fail, but receives nothing in return when things fall apart.

Even post-retirement, the injustice continues. The savings made over a lifetime of work are again taxed in the form of returns, interest, and capital gains. Pensioners are expected to file returns, calculate taxable interest, and sometimes face scrutiny for failing to update PAN or linking documents correctly. In essence, there is no phase in life where the salaried individual is left alone by the tax system. From their first paycheck to their retirement corpus, they are tracked, taxed, and burdened.

The mental and emotional toll of this endless extraction is often ignored. Unlike businesspeople who can afford accountants or investors who hire advisors, most salaried people handle taxes on their own. The constant fear of non-compliance, changing rules, and the pressure to meet deadlines like Form 16, 26AS reconciliation, or AIS verification, all add up to a sense of being watched and penalized for simply earning a legal, declared income. It erodes trust in the system and replaces it with silent frustration.

The salaried class has thus become the perfect taxpayer: easy to monitor, difficult to escape, and psychologically conditioned to accept exploitation. This group funds national development, social schemes, and even government misadventures, yet receives the least gratitude or support. They are the ATM of the Indian tax system—always available, always running, but never acknowledged.

2.3 TDS – Money Taken Before You Even Use It

The concept of Tax Deducted at Source (TDS) might seem efficient on paper, but for the average Indian salaried individual, it represents a deeply unfair principle: the government takes its share of your income before you even get to use it. Unlike in many countries where taxes are paid annually or quarterly based on net income, in India, the employer deducts a chunk of tax every month, irrespective of an individual's immediate needs, liabilities, or life emergencies. The logic behind TDS is that it ensures compliance and reduces tax evasion—but what it also does is eliminate a citizen's control over their own hard-earned income. TDS treats every salaried person as a potential defaulter, not as a responsible taxpayer.

This system punishes the law-abiding citizen with blanket deductions, leaving no room for real-time life adjustments. If someone has a sudden hospital expense, a job loss, or even a natural disaster at home, TDS continues without pause. There's no mechanism to temporarily halt it or reduce it without bureaucracy and employer coordination. Your salary is credited after being filtered through a process you didn't vote for, with percentages and calculations imposed by a remote system. What remains in your hand is not what you earned—it's what the system thinks you deserve to keep. And when the time comes to file returns, you may realize you've paid more than required, but the refund process is slow, complex, and nerve-wracking.

What's worse is that this system of deduction assumes the citizen will go through the pain of proving they deserve their money back. That's the absurdity: you must justify why your own earnings should return to you. Many people skip filing for refunds due to fear of scrutiny, complexity, or lack of awareness. As a result, crores of rupees sit with the government indefinitely, unclaimed, interest-free. This is effectively a forced loan from citizens to the state—without consent, contract, or interest. It's not revenue collection anymore; it's pre-emptive appropriation.

Even the calculations of TDS are prone to error. Employers are often conservative in estimating tax liabilities, leading to higher deductions to avoid being penalized themselves. The employee suffers for the employer's caution. And if the deduction is wrong, the onus is on the employee to fix it—by collecting Form 16, matching it with AIS data, correcting mismatches, and filing the ITR correctly. If something goes wrong, the taxpayer—not the employer or the system—faces the consequences. They may receive a notice, a fine, or have to wait for months for a small refund. It's a process that prioritizes suspicion over service.

The TDS system also extends beyond salaries—banks deduct TDS on fixed deposits, platforms deduct it on freelance payments, and even rent receipts may attract TDS. This means that across multiple income streams, deductions happen automatically, but reconciliation rests with the citizen. The system throws the burden of paperwork, matching, filing, and tracking on the individual, even when the deductions are automated. It's a paradoxical system: advanced in collection, primitive in refunds and support.

For freelancers, gig workers, and contract employees, TDS is even more brutal. Often 10% is deducted on gross income—without accounting for expenses like equipment, travel, rent, or tools required to earn that money. Unlike businesses, they can't deduct these expenses before tax. This means a videographer, designer, or tuition teacher earning ₹5 lakhs a year might lose ₹50,000 in TDS even if their net income after costs is just ₹2.5 lakhs. By the time they claim it back—if they can—they may have faced cash flow issues, delayed payments, or even borrowed money to run their life.

The psychological effect of TDS is significant but rarely discussed. The salaried person feels disempowered—like they're not trusted with their own income. It creates an atmosphere of silent compliance, where citizens adapt their lives to what they are allowed to retain, not what they rightfully earned. The entire salary structure becomes centred on surviving within what remains after deductions. There's no encouragement to earn more, because higher earnings simply mean higher TDS and little improvement in lifestyle unless paired with expert financial planning, which most cannot afford.

TDS also reflects a deeper inequality in the tax ecosystem. Those with wealth stored in property, shares, or businesses can delay or distribute their tax liability. They can hire chartered accountants, use legal loopholes, and claim exemptions under complex rules. But a salaried employee has no such leverage. Their TDS is precise, constant, and merciless. They are the only group in India whose income is fully traceable and whose tax is prepaid. That's not a sign of progress—it's a design of control.

In reality, TDS has become a tool of silent extraction. It bypasses consent, ignores context, and assumes guilt. It treats income as something the government owns first, and the citizen receives later. While it may look organized and efficient in policy documents, in practice it's a system that strips financial autonomy from those who contribute honestly. It ensures tax compliance not through education, participation, or transparency—but through fear, deduction, and default control. In the name of streamlining, it has turned taxation into pre-emptive confiscation.

2.4 Deductions That Barely Help

The Indian tax system often highlights "deductions" as a form of relief, giving an impression that citizens can significantly reduce their tax liability by planning wisely. But when one looks deeper into how these deductions work, it becomes clear that they are more cosmetic than effective—designed to create the illusion of benefit while barely scratching the surface of what people actually need. For the middle-class salaried individual, the deductions provided under various sections of the Income Tax Act, such as 80C, 80D, 24(b), and others, are restrictive, outdated, and disconnected from the realities of modern living costs.

The most commonly cited section is 80C, which offers a deduction of up to ₹1.5 lakh per year for specified investments and expenses. On paper, this seems like a significant amount. But when broken down, it quickly gets exhausted by just a couple of mandatory expenses: school tuition fees, employee provident fund (EPF) contributions, and home loan principal repayments. For someone paying EMIs on a housing loan or sending children to private school, the 80C limit gets filled automatically—without any room for actual investment planning. The deduction, therefore, does not reward additional financial discipline; it simply offsets basic, unavoidable middle-class expenses. Further, many people are forced to invest in schemes they don't fully understand or need—just to claim a tax break. Insurance policies are bought not for protection, but for deduction. This leads to suboptimal investments with low returns, long lock-ins, and poor liquidity. In effect, the citizen is pushed into channeling their money into rigid government-preferred instruments instead of being empowered to plan finances freely. It's not a deduction—it's a restriction masquerading as a benefit.

Health insurance premiums under section 80D are another supposed relief, with limits ranging from ₹25,000 to ₹1,00,000 depending on age. But given the rising cost of healthcare in private hospitals, this is a laughably inadequate figure. A single hospitalization can wipe out ₹5 to ₹10 lakh. Most people either under-insure themselves to save money or buy policies whose premiums are well above deductible limits—meaning the tax benefit is partial at best. For senior citizens, the benefit is slightly higher, but their premiums are much higher too, creating a gap between real cost and deductible value.

Even the interest on housing loans under section 24(b), which offers up to ₹2 lakh per year as a deduction, falls short in urban contexts. With property prices and home loan EMIs soaring in metro cities, the annual interest paid often exceeds this limit, but the tax system caps the benefit. The citizen continues to bleed money in interest while the deduction remains static. Worse still, this limit has not been revised in many years to match inflation, rendering it increasingly irrelevant over time. It's a token relief, not a meaningful policy response.

Then there are deductions for education loans, interest on savings accounts, donations to charity, and expenses for disabled dependents or specified diseases. These are highly specific and apply to narrow cases—most of which require extensive documentation, medical certificates, or bureaucratic approval. For a common taxpayer, the effort required to claim such deductions often outweighs the benefit. In many cases, people are not even aware that they qualify, and government communication does little to educate them. Tax literacy is low, and the system does little to fix that—because complexity benefits the collector, not the payer.

The design of deductions also reveals systemic bias. Businesses can claim a wide range of expenses—office rent, fuel, travel, depreciation, entertainment, meals, phone bills, and more—as business expenditures, reducing taxable income drastically. But a salaried individual has no such leeway. Even if they spend money on work-related needs—like buying a laptop, upgrading internet, commuting long distances, or paying for professional development—these are not deductible. The individual bears the full cost, while the business gets tax benefits. This uneven treatment makes the working citizen a second-class participant in the economy.

Moreover, the process of claiming deductions is cumbersome. Receipts, certificates, declarations, and proofs must be submitted to employers or uploaded in ITR filings. Mistakes or omissions can lead to reduced refunds or even tax notices. Many avoid claiming certain deductions out of fear or lack of time. There's no streamlined interface, no user-friendly system that shows eligible deductions intuitively. You either learn the hard way or pay a consultant to figure it out.

The government often uses deductions to nudge behaviour: save more, insure more, donate more, buy a home, send kids to school. But what it doesn't do is recognize financial diversity. A single mother in a rented apartment, paying high school fees and medical bills, may not benefit the same way as a man with a home loan and insurance policy. The deductions don't adjust for gender, geography, or genuine hardship. They treat all incomes the same and ignore all contexts—making the entire tax relief structure unjust in practice.

The reality is that deductions are not about helping citizens—they're about managing the perception of fairness. They give policymakers talking points and allow the system to pretend it's inclusive. But the ceiling limits, procedural burdens, and narrow categories ensure that most citizens never truly benefit. These deductions are structured to take more from you than they give back. They are a cushion that looks soft but has concrete underneath.

In the end, the story of Indian tax deductions is a tale of controlled relief—offered in measured teaspoons while the system drains buckets. It's not financial empowerment, it's financial pacification. The middle class is lulled into compliance by a handful of deductions that, in reality, do little to improve life or wealth. You work more, pay more, save where they allow, and still remain stuck in the same financial treadmill year after year.

2.5 Stress of Filing Every Year

For the average Indian citizen, especially the middle-class salaried individual, income tax filing has become more than just a financial activity—it's an annual mental burden. What should ideally be a simple, transparent, and user-friendly process turns into a time-consuming, confusing, and stressful ordeal year after year. While the government promotes digital platforms and improved systems, the reality on the ground tells a very different story. Filing taxes isn't just about submitting numbers—it's about navigating a complex bureaucratic maze designed with little regard for user experience or emotional well-being.

To start with, most people dread the season of tax filing. From April to July, a sense of urgency and anxiety builds up. Even though the data is available in payslips, bank accounts, or Form 16, compiling and reporting it correctly on the government portal is far from easy. For someone unfamiliar with taxation jargon or financial nuances, the income tax return (ITR) forms appear more like coded documents than citizen-friendly interfaces. Sections like 80C, 80D, 24(b), 10(13A), 10(14), 80E, and others make little sense to a layperson. One mistake, even unintentional, can invite scrutiny or delay refunds.

While the government has rolled out pre-filled ITR forms and online filing options, they often remain riddled with glitches. The portal frequently crashes near the deadline, updates don't sync properly, and pre-filled data is often incomplete or inaccurate. People have to cross-verify everything manually, leading to mistrust in the system. The burden of proof remains entirely on the taxpayer—if your bank account or Form 16 doesn't match, it's your problem, not the system's. In the end, many give up and seek help from chartered accountants or tax filing agencies, paying them ₹500 to ₹2000 just to make sense of their own income and deductions. This is not convenience; this is dependency.

The stress doesn't stop with filling the form. It extends to calculating the correct tax liability, ensuring deductions are accurately applied, entering correct bank account numbers for refund, and validating the return through Aadhaar OTP or e-verification. If the verification fails or isn't completed in time, the entire filing becomes void. Worse, the person might not even be notified properly, leading to late penalties or loss of refund. All of this adds psychological pressure to an already exhausted citizen—one who is trying to survive rising inflation, stagnant salaries, and insecure jobs.

Even salaried employees, who are assumed to have a simpler tax situation, often struggle due to mismatch errors. Employer-issued Form 16 might not align with the tax deducted at source (TDS) details on the income tax portal. If the PAN was incorrectly reported or deductions wrongly applied, the responsibility again falls on the employee to sort it out. The system does not offer a helping hand—it offers automated notices, delayed corrections, and a robotic grievance redressal that lacks any human empathy or speed.

For self-employed individuals or those with multiple income sources—like rent, freelancing, capital gains—the filing process becomes a mini-audit. They must declare all incomes, maintain invoices, reconcile bank statements, and calculate taxes accordingly. Even minor errors or omissions can be treated as concealment or evasion, bringing additional stress. There's no room for honest mistakes—every issue is presumed guilty until proven innocent.

Then comes the fear of being picked for "scrutiny" or "reassessment." Even after correctly filing the return, there is always a nagging worry—what if a notice arrives months later? What if something small was flagged? What if an unknown discrepancy leads to a demand letter? The mere thought of having to deal with tax officers, submit physical documents, appear for hearings, or write lengthy explanations can send anyone into panic. For many, tax filing doesn't end after submission; the fear continues for years. It's like walking through a minefield even after crossing the border. Also, the psychological toll of comparing your tax payment with what you receive in return is demoralizing. After paying tens of thousands or even lakhs in taxes, what does one get? No guaranteed healthcare, no quality public schooling, no clean roads, no free legal support, and no transparent pension security. The filing stress is compounded by a sense of betrayal—where your duty is taken seriously, but your rights are casually ignored.

For senior citizens, the situation is even worse. Many don't understand online platforms, don't use net banking, and find OTPs, portals, and digital forms to be barriers rather than enablers. They either have to depend on family or hire someone else to file returns. This dependency creates humiliation and frustration—especially when they are still expected to file taxes diligently at age 70 or 80.

To add insult to injury, the process repeats every single year. The structure doesn't learn from your previous data, doesn't improve significantly, and doesn't offer proactive assistance. You begin every year at square one—with the same stress, same confusion, and same fear. Filing becomes a ritual of frustration—celebrated by the government as progress, but experienced by the citizen as punishment.

In a country that claims digital advancement and economic growth, the income tax filing process should reflect those values. But instead, it remains a relic of bureaucratic arrogance. A process that should empower citizens to contribute proudly to the nation instead forces them into yearly cycles of fear and exhaustion. The stress of filing taxes is not just a mental toll—it's a reminder that the system sees you not as a respected contributor, but as a suspect to be constantly monitored and controlled.

2.6 Fear of getting notices

For many Indian citizens, the word "notice" from the Income Tax Department carries more psychological weight than the actual tax burden itself. It doesn't matter whether you're a salaried employee who pays taxes dutifully or a small business owner juggling receipt—an unexpected notice creates instant fear. This fear is not just about monetary penalties; it's the anxiety of navigating a bureaucratic maze, the threat of being presumed guilty until proven innocent, and the looming uncertainty of what could go wrong next. Most people don't even know what triggers a notice. It could be a mismatch in bank interest reporting, or a minor inconsistency in TDS filings by an employer. Yet, the responsibility to clarify, justify, and correct falls squarely on the taxpayer, often under strict timelines and confusing instructions.

The Income Tax system is meant to function as a tool for national revenue, but the way notices are issued makes it feel more like a tool for psychological intimidation. The complexity of the law allows tax authorities to find some technical irregularity in almost any file, especially among those who are not professional accountants or financial experts. Automated notices generated by algorithms flag people based on arbitrary thresholds, without any human understanding of context. For example, receiving money from a relative, which may be non-taxable under the law, could still trigger a notice if it exceeds a certain amount and lacks the proper documentation. This leads to a vicious cycle: people become afraid of doing any transaction outside of their salary, which kills entrepreneurial spirit and financial confidence.

Even more damaging is the lack of clarity in the notices themselves. They're filled with references to sections, sub-sections, and clauses that make little sense to the average taxpayer. Often, there's no specific explanation—just a vague line about "mismatch" or "non-disclosure." This ambiguity compels citizens to rush to chartered accountants or tax consultants, spending money just to understand what went wrong, even if there was no wrongdoing at all. This professional dependence adds to the stress and alienates the average person from their own financial records. Over time, this builds a feeling of helplessness, where even honest taxpayers believe the system is rigged against them and that they could be penalized for following the rules incorrectly.

The fear becomes generational. Young earners, just starting out in jobs or freelancing, are warned by elders to be cautious, to avoid "attracting attention" from the tax department. This advice comes not from guilt but from the widespread understanding that notices are arbitrary and can ruin peace of mind. The tax system should encourage transparent earning, saving, and investment. But when fear becomes the dominant emotion, people avoid legitimate transactions—like buying property, investing in mutual funds, or even accepting freelance work above a certain amount—because they're unsure of the tax consequences. This has a chilling effect on the economy, reducing financial participation and causing artificial suppression of income reporting.

Notices also breed inequality in how citizens experience the tax system. The rich can afford full-time legal and financial advisors. If a notice lands in their inbox, it is forwarded to a team of professionals who handle it seamlessly. But the middle class and the poor do not have this luxury. A single notice could mean missing work to visit a tax office, arranging piles of old documents, and paying consultancy fees that bite into already stretched monthly budgets. Worse, a small slip—like a forgotten investment, misentered PAN number, or non-updated address—can lead to penalties and prolonged harassment. The mental pressure builds up silently and steadily.

In recent years, the government has pushed faceless assessments and online portals as a solution to this fear. While the intention may be good, the execution has created new problems. The portals often crash or show outdated data. Uploading documents becomes a nightmare when file sizes are restricted and formats are non-compatible. The "faceless" system also removes the human touch—there is no one to explain what is expected or why the notice was even issued. In theory, technology was supposed to make things easier. In reality, it has become a wall that isolates the citizen from the tax office and offers no emotional or logical reassurance.

Ultimately, fear of tax notices creates a gap between the citizen and the state. Trust erodes. People stop believing that the system exists to protect them. Instead, they view it as an authority waiting to pounce on errors, real or perceived. This undermines national morale and damages the very goal of tax compliance. A healthy tax ecosystem must balance accountability with fairness. Instead of treating every citizen as a potential fraud, the system must create an environment where clarification is welcomed, assistance is available, and notices are written in plain language with logical justifications. Until that happens, the phrase "You've received a notice" will continue to strike fear into the hearts of millions—driving home the unfortunate truth that in India, paying taxes doesn't end your obligations, it only begins them.

2.7 Rich Escape, Middle Pays More

The irony of India's income tax system lies in how it claims to be progressive yet disproportionately burdens the middle class. The rich—armed with elite tax consultants, shell companies, foreign investments, and legal loopholes—often find legal ways to either reduce their tax liability or avoid paying taxes altogether. Meanwhile, the middle-class citizen, particularly the salaried individual, becomes the most reliable and consistent source of revenue for the government. They have no escape route, no tax havens, and no luxury of structuring their income. Their salaries are taxed at source, their incomes are documented, and their every transaction is traceable—making them sitting ducks in this system.

We often hear the narrative that "those who earn more should pay more," which is the foundation of a progressive tax system. However, the implementation tells a different story. The ultra-rich use investment vehicles like trusts and equity holdings to channel their wealth in ways that are taxed lightly or not at all. They can convert their earnings into capital gains, which are taxed at lower rates, and even offshore income escapes scrutiny in many cases due to the lack of stringent enforcement and international pressure. On the other hand, a salaried person earning Rs. 15–20 lakhs annually pays a higher effective tax rate than a billionaire who reports only business losses and capital gains. This is not just unjust; it is demoralizing.

The data also confirms this disparity. A small percentage of India's population pays income tax, and within that, a vast share of the tax revenue comes from middle-income earners. According to the government's own statistics, the top 1% holds a significant portion of the country's wealth but contributes much less in proportion to their wealth compared to the salaried middle class. Despite earning and spending within the system, the middle class does not get proportional returns in public services, infrastructure, or relief measures. They are made to feel responsible for nation-building while the wealthy manoeuvre their way around contributing anything meaningful.

One of the main enablers of this disparity is the structure of tax exemptions and deductions. The tax code is riddled with clauses that are disproportionately favourable to business owners, investors, and high-net-worth individuals. For instance, depreciation benefits, loss carry-forward provisions, and deductions for research and development disproportionately benefit corporate entities.

These are barely accessible or relevant to the salaried class, whose deductions are limited to standard deduction, Section 80C investments, and housing loan interest—most of which don't offer substantial relief in the face of rising living costs.

Moreover, the compliance burden is far lighter on the rich. They have access to the best chartered accountants and lawyers who can interpret the fine print and manipulate it to their benefit. When notices come, they respond with legal firepower. If needed, they stretch out the process through tribunals and appeals, often dragging cases for years until they are either dropped or settled advantageously. The middle class, on the other hand, trembles at the thought of an IT notice. With fewer resources, they usually end up paying penalties or settling quickly, even when not at fault, just to avoid the hassle.

The political economy of taxation is also rigged in favour of the rich. Tax policies are often influenced by powerful lobbies who ensure that laws are tailored to protect their interests. Be it the removal of wealth tax, the introduction of long-term capital gains tax with loopholes, or the generous tax holidays in special economic zones, each measure ends up benefiting those who need relief the least. The salaried class, with no organized lobbying power, becomes the default target every time the government wants to boost tax collection.

Even in the name of nation-building, the narrative is selectively applied. The rich are celebrated for job creation and investment, and they are given incentives to do so. Meanwhile, the middle class is expected to pay taxes religiously, support subsidies, bear inflation, and still be grateful. Their problems are seldom addressed because they neither fall into the "poor" category that deserves welfare, nor into the "rich" group that commands influence. They are the invisible workforce that keeps the economy running, yet they remain the most ignored segment in tax policy reform discussions.
It's not that the government lacks solutions. The implementation of wealth taxes, inheritance taxes, and more effective capital gains monitoring could bring more fairness to the system. However, these measures are either politically sensitive or actively lobbied against. As a result, the status quo remains untouched. While there's public outcry about tax evasion by the rich, little is done to actually curb it. Instead, more reporting burdens are imposed on the average taxpayer, more penalties are levied for minor errors, and more surveillance mechanisms are introduced—all of which hurt the

salaried and small business sectors the most.

Ultimately, the narrative of "tax justice" becomes hollow when viewed through the lens of the middle class. They are not against paying taxes; they are against paying disproportionately more while receiving disproportionately less. Their discontent is not just about money—it is about the feeling of being exploited by a system that celebrates those who dodge their duties and punishes those who comply. Until this imbalance is addressed with structural reforms and equitable enforcement, the Indian tax system will continue to be a burden carried unfairly on the shoulders of the middle class.

2.8 Work More, Still No Wealth

The dream of working hard and becoming wealthy is a deeply embedded narrative in modern society, especially in a country like India, where the middle class has long believed that upward mobility is achievable through honest effort. Yet, reality shows a grim paradox—despite increasing work hours, professional qualifications, and rising cost of living, the average Indian taxpayer, especially salaried individuals, finds themselves running endlessly on a treadmill that leads nowhere. This is not due to laziness, lack of ambition, or poor choices. It is a direct result of a taxation and economic system that bleeds the middle class dry while offering them very little in return. Working more no longer translates to building wealth. Instead, it often results in deeper entanglement in a loop of consumption, debt, inflation, and taxes that erode any chance of financial freedom.

At the heart of this issue lies the tax structure that penalizes earned income heavily while often leaving unearned or speculative income from the wealthy either lightly taxed or legally sheltered. A salaried individual earning a few lakhs a year is subjected to strict tax deductions, TDS, cess, and compliance requirements, while someone earning crores through capital gains or dividend income often pays far less proportionally, thanks to loopholes, exemptions, and friendly policies. This system doesn't reward hard work—it penalizes it. In fact, the more you work, the more you are exposed to tax liability, without any corresponding increase in net wealth or assets unless you're operating in an elite financial tier.

The taxation system is just one part of the equation. The second dimension is inflation, often referred to as a "silent tax." Prices of essential goods—food, fuel, housing, education—have steadily risen over the years, consuming a larger share of household income. Even when the government claims to keep inflation in check, the everyday experience of citizens says otherwise. A person who earned ₹50,000 a month a decade ago and now earns ₹1 lakh might assume they've progressed—until they realize that their savings potential and purchasing power remain stagnant or have even worsened. The double whammy of taxes and inflation ensures that additional income earned from working harder doesn't translate to wealth but merely keeps the person afloat.

Further exacerbating the problem is the easy availability of loans and credit cards, which promote the illusion of prosperity. Middle-class citizens are subtly pushed into lifestyle upgrades—EMIs for smartphones, homes, vehicles, and even vacations—leading them into long-term debt traps. The taxation system does not offer meaningful relief for these individuals, and in many cases, the interest paid on such debts does not qualify for tax deductions, except in limited cases like housing loans. Working more, in this context, simply funds a life of interest payments rather than asset accumulation. The few tax-saving investment avenues that do exist—like Public Provident Fund (PPF), Employee Provident Fund (EPF), or ELSS mutual funds—are either too slow in returns or carry their own risks and restrictions.

Another critical element is the absence of employer equity or wealth participation models in India. Unlike in some developed nations where employees can accumulate wealth through stock options or profit-sharing plans, most Indian workers are confined to fixed salaries with little to no share in the growing wealth of the companies they help build. Their work increases productivity, efficiency, and profit for the employer, but the resulting wealth largely bypasses them. What remains are routine increments that barely beat inflation and do nothing to close the gap between effort and financial growth. Thus, even after decades of service, many middle-class workers retire with just modest savings and no major assets, living a life that constantly teeters between comfort and crisis.

The government's role in this disparity cannot be ignored. Budget after budget has prioritized corporates, waived massive loans, and provided stimulus packages to big businesses in the name of growth and employment. Meanwhile, the salaried class continues to bear the tax burden with minimal state welfare or support. Basic services like healthcare, education, and public transport—ideally funded through collected taxes—are often substandard, forcing citizens to pay again for private alternatives. This is nothing short of double taxation—one in the name of nationhood, and another for survival. And the worst part is that there's no transparent, accountable system that shows taxpayers where their money is being used or how it benefits them directly.

Additionally, wealth creation in India heavily favours asset ownership—particularly real estate and stocks—which the average salaried person struggles to enter due to exorbitant prices and limited disposable income. Most of their wealth is tied up in depreciating assets or locked-in instruments, while the wealthy expand their portfolios rapidly. Government policies continue to incentivize speculative investments, while failing to protect or promote wage-based earners. The income disparity continues to widen, and those who work the hardest remain trapped in a financially fragile state, just one medical emergency or job loss away from collapse.

Ultimately, the system is designed to keep workers working—not to reward them for it. The middle class, despite its contributions to economic productivity, national revenue, and social stability, remains underappreciated, over-taxed, and financially insecure. They are caught in a cycle, where working more is not a path to wealth but a mechanism of survival in a structure that benefits others. Unless the tax system is reformed to reward actual effort, offer real benefits, and provide equitable opportunities to grow wealth, this silent exploitation will continue—masked as patriotism, duty, or progress, but delivering nothing more than a sophisticated economic trap.

The income tax system in India, instead of becoming a symbol of collective responsibility and fairness, has evolved into a punishing mechanism that targets the very group keeping the economy running—the middle class. Through layers of confusing rules, pre-emptive deductions, annual stress cycles, and a persistent fear of scrutiny, the system ensures that salaried citizens remain bound, compliant, and exhausted. They work more, save less, and live with the constant anxiety of financial instability, even after paying their dues without fail. While the wealthy manoeuvre around taxation and the poor are excluded from its grip, the middle class continues to bear the weight of a nation that gives back little in return. This isn't just taxation—it's institutional exhaustion, masked as duty.

Chapter 3
GST – The Everyday Tax Trap

When the Goods and Services Tax (GST) was introduced in India, it came with grand promises— "One Nation, One Tax," simplified compliance, and reduced tax burden. For a country long plagued by complex indirect taxation, this seemed like a revolutionary step forward. But the reality that unfolded was very different. GST, instead of simplifying, became a new web of complications for both businesses and consumers. Its multi-slab structure, ambiguous rules, and frequent changes created confusion instead of clarity. Small businesses were hit hard, compliance costs skyrocketed, and the common man continued to pay tax on almost every essential. What was meant to unify and ease has turned into an everyday trap, affecting every purchase, every service, and every citizen, silently but relentlessly.

3.1 GST Promised Simplicity, Delivered Pain

When the Goods and Services Tax (GST) was introduced in India, it was marketed as the most ambitious tax reform in the country's post-independence era. The promise was grand—a single, unified tax structure that would eliminate the cascading effect of multiple indirect taxes and make compliance smoother for all. The anticipation was that GST would simplify the tax landscape and enhance transparency, enabling businesses to flourish and consumers to benefit from uniform pricing. However, as the system unfolded, the reality turned out to be far more complex, bureaucratic, and punishing, particularly for small traders, start-ups, and the common man. What was meant to be a revolutionary reform ended up becoming a maze of slabs, returns, and inconsistencies that defeated the very purpose it claimed to serve.

At its core, GST was introduced to consolidate a number of taxes—central excise, service tax, VAT, and more—into a single indirect tax, creating a common national market. But instead of implementing a single flat rate, the government introduced multiple tax slabs—0%, 5%, 12%, 18%, and 28%—each with its own list of inclusions and exemptions. The complexity of determining which product or service falls under which slab became a nightmare for businesses. Even minor differences in product characteristics could shift a good from one slab to another, thereby drastically changing the tax implications. For example, unbranded snacks may be taxed at 5%, but the moment a brand label is added, the rate jumps to 12% or even higher. This lack of clarity leads to misclassification and legal confusion, especially for small players who cannot afford legal counsel or tax professionals to navigate the system.

The GST Network (GSTN), which was supposed to simplify the entire compliance process through digitization, has instead become an added burden. Businesses are now required to file multiple returns every month—GSTR-1, GSTR-3B, annual returns, reconciliation statements, and more. A single missed deadline can invite penalties and interest, pushing already stretched entrepreneurs into the hands of consultants. For a small business that once managed tax filing with pen and paper or at most a local accountant, adapting to GST has meant purchasing expensive software, learning a new vocabulary of codes and forms, and living in constant fear of compliance errors.

A major blow came in the form of input tax credit (ITC), a mechanism that was supposed to make GST truly non-cascading. In theory, ITC allows businesses to claim credit for the tax paid on inputs, thus reducing the overall tax burden. But in practice, ITC has become one of the most contested and opaque aspects of the GST regime. If the supplier fails to upload their invoices correctly or defaults in paying their taxes, the buyer is penalized by denial of credit. This means a business can pay taxes honestly, but still get punished because their vendor failed in compliance. This dependency chain discourages small business networks, fosters mistrust, and increases litigation.

Moreover, the arbitrary and frequent changes in GST rates have added another layer of uncertainty. What is taxed at 18% today might shift to 12% or 28% next month, making it difficult for businesses to set long-term pricing strategies. These rate shifts are often politically motivated or done under pressure from lobbying groups, instead of being based on sound economic principles. This unpredictability does not just confuse businesses—it also hurts consumers who never know whether the price of their daily use items will remain stable. The promise of simplicity gets shattered every time the GST Council holds a meeting and releases a new set of notifications, circulars, and amendments.

The irony lies in how the GST's original aim of removing tax barriers between states has not been fulfilled in spirit. The e-way bill system, which was introduced to monitor the movement of goods across state lines, has effectively recreated a new version of border checking, albeit digitally. Transporters and suppliers often face harassment from tax officials if there are minor mismatches in documentation. Goods are detained, penalties are imposed, and perishable stock gets wasted in transit. The digital backbone may have replaced physical check posts, but the bureaucracy continues to act as a choke point in commerce. This affects not just the big players with nationwide logistics chains but also the local distributor trying to send goods to a nearby state.

One cannot overlook how GST has harmed sectors like textiles, MSMEs (Micro, Small & Medium Enterprises), and handicrafts—areas that were previously either exempt or lightly taxed. These industries form the backbone of employment in India, especially in rural and semi-urban regions. GST forced them into formalization without adequate training or support, resulting in widespread closures and job losses. A small handloom weaver now has to compete on the same tax terms as a big textile factory. This one-size-fits-all approach undermines the unique strengths of India's local economies and promotes monopolization by larger corporations that can afford compliance.

Finally, the consumer—the supposed beneficiary of GST—finds themselves paying taxes on everything from toothpaste to insurance, without understanding how much tax is being embedded into the final price. Retailers and service providers rarely issue invoices with detailed tax breakdowns, and the average citizen has no idea whether they're paying 5%, 12%, or 28% on the goods they consume. The idea of transparency becomes meaningless if the citizen cannot decode it. What was envisioned as a citizen-friendly reform is now a system understood only by chartered accountants and tax consultants.

3.2 Tax on Essentials Still Exists

GST was introduced with grand assurances of a fair tax system that would spare essential commodities from heavy taxation, either exempting them or applying only nominal rates. However, the practical reality paints a very different picture. Many everyday items that form the core of basic human survival—such as food grains, soaps, cooking oils, personal hygiene products, and sanitary napkins—continue to fall under various tax slabs. While some unbranded or unpackaged items may be exempted, the moment they are packaged, branded, or processed even slightly, they enter the taxable bracket, often at 5% or 12%. This artificial distinction created by bureaucratic definitions makes life harder for the common citizen, especially the lower and middle classes who rely heavily on packaged essentials for safety, hygiene, and convenience. What was claimed to be a pro-poor taxation model is now exposing its structural bias towards maximizing government revenue over citizen relief.

The invisible burden created by taxing essentials disproportionately affects women, children, and senior citizens. For instance, the tax on sanitary napkins—though removed later after public protests—initially signaled how the system views gender-sensitive necessities as luxuries until massive public pressure forces reconsideration. Even now, many medical and hygiene-related products such as diapers, adult incontinence pads, thermometers, hand sanitizers, and basic medical tools are taxed under GST. This not only discourages the use of health-enhancing goods but also forces poor families to make trade-offs between nutrition, cleanliness, and other vital expenses. The systemic failure to classify such items as essential arises from a decision-making ecosystem disconnected from the ground-level realities of household economics in India. As a result, the most vulnerable population silently pays extra every single day, without even realizing that a large portion of their budget is being siphoned off in small chunks through indirect taxation.

Furthermore, the cascading effect of taxation on essentials doesn't end at the product level. Every service and supply chain involved in the production, transport, packaging, and marketing of these goods is taxed under GST, and that cost is passed down to the end consumer. So, a loaf of bread, a school notebook, or a simple comb may appear affordable on the shelf, but hidden within that price are multiple layers of GST charged across the value chain. This effect is especially damaging in rural and semi-urban areas where alternatives are few and prices are less competitive. People in such regions end up paying more for basic needs than some in metro cities, even though their incomes are significantly lower. The promise of "One Nation, One Tax" thus rings hollow for those who must navigate survival with little support and disproportionate taxation on items essential to their dignity and well-being.

A deeper issue is the lack of public awareness about how GST affects daily expenses. Since the tax is embedded in the final price of the item, unlike income tax, people don't get a receipt showing how much they paid in taxes. This invisibility makes it easier for the system to continue taxing even the most basic commodities without resistance. The psychological design of GST, where tax is silently integrated into every purchase, ensures compliance through ignorance. People don't protest what they don't clearly see. This quiet bleed is more dangerous than visible taxation because it offers no space for dissent or awareness. The citizen pays blindly, believing it's the actual price of the product, unaware that 5% to 28% of it is government extraction disguised as retail pricing.

What makes the taxation of essentials more unjust is the stark contrast in policy treatment when compared with luxury goods. High-end makeup products, branded watches, high-tech gadgets, or even luxury SUVs are often taxed at 18% to 28%, which is comparable to or just slightly higher than taxes on certain essential services like mobile data or packaged foods. In some cases, lower-end phones or power banks used by common people attract higher tax than imported watches. The lack of strong moral or policy logic behind tax categorization exposes the regressive nature of the GST regime. Instead of making the system equitable and reflective of human needs, it often rewards consumerism and penalizes survival. In a welfare-oriented democracy, such a policy direction is a betrayal of public trust.

Even school-related products are not spared. School bags, geometry boxes, writing instruments, and exam stationery all attract GST. Education is touted as a fundamental right, but the items needed to fulfil that right are treated as taxable commodities. This hypocrisy strikes directly at the heart of equality. How does a poor child compete in school if the most basic tools of learning come with an added burden of taxation? The gap between educational ideals and ground realities gets wider when taxation policies do not account for access, affordability, and the rising cost of schooling. Essentials are no longer just food and hygiene; they include tools for mental, emotional, and developmental well-being, all of which fall prey to the relentless net of GST.

Moreover, attempts to rationalize these taxes through temporary exemptions or reliefs during election seasons are nothing more than political gimmicks. Often, states reduce or remove GST from select items to woo voters, only to reinstate or adjust slabs later. This seesaw of fiscal populism creates an unstable pricing environment and furthers citizen distrust in the tax framework. People no longer know what to expect next. A policy meant to be stable and predictable becomes a tool of manipulation, used as a reward for compliance or punishment for political disobedience. When taxation loses neutrality and becomes a vote-catching tactic, the credibility of the entire economic system falls into question.

3.3 Small Traders are the Worst Hit

When GST was rolled out, it was hailed as a transformative reform meant to simplify India's tax structure. But beneath that shining slogan lies a bitter reality for India's small traders, retailers, and shop owners. The very backbone of India's informal and semi-formal economy—the Kirana store owner, the small textile trader, the mobile shop dealer—is now caught in a maze of paperwork, filing deadlines, tax classifications, and software mandates they neither understand nor can afford to navigate. These traders, often working with limited margins and small capital, find themselves facing a system designed with corporates in mind but imposed equally on micro-level operations. GST might have streamlined tax for multinationals and large businesses, but for small traders, it introduced a web of fear, confusion, and survival anxiety.

Before GST, most small traders dealt with VAT or local taxes that, while fragmented, were more manageable. There was familiarity, flexibility, and often some room to negotiate delays or confusion with local officers. Now, with GST's centralized digital framework, there is little space for errors, and penalties are swift. Many traders are not digitally literate, nor do they have regular access to chartered accountants or compliance professionals. Yet, under the GST regime, they must understand HSN codes, input tax credits, reverse charges, e-way bills, and file multiple returns every quarter. Each failure or delay in compliance invites fines, interest, and notices. For a trader who earns by selling a few thousand rupees' worth of goods daily, even a minor penalty could mean wiping out a week's profit.

The real irony is that these traders are not tax evaders. They are hard-working individuals trying to earn an honest living. But GST has labelled them "non-compliant" not because of any intention to cheat the system, but because the system is far too complex for their scale. The assumption that technology would level the playing field ignores India's digital divide. In towns and semi-urban areas, internet access remains patchy, and computer literacy is far from universal. Mobile apps and cloud-based accounting platforms are luxuries, not realities. But the GST portal assumes everyone is a trained techie, or at least can afford one.

Another blow came in the form of constant updates to rules and return formats. The government has tweaked filing procedures, changed tax slabs, added new compliance layers, and issued circulars at a bewildering pace. For small traders, this means they are always in doubt about whether they're doing things right. One month, a product is taxed at 12%, next month it's 18%. Transporting goods even within a state may require e-way bills, even for low-value consignments. Missing an e-way bill or a mismatch between seller and buyer records results in withholding of input tax credit or blockage of working capital. And for a trader, working capital is not just liquidity—it's survival.

The pressure to remain compliant has pushed many small traders to hire accountants, not just for filing returns, but for daily guidance. This adds to their operating cost without adding any productive value. In many cases, compliance cost eats up any potential benefit from input tax credits. Small traders also find themselves at the mercy of their suppliers and buyers, as the entire chain has to match GST filings. If a supplier fails to upload the invoice, the buyer can't claim credit. This interdependence has led to delays, disputes, and broken trust between previously close-knit trading networks.

Even worse, there's a psychological tax. The fear of receiving notices, the panic before filing deadlines, and the helplessness in front of GST officials have taken a toll on the mental health of traders. Many who were once self-reliant and proud of their businesses are now constantly worried. Confidence has eroded. Some have shut shop, unable to bear the compliance burden. Others have scaled down operations, laid off workers, or moved to cash-only transactions in hopes of staying below the radar. This push toward informality defeats the very purpose of GST, which was to widen the formal economy.

Instead of fostering entrepreneurship, GST has, in many cases, become a roadblock to it. Young people who once dreamed of starting small trading ventures are discouraged by stories of harassment, errors, and penalties. The entry barrier has increased, not because of market challenges, but due to regulatory complexity. This chokes innovation at the grassroots level. And unlike large firms, small traders can't lobby for reforms or have the ear of policymakers. Their complaints are often dismissed as teething problems or lack of understanding, rather than valid system-level grievances.

The contrast is evident when we compare how GST impacts a local cloth trader versus a branded apparel chain. The latter has ERP systems, tax consultants, dedicated compliance teams, and bargaining power. The former has none of these, yet both are expected to navigate the same regulatory ocean. This is not equity—it is systemic discrimination wrapped in the language of modernization.

There's also the irony of timing. GST came right after demonetization, when small traders were already gasping for breath. That one-two punch damaged their capital cycle, eroded their cash reserves, and weakened customer footfalls. GST was supposed to be a healing reform. Instead, it deepened the wound.

For small traders in India, GST is not just a tax system—it's a daily obstacle. It demands their time, energy, money, and peace of mind. It forces them to divert attention from growth to compliance, from strategy to survival. And it gives them no rewards in return—no benefits, no stability, and no dignity.

3.4 Filing is a Nightmare for Businesses

GST filing today feels less like compliance and more like navigating a maze of never-ending formalities. For many business owners, especially in the small and medium sector(SMEs), the process has become a relentless cycle of data entry, verification, and technical hurdles. The process of GST filing is riddled with layers of digital bureaucracy, constant technical glitches, and burdensome compliance requirements that have turned tax filing into a recurring nightmare. Unlike the old tax regime where traders dealt with a few local officials, now they're up against a nationwide digital system that demands pinpoint accuracy, timely uploads, and compliance with a schedule that rarely allows breathing room. The filing structure includes multiple returns such as GSTR-1, GSTR-3B, and annual returns, among others. For the average trader or manufacturer, this system has introduced stress, delays, and dependence on expensive chartered accountants or tax professionals to just stay afloat. What was projected as a user-friendly mechanism has turned into a time-consuming monthly ritual that eats into productivity.

Every month, a registered GST business is expected to file GSTR-1 to report all outward supplies—essentially a record of every sale made. Then comes GSTR-3B, which is used to pay the tax liability, but only after reconciling invoices with vendors and buyers. This matching process sounds easy on paper but is nightmarishly complex in practice. Input tax credit (ITC), which is supposed to be a major benefit under GST, becomes inaccessible if the buyer or supplier fails to upload or verify matching invoices. This means a business owner could pay for goods or services and not be able to claim a tax credit unless their supplier files returns correctly. In this tangled setup, the compliance of one business is directly dependent on another's punctuality and precision, creating a chain of stress and uncertainty across the market. It is not rare for businesses to be penalized or lose credit due to no fault of their own—just because another party failed in their GST duty.

Then there is the technical side of things, where the digital GST Network (GSTN) platform, though ambitious in design, often fails in execution. The website experiences downtime during peak filing periods, glitches while saving data, and delays in processing. The complexities are multiplied for businesses operating in multiple states or dealing in a combination of goods and services, as each registration needs to be maintained and filed separately. A business with operations in five states needs five GST registrations and has to file separate returns for each jurisdiction, every month, without fail. This multiplies the cost and administrative burden. Even small delays attract penalties, and interest begins accruing almost immediately. The pressure to meet these technical requirements forces small businesses to divert resources from core operations into administrative firefighting.

The government also keeps shifting deadlines and rule interpretations, which adds another layer of unpredictability. Frequent changes in GST rules, such as rate changes or format modifications, make compliance a moving target. What was compliant one month may be outdated the next. The introduction of e-invoicing and mandatory HSN code disclosures for even small businesses has further increased the mental load. In this environment, businesses often make honest mistakes but are treated with the same rigor as wilful defaulters.

Even minor mismatches or delays result in show-cause notices, late fees, or blocked ITC, creating a culture of fear and suspicion rather than trust. Tax officers, instead of guiding and enabling compliance, are seen as enforcers waiting for errors to strike with penalties.

One of the biggest casualties of this over-complicated filing regime is time—something invaluable for entrepreneurs. The constant demand to monitor invoices, match credits, respond to queries, and keep up with evolving compliance requirements transforms taxation into a full-time concern. This is especially problematic for sole proprietors or family-run businesses, who lack the manpower to dedicate an entire resource to GST compliance. Hiring a tax consultant is an additional cost that not all businesses can afford, and yet without professional help, errors are inevitable. This results in a lose-lose scenario where business owners either overpay for compliance or underperform and get penalized. The mental toll is as damaging as the financial burden, pushing many entrepreneurs to the edge of burnout.

While large corporations may have in-house tax departments, automated accounting software, and legal teams to handle such complexities, the majority of Indian businesses do not. Nearly 95% of Indian enterprises are micro, small, or medium in scale. These businesses are the backbone of local economies and employment, yet they are the worst affected by GST filing hurdles. Many have chosen to remain under the threshold for GST registration just to avoid the compliance burden, even if it means limiting their business growth. Others have shifted to cash transactions and informal dealings, weakening the goal of formalizing the economy. Ironically, the tax system meant to bring transparency and uniformity has, in many ways, reinforced the shadow economy by making compliance unattractive and punishing.

The bureaucratic rigidity of GST filing, its lack of ground-level support, and the never-ending technical updates have turned it into a punishing exercise. Businesses spend disproportionate amounts of time worrying about whether they've uploaded every invoice, reconciled every credit, and met every filing deadline. Even basic activities like checking return status or downloading data involve navigating jargon-heavy dashboards and following a multi-step digital trail. There is no physical helpdesk, no local assistance that can instantly resolve issues. This detachment creates a sense of alienation for the average business owner, making them feel like cogs in a machine rather than stakeholders in a national tax framework.

3.5 Common People Pay Tax on Everything

The idea that GST would reduce the tax burden for the common man was central to the government's narrative at the time of its rollout. Yet, a closer look at everyday expenses reveals that the average Indian continues to bear the brunt of indirect taxation on nearly every product and service they consume. Whether it's buying a toothbrush, booking a cab, eating out, or even purchasing essential household items, GST is silently embedded into the final price. It doesn't appear separately in most consumer bills, especially in retail and small shops, making it nearly invisible. But this invisibility doesn't mean it's absent—it just means people don't realize they're paying taxes on almost everything, even things that are essential to daily survival. For a nation where the majority still earns modest incomes and lives with minimal financial safety nets, this widespread tax imposition is a silent extractor of wealth from the poorest to fund the state machinery.

In the GST regime, the tax rates range from 0% to 28%, with most consumer products falling in the 5% to 18% slab. Basic food grains like rice and wheat are exempted, but the moment these raw materials are processed, branded, or packaged, they fall under a taxed category. A packet of branded atta carries 5% GST, even though the grain itself is exempt. The same logic applies to pulses, spices, and oils—if they're unbranded, they may escape tax, but branding or simple packaging immediately brings them under the GST umbrella. The end result is that common consumers, who mostly buy from organized retail chains and prefer trusted brands for health and safety reasons, pay tax on products that should ideally be tax-free as daily necessities. This contradiction between policy theory and market practice disproportionately affects middle- and lower-income households, whose consumption patterns are mostly limited to basics.

Even children's items—once considered tax-exempt or minimal taxed in the pre-GST era—are not spared. School bags, notebooks, and even pencils are subject to GST. A simple birthday celebration or a family dinner at a restaurant becomes an expensive affair when you factor in the 5% or 18% GST added to the bill. Entertainment services, such as movie tickets or OTT subscriptions, are taxed at high rates, making leisure a luxury for many. The irony deepens when one realizes that luxury items like diamonds and gold jewellery have lower tax rates in some cases compared to products like soaps, shampoos, or sanitary napkins. While GST was marketed as a progressive tax, its application often leans regressive—affecting those with less money more severely. There is no option for a low-income earner to escape GST. Unlike income tax, which is levied only if earnings cross a certain threshold, GST applies to all purchases, regardless of a person's income.

Services, too, are taxed in a way that hits the common citizen relentlessly. Mobile phone bills, electricity for commercial purposes, insurance premiums, online education platforms, hospital room rents (above ₹5,000), and even train and air travel come under GST. For many working-class individuals, even the smallest increase in the cost of living caused by such taxation impacts monthly budgeting. A middle-class family sending their child for after-school coaching or using online tools during pandemic-era education ended up paying 18% GST on such services. Even in cases where services are zero-rated or exempted, the service providers still pay GST on their inputs, and this cost is eventually passed on to the consumer through inflated pricing. Thus, the exemption is only superficial—the financial burden still flows downstream to the public.

In rural and semi-urban areas, where awareness about GST is low, most consumers don't even realize they are paying taxes. They just see that prices have gone up steadily since 2017. Inflation is often blamed on fuel or other global factors, but GST silently amplifies it in the background. A ₹100 product now costs ₹118 in many cases because of GST, and consumers accept it as market pricing without realizing the embedded taxation. The tax is baked into the supply chain at multiple stages—manufacturing, wholesaling, retailing—and while businesses may claim input tax credits, the end user does not benefit from that mechanism. The cascade ultimately culminates at the final consumer's pocket, with no recourse or awareness of how much of the price they paid was actual cost and how much was tax.

Even funeral services have not been spared by GST. Cremation services might be exempt, but items like coffins, urns, and religious offerings used during final rites attract tax. The idea that one has to pay a government-imposed tax during birth, life, and death forms a deeply unsettling commentary on modern governance. The spiritual and emotional moments in human life—marriages, funerals, temple visits, and even pilgrimages—are often tax-tagged through hotel bookings, priest services, vehicle rentals, or packaged offerings. Thus, taxation under GST is not limited to economics but extends into the cultural and social fabric of life, subtly altering how people live and experience even their most sacred moments.

From a policy perspective, the government's defence lies in the logic of broadening the tax base, curbing black money, and increasing revenue for infrastructure and welfare. But when these goals are pursued without creating safeguards for the economically vulnerable, the tax system ends up being a tool of extraction rather than equity. The burden borne by the consumer is rarely acknowledged in political debates or mainstream economic narratives. The silence around indirect tax suffering is partly because it's less visible than direct taxation, and partly because it affects everyone equally, giving the illusion of fairness. But in a country marked by vast income disparities, equal imposition is not the same as equitable impact. In effect, the poor and middle class pay a higher percentage of their income in GST compared to the rich.

3.6 Refunds Delayed, Businesses Hurt

One of the foundational promises of the GST regime was the assurance of timely refunds, especially for exporters and small-to-medium enterprises (SMEs), who depend heavily on consistent cash flow for survival. The logic was that input tax credits (ITC) would be promptly processed, allowing businesses to avoid unnecessary capital blockage. However, the ground reality has been far removed from this optimistic projection. Across India, businesses have consistently reported excessive delays in receiving GST refunds, often extending into months or even years. This lag effectively transforms what should have been a neutral tax system into a cash-guzzling maze, draining liquidity from the veins of the economy. For small businesses operating on thin margins, delayed refunds are not just an inconvenience—they are a crisis that threatens continuity, employment, and expansion.

The process of claiming a refund under GST is theoretically streamlined but practically nightmarish. It requires a maze of documentation, cross-verification, portal navigation, reconciliations between GSTR-1 and GSTR-3B, and bank details matching with invoices. In cases where even a minor mismatch occurs, the refund gets stuck in processing without any automatic alerts or corrective action pathways. While the GST Network (GSTN) was supposed to automate and simplify tax compliance, its interface often crashes, shows outdated records, or experiences lag during peak hours, further frustrating users. For many businesses, hiring a dedicated team or professional just to manage refunds has become a necessity, adding to operational costs. And despite doing all this, they still face delays, queries from tax officers, or random rejections—often without proper explanation or remedy.

The most heavily affected sectors are export-oriented industries such as textiles, gems and jewellery, leather, and agriculture-based SMEs. These industries are typically entitled to refunds due to their zero-rated supply status. But instead of receiving fast disbursals, exporters often experience a never-ending wait. In the meantime, they continue to pay wages, import raw materials, and meet overheads without the benefit of funds rightfully owed to them. The irony is that the government uses taxpayer money to run welfare schemes and infrastructure while withholding returns due to those who generated the tax in the first place. This creates a paradox where businesses fund the state but are starved of their own liquidity—an inversion of fair economic logic. When refund delays become the norm, trust in the system erodes, and many small exporters are pushed out of business or forced into informal dealings to stay afloat.

The delays have also had a chilling effect on foreign trade confidence. For a nation aspiring to become a global manufacturing hub, making its exporters wait indefinitely for their refunds sends a counterproductive message to international buyers and trade partners. Several international contracts get jeopardized because Indian exporters can't ensure consistent delivery or are forced to increase prices to cover capital shortfalls. This reduces India's competitiveness on the global stage, especially when compared to other countries with faster refund mechanisms and lower compliance hurdles. Rather than being a facilitator, the GST refund system in its current form becomes a bottleneck, creating an image of bureaucratic inefficiency and unpredictability that repels long-term investments.

The issue becomes more complex when you look at the behaviour of state tax authorities. GST is a dual system involving both central and state jurisdictions. There have been cases where the state authorities delay their portion of the refund while the central portion is cleared, or vice versa. This fragmented processing undermines the very idea of a unified tax system. Even within states, refund behaviour varies—some states are known for prompt disbursals, while others sit on refund claims endlessly. Businesses operating across multiple states face the additional burden of dealing with different levels of administrative inertia. In many cases, the delays aren't due to system errors but deliberate foot-dragging by officials who want to meet revenue targets or avoid audit flags by releasing large sums. The net effect is the same—businesses lose valuable time, money, and peace of mind.

Another dark side to delayed refunds is the emergence of corruption and underhand dealings. There have been widespread reports of officials unofficially demanding bribes to process refunds faster, especially for large claims. This takes the GST system back to the very corruption it promised to eliminate. The more complex and delayed the process, the more it incentivizes unethical shortcuts. Businesses that refuse to pay bribes are left waiting indefinitely, while others with connections or "facilitation" manage to speed up their refunds. Such inconsistencies harm honest taxpayers and reward manipulation, further weakening the moral and operational fabric of the tax system.

From a financial standpoint, blocked refunds translate into reduced working capital, which limits the business's ability to purchase inventory, pay salaries, expand operations, or invest in innovation. Many small manufacturers and exporters rely on loans to bridge the gap caused by delayed refunds, pushing them into debt cycles. Banks, too, are wary of financing businesses that show sluggish cash flow, leading to a shrinking of credit access. Thus, refund delays don't just hurt the business but also ripple into the banking sector, job market, and regional economies. The stress accumulates, leading to shutdowns, layoffs, and declining tax morale across the board.

The government occasionally rolls out "refund drives" or promises faster settlement during budget sessions, but these are often temporary and superficial measures. Structural reform remains lacking. An automated, time-bound refund system with real-time tracking, reduced human interference, and built-in grievance redressal is essential to fix the current mess. But until such systemic corrections are made, the dream of GST as a simple and fair tax remains unfulfilled for the very businesses it was meant to empower. Instead of easing trade and boosting growth, delayed refunds under GST have become an invisible chokehold around the necks of Indian enterprises.

3.7 Still a Cascading Tax in Disguise

One of the primary justifications for introducing the Goods and Services Tax (GST) in India was its promise to eliminate the cascading effect of taxation—commonly known as "tax on tax." The system it replaced, comprising excise duty, service tax, VAT, entry tax, and other state-level levies, was criticized for compounding tax liabilities at every stage of the supply chain. GST was presented as the panacea that would consolidate all these into a unified creditable chain, ensuring seamless input tax credit (ITC) and preventing duplication of taxes. However, years after its implementation, it has become increasingly evident that GST has not entirely eradicated the cascading effect. In practice, certain structural limitations, exclusions, and compliance hurdles continue to perpetuate the very tax-on-tax scenario it sought to abolish.

A particularly striking illustration of the continuing tax-on-tax problem under GST is the exclusion of petroleum products—such as petrol, diesel, natural gas, and aviation turbine fuel—from the GST framework. These essential commodities remain subject to central excise and state VAT, which are non-creditable under GST. This means that when businesses use petroleum products for production or transportation, the taxes they pay on fuel become part of their cost structure, with no possibility of claiming input tax credit. These costs are then embedded into the final price of goods or services, creating a ripple effect of non-creditable taxation across the value chain. As a result, the cascading tax burden returns through the backdoor, impacting pricing, competitiveness, and profit margins.

Another significant contributor to the disguised cascading effect is the restriction or denial of input tax credits in certain sectors and transactions. The GST law includes a long list of blocked credits under Section 17(5) of the CGST Act. These include taxes paid on items such as motor vehicles, construction services, works contracts, employee-related benefits like food and health insurance, and personal use expenses. While these may appear to be rational exclusions on the surface, in reality, they impose a hidden tax on businesses. Companies providing employee welfare facilities or operating in infrastructure-heavy industries cannot claim credits on a significant portion of their input costs. As a result, these costs are taxed again when embedded into output pricing, triggering the very cascading effect GST was meant to remove.

The complexity deepens when inter-state transactions and differing rates across states are considered. While IGST (Integrated GST) was designed to harmonize interstate trade, discrepancies still arise in terms of time lags for credit availability, reconciliation errors between buyers and sellers, and the mismatch of GSTR forms. Businesses often face problems when suppliers fail to upload invoices properly, resulting in blocked credits for the purchaser. This incomplete credit chain leads to businesses absorbing extra costs, which again forms part of the tax base for subsequent sales. Thus, due to technical lapses, credit mismatches, or software delays, cascading effects continue to persist in the system.

Small businesses and unregistered suppliers also feed into this hidden cascading structure. A registered dealer procuring goods or services from an unregistered entity cannot claim input tax credit on such purchases. This compels many small enterprises to register under GST even when they don't cross the threshold, just to remain relevant in the supply chain. Alternatively, when businesses deal with unregistered vendors—such as local artisans, transporters, or contractors—they are forced to bear the entire tax liability under reverse charge mechanisms. This breaks the seamless input credit chain and reintroduces additional tax costs that cannot be neutralized.

The situation worsens in industries like construction, hospitality, or education, where multiple tax rates, exemption categories, and composite schemes lead to fragmented taxation. For example, a real estate developer cannot claim ITC on materials used for constructing exempt properties such as affordable housing. Similarly, education institutions offering exempt services cannot offset taxes paid on administrative or infrastructural inputs. This again results in embedded tax costs that get passed on to the end consumer, reinforcing the disguised cascading effect under the veil of compliance.

Adding to the problem is the inconsistent treatment of exempted goods and services. While exempt supplies attract no GST, the input taxes incurred in producing them are not creditable, thereby increasing the cost base of exempted sectors. In healthcare, for instance, hospitals are exempt from charging GST to patients. However, they pay GST on medical equipment, consulting services, and consumables, with no provision to offset these taxes. This not only makes healthcare more expensive but creates an indirect burden on consumers who were supposedly protected by exemptions.

The lack of a universal GST rate or a flatter slab system also contributes to cascading by complicating compliance and credit eligibility. India's GST regime has multiple tax slabs—0%, 5%, 12%, 18%, and 28%—along with cess on luxury and sin goods. This tiered structure results in classification disputes, litigation, and uneven credit flow across sectors. A mismatch in input-output tax rates leads to accumulation of input credits in some cases, which cannot be fully utilized or refunded, particularly for businesses operating at the lower end of the tax chain. This credit blockage becomes an invisible cost, ultimately passed on to customers.

Even the mechanism for availing credit itself introduces challenges. The monthly filing requirements, invoice matching, GSTR-2B dependency, and complex reconciliation make ITC utilization a cumbersome task. Errors in filing or delay by the counterparty leads to automatic disallowance of credit, thereby invalidating the intended seamless chain. The penalties for erroneous credit claims are harsh, and rectification procedures are opaque and time-consuming. For micro and small enterprises with limited accounting resources, this complexity results in the forfeiture of eligible credits, indirectly creating cascading taxation on their operations.

In essence, while GST aimed to be a clean and efficient value-added tax system, its execution has retained and reproduced many elements of cascading through exclusions, compliance gaps, and policy loopholes. It has created a new form of embedded taxation—less visible but equally burdensome. The idea of "One Nation, One Tax" is undermined when credits are blocked, refunds are delayed, and core inputs like fuel are kept outside the net. The cascading effect may have changed its appearance, but it still exists—lurking in policy gaps, technical faults, and sectoral exclusions—making GST a refined yet incomplete departure from the older tax regime.

3.8 Politics of GST Council

The GST Council, envisioned as the apex decision-making body for the implementation and evolution of the Goods and Services Tax in India, was initially praised as a cooperative federal innovation that balanced the interests of both the Centre and the States. It was meant to be a consensus-driven platform where decisions would reflect a collective national interest. Yet, the practical functioning of the Council has steadily revealed a disturbing trend—the growing influence of political motives and power imbalances. Instead of operating as a neutral body for economic harmonization, the GST

Council has increasingly become a site of political bargaining, competitive populism, and tactical policy manoeuvring, often at the expense of sound fiscal reasoning and equitable governance.

At the structural level, the GST Council consists of the Union Finance Minister as its chairperson, along with the Ministers of Finance or Taxation from each state. While this appears democratic on paper, the actual voting mechanism grants the Central Government one-third of the total voting power, with the remaining two-thirds divided among all the States collectively. This disproportionate weight ensures that the Centre can easily tilt decisions in its favour, especially if politically allied states support its stance. In practice, the central government has used this leverage to push policy changes and rate modifications that align with its fiscal and political agendas, even when states have raised dissenting voices. This power asymmetry undermines the federal spirit the Council was supposed to uphold.

The politicization becomes especially visible during election cycles. There have been multiple instances where GST rate cuts or exemptions are announced just before state or national elections—ostensibly to provide relief to the public but in reality, aimed at gaining voter favour. Such politically-timed decisions often ignore the long-term revenue implications for states, which heavily rely on GST collections to fund social programs and infrastructure. States with fragile fiscal conditions find themselves caught between the need to maintain public support and the compulsion to abide by Council decisions that reduce their tax base. Consequently, this populist tinkering weakens both the revenue stability and policy credibility of the GST framework.

Another politically driven fault line is the persistent demand by opposition-ruled states for higher compensation and extended financial support, especially in times of economic downturn. The compensation mechanism, which assured states a 14% annual revenue growth post-GST, became a flashpoint during the pandemic when the Centre delayed payments citing fiscal constraints. States like Kerala, Punjab, and West Bengal, ruled by opposition parties, accused the Centre of breaching trust and unilaterally altering the compensation terms. This crisis not only exposed the Council's limited ability to ensure fairness in fiscal transfers but also highlighted how centralization of power can destabilize cooperative structures when political consensus breaks down.

The delay in including critical sectors like petroleum, electricity, and alcohol within the GST ambit also reflects the Council's political paralysis. While it is universally acknowledged that bringing these sectors under GST would streamline input credit chains and rationalize pricing, states continue to resist such integration. Their reluctance is rooted in the fear of losing discretionary revenue control—especially over petroleum products, which constitute a large share of state revenues. The Centre, rather than resolving these concerns through dialogue and compensation mechanisms, often avoids forcing a resolution to maintain political goodwill with state allies or to avert regional backlash. As a result, the larger vision of GST as a comprehensive tax remains compromised due to short-term political calculations.

Even the Council's decision-making process lacks the transparency expected from such a crucial economic institution. Meeting minutes are not always made public, voting patterns are opaque, and dissenting opinions often get buried under vague consensus resolutions. This information asymmetry erodes public trust in the Council's objectivity and shields politically motivated decisions from scrutiny. States that disagree with central proposals find themselves constrained by the lack of procedural clarity and the difficulty of mobilizing enough support to challenge the Centre's influence. Over time, this cultivates a climate of passive compliance rather than active cooperation.

One of the subtler effects of political dominance in the Council is the skewed prioritization of sectors for tax rate changes. Sectors with significant lobbying power or electoral relevance—such as consumer goods, automobiles, or real estate—tend to receive faster and more favourable adjustments. Meanwhile, sectors critical for long-term national development—such as education tools, medical equipment, or renewable energy—often wait indefinitely for rational tax relief. This lopsided decision-making favours short-term political returns over strategic economic planning. The Council thus risks becoming reactive rather than visionary, governed more by the headlines of the day than the principles of sound tax policy.

States with smaller populations and weaker political leverage suffer further from the Council's majoritarian structure. Their voices are often overshadowed by the dominant interests of larger states or central mandates. This has led to repeated complaints about the "one-size-fits-all" approach of GST, which fails to accommodate regional economic realities, consumption patterns, or administrative capacities. For instance, north-eastern states have unique logistical challenges and revenue needs, but they are often forced to comply with policies crafted around the realities of metropolitan economies. This disconnect between central policy and local execution amplifies governance inefficiencies and deepens fiscal inequities across the country.

Even when the Council aims to reform procedures—such as simplifying returns or adjusting rates—it struggles to build lasting consensus due to political polarization. Reforms proposed by the Centre are viewed with suspicion by opposition-ruled states, and vice versa. This antagonism delays crucial decisions and introduces regulatory uncertainty, which negatively affects businesses, especially small and medium enterprises that rely on policy predictability. Instead of acting as a technocratic body shielded from political influence, the GST Council has become a microcosm of India's broader political landscape—divided, contentious, and often more focused on ideological alignment than economic efficiency.

In sum, the GST Council, while structurally designed for cooperative federalism, has been gradually hollowed out by political calculations. The ideal of balanced governance has given way to strategic dominance, electoral opportunism, and competitive populism. The spirit of consensus that once defined its initial meetings has now been diluted by mistrust and tactical positioning. What could have been a bold and rational economic experiment in unified taxation is now often a theatre of political choreography, with states and the Centre pulling in divergent directions under the pretence of unity.

3.9 Local vs Imported: A Tax Bias

One of the most paradoxical and frustrating outcomes of the Goods and Services Tax (GST) regime in India is the unintentional but significant disadvantage it creates for local products when compared to their imported counterparts. While GST was designed to create a level playing field by unifying tax structures, it has instead allowed for an invisible but highly impactful tax bias that favours imports over domestic goods. This disparity is not a consequence of the GST rates themselves but is a result of a series of structural issues, including loopholes in the system, input credit mismatches, and the way taxes are applied unevenly across various sectors. As a result, local manufacturers—especially small and medium enterprises (SMEs)—are placed at a considerable disadvantage when competing with imported goods, which often arrive at similar or even lower prices despite incurring customs duties.

The first and perhaps most glaring cause of this discrepancy lies in the application of input tax credits. While imported goods are subject to customs duties and integrated GST (IGST), the tax paid on such imports is creditable when the goods are sold in the domestic market. This provides a distinct advantage to imported goods, as businesses can pass on the tax paid at the import stage to consumers without any cascading effect. In contrast, locally manufactured goods face a different set of challenges. While the raw materials and components used in the production of local goods are taxable under GST, the credits that manufacturers can claim are often limited, especially if they operate in sectors that do not benefit from input credit on key inputs or services. This creates an invisible tax gap, where the cost of local production is inherently higher due to the inability to fully offset taxes on inputs, forcing local goods to carry a heavier cost burden than imported alternatives.

The challenge is exacerbated when it comes to the treatment of small businesses. Many small manufacturers and local vendors, who form the backbone of India's domestic production, are often unable to fully utilize the benefits of the GST system. Small traders and manufacturers, especially those in the unorganized sector, often struggle with compliance issues, lack of access to robust tax credit mechanisms, and limited accounting capabilities. They frequently end up paying higher taxes on their inputs, as they cannot claim input tax credit due to gaps in their supply chains or the inability to register for GST. In such cases, the higher cost of production for local goods leads to an unintentional price hike, making them less competitive against imported products, which, in many instances, benefit from more streamlined credit mechanisms at the customs level.

The problem becomes even more pronounced in sectors like textiles, electronics, and consumer goods, where imported products are often priced similarly to locally produced items, despite the added costs of freight, customs duties, and handling charges. For instance, a foreign electronics brand may arrive in India at an effective price that is close to or even cheaper than the price of a domestically manufactured product. This is primarily due to the fact that the local manufacturer may be paying higher taxes on the materials and components used to assemble the product, while the imported counterpart is benefiting from the IGST system that allows for the passing on of duties without the hidden costs that plague local manufacturers. The result is an uneven playing field where imported goods can be sold at the same price as, or even cheaper than, their locally made counterparts—undermining the viability of domestic production and encouraging imports over homegrown solutions.

Moreover, many imported goods enjoy preferential treatment through Free Trade Agreements (FTAs) and other international trade arrangements that lower or eliminate tariffs, making it even easier for foreign goods to enter the Indian market at a competitive price point. In some cases, these imports are further incentivized by low manufacturing costs in countries with more favourable tax regimes or government subsidies. As a result, local manufacturers, who have to contend with India's complex tax system and higher compliance costs, find themselves unable to compete on price, even though the goods are identical or of similar quality. This creates a vicious cycle where domestic products are penalized by hidden tax inefficiencies while foreign imports continue to enjoy an advantage, further eroding the prospects for local manufacturing and innovation.

At the same time, the political economy surrounding the taxation of imports versus domestic products plays a significant role in perpetuating this imbalance. Import duties on certain items are subject to frequent policy changes, often driven by global trade dynamics or political interests, which can further complicate the equation. For example, changes in tariff rates, the introduction of anti-dumping measures, or the negotiation of new trade deals can create sudden shifts in the competitive landscape, impacting local manufacturers more than foreign competitors. Moreover, the lack of a consistent approach in terms of local taxation policies further adds to this unpredictability, as GST rate cuts or changes in input credit eligibility do not always reflect the realities of domestic production, leaving local businesses in a constant state of adjustment.

The consequences of this invisible tax bias are far-reaching. For local manufacturers, the higher cost of compliance, along with the inability to recover input taxes fully, leads to lower profit margins, which in turn stifles investment in innovation, quality improvements, and expansion. Small traders and businesses, who already face a tough competitive environment, are disproportionately impacted. These businesses, which form the backbone of India's job market and rural economy, find themselves unable to scale or thrive under the weight of higher tax burdens, thereby contributing to stagnation in the domestic economy. Additionally, this imbalance also discourages foreign direct investment (FDI) in local manufacturing, as investors may be more inclined to partner with businesses that import finished goods rather than support local production, further exacerbating the dependency on foreign imports.

Despite its promise of unifying the tax structure, GST has silently become a trap that tightens its grip on every citizen, every trader, and every creator in the nation. It punishes local enterprise while rewarding global imports, taxes survival while pretending to be progressive, and forces the smallest hands in the economy to carry the heaviest burdens. From the vegetable seller to the small-scale artisan, from the rural trader to the urban manufacturer, GST has become less about simplicity and more about silent control. It isn't just a tax system—it is a mechanism of quiet economic suppression, masked as reform. In the name of one nation, one tax, it has created one invisible cage.

Chapter 4
Hidden and Everyday Taxes

For the average Indian citizen, taxation is not confined to the well-known categories like income tax or GST. A large portion of the population unknowingly contributes to the national revenue through an intricate web of hidden and daily taxes that quietly erode their disposable income. These taxes are embedded in services and commodities used every day, from filling up fuel to paying electricity bills, buying groceries, or enjoying basic entertainment. While they may seem insignificant in isolation, their cumulative effect is financially burdensome. People often don't realize how much they are paying because these charges are not transparently shown, yet the impact is constant and unavoidable. These covert taxes operate in the background of everyday life, draining citizens slowly and systematically under the illusion of necessity, while providing little to no return in public services. This chapter sheds light on the mechanics of these hidden taxes, their impact on household budgets, and how they reinforce a taxation system that exploits the unaware.

4.1 Fuel Taxes – Paying Three Times Over

The cost of fuel in India is a classic example of how taxation gets buried within a basic necessity, turning mobility into a recurring financial liability for common citizens. At the core of this issue is the complex structure of fuel pricing, which includes central excise duties, state value-added tax (VAT), and dealer commissions, all of which get stacked on top of the base price of petrol or diesel. When citizens pay for fuel, they aren't just covering the cost of refining and distribution—they are paying a disproportionate amount in taxes that often constitute over 50% of the pump price. For instance, even if global crude prices drop, the Indian government often maintains or increases tax components to retain high revenue flows. This reveals the state's over-reliance on fuel as a guaranteed source of income.

The irony is that fuel is taxed heavily despite being an essential good. It powers not only personal vehicles but also public transportation, agricultural machinery, delivery networks, and emergency services. When fuel becomes expensive due to tax loading, the resulting price hikes ripple through every sector that depends on transport, which includes virtually everything from vegetables to electronic goods. This leads to inflation across the board, making life harder for every income group, especially the poor and middle class, who experience the sharpest pinch. Yet they rarely link their suffering to fuel taxation, as it remains hidden in layers of bureaucratic complexity.

To make matters worse, fuel taxation happens at multiple levels. First, there is the central government excise duty, which is uniform across the country. Second, each state imposes its own VAT, leading to varying fuel prices depending on location. This disparity causes logistical inefficiencies and drives up transport costs unnecessarily. Additionally, citizens also bear the brunt of cesses, surcharges, and development levies—all of which are technically taxes but are excluded from revenue sharing with states, creating friction in fiscal federalism. These charges are not transparently communicated to the public. Instead, they are quietly absorbed into the price displayed at petrol pumps, leaving consumers with no understanding or power to question their burden.

Another disturbing aspect of this tax structure is its regressive nature. Unlike income tax, which is progressive and linked to earnings, fuel tax affects everyone uniformly. A daily wage labourer using a scooter for work pays the same tax rate on fuel as a wealthy industrialist driving a luxury car. This structure violates the very principle of tax justice, where contributions to state revenue should be aligned with one's financial capacity. In essence, fuel taxes function as an equalizer in reverse, disproportionately hurting the lower strata of society who can least afford it.

Despite repeated debates and promises of rationalizing fuel taxes, little has changed. Inclusion of petrol and diesel under the GST regime has been discussed but never implemented, likely because it would significantly reduce tax revenue for both the center and the states. The reluctance to reform fuel taxation reflects the deeper problem of political unwillingness to shift away from easy, non-transparent revenue mechanisms. In fact, during election seasons, states often temporarily lower VAT or offer subsidies, which proves that prices are artificially inflated through tax structures rather than market forces. Such manipulations are symptomatic of a broader system that weaponizes essential commodities for fiscal convenience.

Fuel taxes also expose the broader failure of India's public transport policies. Ideally, high taxes on fuel should be offset by investment in efficient, reliable, and affordable public transport options. But India's public transit infrastructure, especially outside major cities, remains inadequate and inconsistent. As a result, people are forced to rely on personal vehicles, which increases fuel consumption and, by extension, tax revenue for the government. This cyclical dependency traps citizens in a loop where their necessity becomes the state's opportunity for silent taxation. The absence of reliable alternatives means that resisting this taxation is nearly impossible.

Even those who use public transport indirectly pay fuel taxes, as bus operators and service providers factor the cost of diesel into ticket prices. Similarly, food delivery, ride-hailing services, and cargo transport—all of which are integral to modern life—adjust their pricing based on fluctuating fuel charges. This means the tax burden is passed along the chain, ultimately reaching the end consumer in disguised forms. The sheer pervasiveness of this tax makes it one of the most powerful tools of silent economic control.

Fuel taxes in India represent a quiet but significant form of systemic financial extraction that affects every citizen, regardless of awareness or consent. Their impact is far-reaching, inflationary, and socially regressive. Yet their invisibility within the broader taxation discourse allows the government to continuously use them without facing widespread resistance or accountability. The result is a nation where people pay three times for the same fuel: once through direct purchase, again through inflated prices of transported goods, and finally through long-term economic stagnation caused by regressive fiscal policies.

4.2 Taxes in Mobile, Internet, and Entertainment

In today's digital age, mobile connectivity, internet access, and digital entertainment are no longer luxuries—they are basic utilities, necessities without which modern life would collapse into dysfunction. Yet, hidden beneath the surface of every mobile recharge, every data plan, and every streaming subscription lies a network of taxes that most users are barely aware of. This tax structure has quietly converted essential digital consumption into a lucrative revenue stream for the government. Every time someone recharges their prepaid phone, pays a post-paid bill, subscribes to an OTT platform, or downloads a paid app, they are not just paying the service provider—they are indirectly paying the government through multiple layers of taxation embedded into the cost. What appears to be a simple price tag is, in truth, the result of carefully layered taxation that maximizes extraction without drawing attention. The mobile-internet-entertainment ecosystem has thus become a digital goldmine of taxation, impacting every citizen while remaining under-discussed in mainstream narratives about tax justice.

The introduction of the Goods and Services Tax (GST) drastically altered the taxation landscape for digital services. Before GST, telecom services were subjected to service tax at around 15%. With the implementation of GST, telecom and internet services were placed under the 18% tax slab. This shift, while seemingly marginal, resulted in a noticeable increase in the final cost of services for the end user. The key issue is not just the rate but the blanket application of this tax to every bill, regardless of the income or economic status of the consumer. Whether it's a student recharging with Rs. 100 or a corporate paying thousands for high-speed internet, the tax rate remains the same, showing no regard for affordability or necessity. This is fundamentally regressive—imposing a flat tax on an essential service used across social classes punishes the poor disproportionately. For individuals who rely on mobile internet for education, job applications, or basic communication, this 18% is not just a number—it is a barrier.

The digital entertainment sector faces a similar problem. Subscriptions to platforms like Netflix, Amazon Prime Video, Spotify, and others attract an 18% GST, categorizing them as luxury services despite their widespread use. The irony is stark: the same digital entertainment that the government encourages under 'Digital India' is treated as a taxable indulgence. Even domestic content creators and platforms trying to reach Indian audiences are subject to these high taxes, making their pricing less competitive. Furthermore, foreign platforms providing services in India are also required to comply with Indian GST regulations, collecting and remitting taxes on their earnings from Indian users. This effectively ensures that no digital space remains outside the reach of taxation. Add to this the micro-transactions involved in gaming apps, e-books, e-learning platforms, and even cloud storage services—all of which fall under the GST net—and the picture becomes clearer: the entire digital ecosystem has been monetized as a consistent and expanding source of tax revenue.

Another hidden dimension of taxation in digital services is the indirect cost passed down from corporations to consumers. Telecom companies and content platforms must pay compliance costs, licensing fees, and regulatory charges—many of which are effectively taxes or government-imposed levies in disguise. For instance, telecom spectrum charges and licensing fees are substantial, and companies recover these amounts through the pricing of their plans. These costs are not labelled as taxes in the consumer bill, but they are embedded in the total price, making them invisible yet impactful. A user who pays Rs. 500 for a data plan may think they are only paying for internet usage, but in reality, a significant chunk of that amount is feeding into government coffers in one form or another, either directly as GST or indirectly through adjusted corporate charges. This indirect tax structure allows the government to maintain the appearance of stable or reduced tax rates while still increasing total revenue collection.

The advertising-based digital economy also plays into this scheme. Platforms that offer free services often monetize user data and attention through advertising, which is also taxed. Advertisers pay GST on digital ads, and digital marketing firms pass this cost to their clients, who in turn inflate product prices. The average consumer, unaware of this chain, ends up paying more for products and services that use digital platforms for promotion. Thus, the very act of using an "ad-supported free service" is indirectly costing the user money through higher prices elsewhere. It creates an elaborate web where consumption of digital content leads to ripple-effect taxation, all ultimately funnelled back to the state.

Even international digital payments are not exempt. When Indian users subscribe to foreign platforms in dollars, their banks or payment gateways often charge currency conversion fees, on which GST is also levied. This means users are being taxed not just for using the service but also for the act of converting currency—another subtle extraction that goes unnoticed by the majority. While these charges may seem minor on paper, they accumulate significantly at scale, especially when multiplied by millions of daily transactions in India's massive digital user base. In essence, the modern Indian citizen is paying a digital toll every time they interact with the online world, whether for work, learning, entertainment, or connection.

This continuous siphoning of money through digital taxation is made even more problematic by the lack of any direct public benefit tied to it. Unlike road taxes that at least promise infrastructure, or property taxes that claim to fund local civic services, digital taxes are absorbed into the general revenue pool. There is no accountability or visibility on how this massive stream of revenue from digital consumption is being used. Are internet services becoming more affordable as a result? Are rural digital infrastructure projects being adequately funded? The answers are either vague or disappointing. What is clear, however, is that the government sees digital consumption not as a right, but as a revenue source to be tapped relentlessly.

The net effect is clear: what should have been a tool of empowerment—the internet, the smartphone, the global access to information and expression—has been gradually turned into a mechanism of silent financial control. The taxation of mobile, internet, and entertainment services under GST, coupled with invisible levies and compliance burdens, ensures that no click, call, or stream is ever truly tax-free. Digital life in India comes with a hidden price tag, paid daily by its billion-plus users, often without their knowledge or consent.

4.3 Alcohol and Cigarettes – Easy Targets

Alcohol and cigarettes have long stood at the intersection of morality, health policy, and fiscal revenue. Governments across the globe have found these two commodities to be politically convenient punching bags—easy to demonize and even easier to tax. In India, this tactic has been elevated into a structured strategy where alcohol and tobacco are deliberately kept outside the Goods and Services Tax (GST) regime, giving state governments full liberty to levy their own taxes. This creates a dual benefit for the system: immense revenue generation and minimal public backlash. Since these products are considered "sin goods," any increase in their price is rationalized as a public health move, shielding policymakers from deeper scrutiny. But behind this justification lies a different truth: the taxation of alcohol and cigarettes is not about discouraging use—it's about maximizing income from a captive, habitual consumer base that has no real alternatives.

Tobacco products, including cigarettes, beedis, and chewing tobacco, are taxed through a combination of central excise duties, state-level VAT, and cess under GST. In the case of cigarettes, the effective tax burden often exceeds 50% of the retail price. Every puff of smoke a consumer takes is not just filled with nicotine—it's infused with tax. The layers of taxation are designed so that the longer the product, the higher the tax, thus increasing revenue from premium cigarette brands. Ironically, this system hits middle and lower-income users harder. While luxury goods or speculative investments often find tax loopholes, cigarette users—especially in rural or semi-urban areas—are disproportionately contributing to the government's revenue, unknowingly participating in an addiction-driven fiscal model.

Alcohol taxation reveals a similar yet more fragmented reality. State excise duties on alcohol vary dramatically from one state to another, but what remains constant is the enormous contribution liquor sales make to state budgets. In states like Tamil Nadu, Uttar Pradesh, and Karnataka, alcohol taxes contribute anywhere between 15% to 25% of total state revenues. Liquor is not just a product—it is a financial lifeline. This dependence is so deep that attempts at prohibition in various states have often collapsed not because of social unrest, but due to fiscal crisis. The state becomes paradoxically dependent on something it publicly labels as harmful. This contradiction allows governments to expand alcohol retail networks, promote government-run liquor shops, and even run ad campaigns for "responsible drinking"—all while steadily increasing taxes under the pretext of social good.

What's rarely spoken about is the regressive nature of this model. The poor spend a higher proportion of their income on alcohol and tobacco, either due to addiction, social influence, or cultural factors. When the tax rate on these products keeps rising, it squeezes their already limited disposable income. Unlike income taxes or capital gains taxes, which the wealthy can manage through planning or evasion, consumption taxes on alcohol and cigarettes are unavoidable for users. The poorest segments of society thus end up paying a larger chunk of their income to the state without receiving proportionate public benefits. In this sense, the 'sin tax' becomes less about reform and more about silent exploitation of human weakness.

The industry structure further adds complexity. Most state governments run liquor monopolies or tightly control licensing, thereby centralizing profit and regulation. Private players in the tobacco and alcohol industries are subjected to heavy compliance, labelling norms, and mandatory health warnings—all of which, while sounding ethical, are also part of a system designed to protect revenue flow without killing demand. On one hand, governments campaign against tobacco use through health awareness ads; on the other, they budget for and anticipate massive tax collections from the same product. This hypocrisy is not accidental—it is engineered. It allows the government to appear morally upright while behaving economically opportunistic. It plays well in public discourse and even better on the balance sheet.

Another underreported consequence of this taxation model is the rise of the illicit and unregulated alcohol market. When legal liquor becomes too expensive due to high taxes, black-market brews, spurious liquor, and smuggling gain traction. These products evade tax entirely, posing severe health risks and safety concerns. Yet the state often turns a blind eye, unwilling to lower taxes but aware that the demand will find a way. The very taxation policy meant to discourage harmful consumption ends up driving vulnerable populations into more dangerous alternatives. Tragedies from toxic alcohol are often framed as enforcement failures, but the root cause lies in the economics of exclusion—the poor are priced out of safety.

In parallel, cigarette companies face similar distortions. As branded cigarettes become more expensive, the market for unbranded beedis and illicit cigarettes thrives. These alternatives rarely comply with health standards or tax laws but flourish because they fill the demand gap left by heavily taxed legal options. Thus, the intent of reducing consumption through high taxes backfires—it fragments the market, compromises public health further, and creates an underworld of tax evasion that the system fails to contain. While the rich can quit or switch to imported cigars and vapes, the poor are left navigating the risky margins of addiction and affordability.

The irony of the alcohol and tobacco tax model is that it is built on a contradiction. If the state truly wanted to eliminate the harm caused by these substances, it would invest its revenues into robust de-addiction programs, alternative livelihood projects, and health infrastructure. But the ground reality is that little of the massive revenue from these "sin taxes" is earmarked for public health. Instead, the money vanishes into general expenditure, often funding political propaganda, bureaucratic salaries, and debt servicing. The state becomes a silent partner in the very addictions it claims to oppose, exploiting them for steady income without meaningful accountability. In the final analysis, alcohol and cigarettes are not just consumer goods—they are instruments of economic control. They allow the state to present itself as a moral guardian while behaving as a financial predator. Taxation on these items is not about public health or ethics—it's about predictability, convenience, and profit. The government doesn't want you to quit smoking or drinking entirely—it wants you to keep consuming, just enough to keep the cash flow alive. And in that unspoken pact, the citizen remains trapped—paying with their lungs, liver, and life, while the state counts the profits.

4.4 Road Tolls After Road Taxes

Every vehicle owner in India pays a road tax at the time of registration—often a sizable amount calculated as a percentage of the vehicle's cost. This tax is supposed to fund the construction, maintenance, and expansion of road infrastructure. However, the reality faced by the average commuter paints a starkly different picture. In practice, this initial road tax is just the beginning of a long financial drain. With the proliferation of toll booths across national and state highways, as well as some city expressways, citizens are forced to pay repeatedly for the same infrastructure. This dual taxation—one upfront and another ongoing—creates a situation where the public is essentially leasing roads that were claimed to be paid for already.

The justification given for toll collections hinges on the Build-Operate-Transfer (BOT) or Public-Private Partnership (PPP) model, where private entities construct highways and recover their investment through tolls over a concession period. In theory, this sounds fair. In reality, many of these contracts are poorly regulated, often extended beyond their original terms, and rarely audited for actual traffic-based revenue. As a result, citizens continue to pay tolls on roads whose construction costs were recovered years ago. In many cases, the toll remains not because the road still needs funding, but because the collection process itself has become a profitable, self-perpetuating business. The original logic of time-bound tolling dissolves into a permanent tax-on-the-move.

The logic becomes even more questionable when urban roads and bypasses begin carrying tolls. These routes, used for daily commuting rather than long-distance transport, make tolls an everyday burden rather than an occasional fee. For a salaried employee traveling through one or more toll booths to work and back, the monthly toll cost can rival or exceed what they spend on fuel. This regressive model ensures that the working class, especially those living in city outskirts, bear the brunt of toll taxation. Wealthier residents in central urban zones with better infrastructure avoid tolls altogether, effectively passing on the cost of development to the less privileged.

Even more problematic is the opacity of toll revenue and contract management. Most citizens have no idea how long a toll booth is legally permitted to operate, what the project cost was, or how close it is to recouping that investment. Information about toll contracts is buried in technical documents or hidden behind bureaucratic walls. There's no public mechanism for real-time tracking of collected revenue versus cost recovery. Despite the presence of regulatory bodies, the system conveniently ignores calls for transparency, relying on citizen fatigue and lack of organized resistance to continue uninterrupted collections. Toll booths, in this sense, become cash cows for private operators and a symbol of state indifference to accountability.

Moreover, technology has added another layer of complexity without easing the financial burden. With the advent of FASTag, toll payments have become more efficient, but not cheaper or fairer. FASTag merely automates the revenue stream, removing human contact while increasing surveillance. Every time your vehicle crosses a toll plaza, data is collected—vehicle number, time, frequency of travel. This real-time profiling adds to the already growing database of citizen movement under the guise of efficiency. Yet, while the government collects tolls more smoothly, citizens still face no clarity on where that money is going or how it's being used. The digital shift masks the deeper issue: monetizing mobility through coercion, not consent.

There's also the environmental angle. Long queues at toll plazas, even with FASTag, cause fuel wastage and air pollution. Ironically, roads that are meant to improve transportation efficiency end up slowing down traffic and increasing emissions during toll congestion. In essence, the system penalizes users not just economically, but ecologically as well. The promise of seamless, fast transport turns into a cycle of stops, fees, and delays. The very infrastructure meant to enable progress ends up becoming a recurring point of friction, both financial and physical.

Rural and remote regions face a different but equally unjust scenario. When new highways are built through previously untolled areas, they become economic barriers. A farmer transporting goods, a villager commuting for work, or a school bus on a daily run suddenly encounters financial obstacles in the form of toll charges. For such users, who already operate on tight margins, toll fees become a significant percentage of monthly expenses. There is no differentiation based on income or locality—just a flat fee that assumes everyone can afford to pay the price of infrastructure. This is taxation without sensitivity, and it goes against the spirit of inclusive development.

Another concern arises from the systemic nature of toll collection expansion. New expressways and bypass roads are designed from the beginning with toll collection in mind, not public service. Instead of building free access routes and charging only for express alternatives, governments and contractors now use the toll model as the default. This shifts infrastructure development from being a public good to a market commodity. The road becomes a service for sale, not a right of the taxpayer. What's worse, alternatives are often deliberately neglected, making toll roads the only feasible option. The citizen is boxed into a corner—either pay, or waste time and fuel on neglected, pothole-ridden routes.

The ideological question here is fundamental. When a citizen pays road tax at vehicle registration, pays GST on fuel, and also pays toll every time they travel, where is the concept of fair taxation? How many times must a person pay for the same kilometer of road? The multi-layered taxation on mobility is not only unjust—it's a blueprint for silent economic extraction. It's engineered in a way that no single point feels like a major theft, but the accumulated burden is massive. It punishes movement, discourages decentralization, and reinforces inequality by making the cost of distance a permanent penalty.

4.5 Stamp Duty and Property Tax Together

When a citizen decides to purchase a piece of land or a home in India, the moment of financial strain does not end with negotiating the purchase price. In fact, it often intensifies when the buyer encounters the barrage of taxes layered onto real estate ownership. Two major contributors to this hidden pressure are stamp duty and property tax. These are not just random administrative fees but significant financial obligations that exist simultaneously—often without providing the kind of tangible public services or infrastructure one might expect in return. The burden is so seamlessly integrated into the process that most buyers accept it as inevitable, not realizing they are paying for the same asset multiple times under different tax labels.

Stamp duty, imposed at the time of property registration, is essentially a one-time tax calculated as a percentage of the transaction value. Depending on the state, it can range anywhere from 4% to 10%, and when registration charges are added, the total cost can easily push the effective rate even higher. The rationale behind stamp duty is supposedly to authenticate and legalize the property transaction—but when we dissect its logic, it becomes apparent that it's nothing more than a high entry fee to exercise ownership of one's legally purchased land or house. Unlike a service tax that guarantees a deliverable, stamp duty gives you nothing in return except a stamped document—something that the digital age could easily automate at a fraction of the cost.

But the tax toll does not end there. Once the stamp duty is paid and the property registered, the homeowner is immediately liable to pay annual property tax to the local municipal body. This tax is levied perpetually for as long as the property is held, calculated based on built-up area, location, usage, and rental value, among other variables. The logic of property tax is ostensibly linked to urban development, public services like garbage disposal, street lighting, and water supply. Yet in many cities, these services are either grossly inadequate or entirely absent, making the property tax feel like a fee extracted for promises never kept. Ironically, even slum dwellers—many of whom have no formal property rights—are charged under makeshift versions of this tax regime.

When examined together, stamp duty and property tax form a cleverly disguised double taxation model. One extracts a heavy toll at the point of purchase, and the other establishes a recurring revenue stream that lasts indefinitely. What's especially problematic is that there is no meaningful policy dialogue around why both taxes need to coexist in their current forms. If the government insists on levying a one-time stamp duty to process the transaction, shouldn't the annual property tax be significantly reduced or eliminated in return? Or vice versa? Instead, citizens are forced to pay both without justification, and neither tax comes with accountability or transparency about where the money goes.

This dual-tax system also has a chilling effect on mobility and market fluidity. People often hesitate to buy, sell, or transfer properties due to the sheer cost of stamp duty. In turn, this freezes the real estate market, creates artificial scarcity, and drives up prices. Those who inherit property face another level of taxation, with nominal or full-value stamp duties even on gifts or family transfers in certain states. The state's intention to generate revenue from land and buildings has effectively turned into a stranglehold on the very concept of private ownership. Instead of being a liberating milestone, owning property becomes an ongoing financial liability.

Moreover, property taxes are deeply flawed in execution. Valuations are often outdated, arbitrary, or misclassified, leading to disputes and inflated bills. Assessment methods differ widely between cities, and there is little effort to standardize or correct the anomalies. This lack of consistency opens the door for corrupt practices, under-assessments, and bribes. A wealthy individual with a large bungalow in a posh area may end up paying less tax than a middle-class family in a denser locality—purely because of flawed valuation formulas or political influence. And despite these systemic inefficiencies, penalties for late payment are harsh, often compounding monthly and creating a debt trap.

Digital systems and municipal apps have only added layers of confusion without true reform. While they make it easier to pay taxes, they do not improve the quality of services linked to them. You may now receive automated reminders and pay through UPI, but the leaking drainage system in your street remains unrepaired. Essentially, technology has helped the government collect taxes more efficiently without enhancing delivery. The citizen, already overburdened, is left wondering if any part of their financial contribution is making a difference on the ground.

There's also an inherent contradiction in charging property tax in areas with little or no public infrastructure. In underdeveloped urban fringes or villages transitioning into towns, the property tax is introduced even before basic amenities arrive. Roads remain unpaved, garbage collection is sporadic, and power or water lines are irregular—but the tax invoice still finds its way to every doorstep. This is taxation without representation in its most blatant form. The logic that one must pay taxes to fund development falls flat when development never follows the tax.

At the policy level, successive governments have failed to rationalize the coexistence of stamp duty and property tax. Neither is progressive, and both disproportionately impact the middle class. The wealthy often circumvent stamp duty through power-of-attorney transactions or underreporting, and property tax becomes an afterthought when the bill is insignificant compared to their portfolio. But for a first-time buyer or a small business investing in commercial space, these taxes can eat up savings and cash flow. It is the economically weaker sections who get squeezed the most—because they don't have the means or networks to navigate these costs, yet must comply or face legal consequences.

The deeper problem is philosophical. Property ownership should be a pillar of economic independence and dignity. Yet, the government treats it as an opportunity to extract revenue at every stage. From the moment of purchase to every year of ownership, the citizen is made to feel like a tenant in their own home. This mental shift—where ownership does not equal freedom but continued obligation—is a subtle yet powerful tool of control. It normalizes financial servitude in the name of civic responsibility, while giving very little in return.

4.6 Electricity and Water Bills Include Hidden Taxes

Electricity and water—two of the most fundamental resources for survival—are no longer just utilities in India. They've become quiet revenue channels through which governments extract money from citizens without them even realizing it. On the surface, these bills appear to reflect the simple cost of consumption: units used, multiplied by a set rate. But a closer examination reveals a complex layering of hidden taxes, surcharges, and cross-subsidization mechanisms that go unannounced and unexplained. These covert financial extractions are masked behind technical jargon like "fuel surcharge," "regulatory duty," "infrastructure cess," and "urban development fee," which makes it difficult for the average household to understand why their monthly bills continue rising despite relatively stable usage patterns.

Take the electricity bill, for instance. It's common for the consumer to assume that the amount is based solely on the number of units consumed multiplied by a fixed per-unit rate. However, the actual bill includes an array of supplementary charges that inflate the final amount. There is the electricity duty, a state-imposed tax that varies significantly across states, sometimes as high as 15% of the bill. Then comes the fuel adjustment charge (FAC), which is supposed to compensate for changes in fuel costs but is often calculated in opaque ways. Add to that fixed charges, wheeling charges, and transmission losses, and suddenly, the bill becomes a dense matrix of costs that few can decipher.

These are not minor fees. In many states, over 25% of a household's electricity bill consists of taxes and surcharges. Yet this indirect taxation is never declared publicly or debated in policy discussions. Citizens are essentially taxed for using electricity, which is no longer a luxury but a necessity. What's worse, these taxes are imposed even when the quality of service is poor. Frequent power cuts, voltage fluctuations, and delays in complaint resolution plague urban and rural areas alike. It creates a paradox where people are paying more for something that remains unreliable. There is no accountability mechanism to justify these charges—just silent compliance enforced through digital billing systems and automated penalties.

Water bills are no different. In municipalities where metered water supply exists, the bill usually includes a "water tax" or "sewerage charge" that quietly adds a substantial percentage to the total. In areas where water is not metered, a flat fee is levied, which often does not reflect actual usage but is still layered with unexplained levies. The irony is sharpest in states facing severe water shortages or irregular supply. People are paying a water tax for services that arrive for only a few hours a week or require them to install private motors and tanks to store the meagre supply. Meanwhile, tanker mafias operate with impunity, further monetizing water in ways that bypass any form of taxation or regulation, while the legitimate taxpayer continues to be squeezed.

These hidden taxes serve multiple political agendas. First, they create a revenue stream that requires no public announcement or legislative scrutiny. Second, they keep the illusion alive that income tax or GST are the only forms of taxation. Most people do not question their utility bills because these payments are normalized as part of household expenses. The hidden taxes buried within them are thus the most efficient form of invisible taxation—constant, automated, and unresisted. Governments across party lines have found this method extremely useful, especially in the face of fiscal deficits. Why propose new taxes that may provoke backlash, when the existing utility system can extract money silently?

This model of hidden taxation disproportionately affects the poor and lower-middle class. For them, the electricity and water bill form a significant chunk of monthly expenditure. They often live in densely populated areas where government supply is irregular, forcing them to rely on alternatives like generators, UPS systems, and bottled water—none of which are subsidized. Thus, not only are they paying for faulty government service laced with hidden taxes, but they are also forced to invest extra just to make up for those service gaps. This leads to a double economic hit that remains unaddressed in mainstream policymaking.

Cross-subsidization makes things even worse. Industrial users or commercial properties often pay a reduced rate, and the shortfall is recovered from residential users through adjusted tariffs. In simple terms, the common man is paying more so that malls, factories, and IT parks can pay less. This unfair structure is rarely discussed in public forums because it benefits powerful lobbies. Even when states do announce reforms or subsidies, the burden eventually shifts to the average user in subtle, untraceable ways. A government may claim to offer "free electricity" up to a certain limit, but they quietly raise the surcharge for those consuming just beyond that threshold. It's a bait-and-switch game that punishes efficiency and rewards political narrative.

The technological infrastructure used to manage electricity and water billing has made the system even more skewed. With digital meters and centralized data collection, it has become easier to overcharge, auto-deduct, and penalize users without human intervention. Disputing a bill has become an arduous process involving online forms, automated helplines, and municipal apathy. The citizen has been completely disempowered—reduced to a passive payer in a system that does not explain, justify, or reform itself. The digitization of corruption has ensured that theft is no longer done with bribes, but with algorithms.

If these taxes and surcharges were being used to improve infrastructure, the narrative might be different. But in many places, the funds collected through electricity duty and water taxes disappear into opaque budgets, mismanaged utilities, or political schemes that have little to do with utility improvements. The water pipeline project that never gets completed; the power substation that never gets upgraded—these are the lived realities of taxpayers who silently fund a broken system. And because these taxes are embedded in bills rather than levied separately, they escape public scrutiny, media attention, and electoral debate.

This invisibility is what makes them the most dangerous. Hidden taxes on electricity and water are not just financial tools—they are instruments of control. By turning basic needs into taxable commodities with unclear structures, the state keeps its population in a perpetual state of economic vulnerability. It's a system where the poor cannot escape dependence, the middle class cannot build stability, and the rich navigate through loopholes. The illusion of cheap utilities hides the reality of an expensive survival, where every drop of water and every unit of electricity carries a cost far beyond its stated price.

4.7 Taxing What You Eat, Use, and Wear

Everyday consumption—the basic act of living—is quietly being taxed in ways that many citizens neither notice nor understand. The things you eat, wear, and use daily are embedded with layers of taxation that often go unnoticed due to the lack of transparency in pricing. From packaged food and toiletries to school uniforms and kitchen utensils, hidden GST slabs and cascading input costs result in a systematic extraction of money from consumers, disguised within the price tag. What was once considered accessible and essential is increasingly turning into a revenue source for the state, making basic survival an expensive affair for the average Indian.

When the Goods and Services Tax was introduced, it promised uniformity and the removal of cascading taxes. However, it ended up creating a complex web of tax rates on items that should ideally be exempt or taxed minimally. Basic food products like biscuits, cereal, ghee, ready-to-eat meals, pickles, sauces, and even frozen vegetables attract GST ranging from 5% to 18%. Toiletries such as soaps, shampoos, toothpaste, and sanitary napkins often fall under 12% or 18% slabs, which directly affects the poor and middle class who already spend a large portion of their income on household maintenance. This tax burden is not only financial—it's psychological. It forces families to downgrade their lifestyles, compromise on nutrition, and cut down on hygienic essentials to stretch their limited incomes.

The GST Council once argued that unbranded or unpackaged goods are exempt, but in an urbanized economy where branding and packaging are necessary for safety and compliance, this exemption holds little value. A rural family might buy unpackaged flour or rice, but in cities, consumers are compelled to buy sealed, branded alternatives to avoid adulteration. Thus, in practice, most urban consumers pay tax even for food grains. Items like honey, jaggery, butter, cheese, and dry fruits, though culturally linked to Indian health systems and everyday diet, are taxed as luxuries. Even baby food, feeding bottles, and children's clothes beyond a certain price attract

GST. The message is clear—unless you're poor enough to eat and wear only the most basic and unprocessed products, the state will treat your survival as a taxable event.

Clothing, another fundamental human need, has not been spared either. While garments under ₹1000 are taxed at 5%, anything above that threshold is hit with 12% GST. This blanket treatment ignores the fact that ₹1000 barely buys a single piece of decent clothing today. Middle-class families looking to purchase uniforms, winter wear, or festival clothes end up paying disproportionately high taxes. Footwear follows a similar regime. Slippers and shoes costing under ₹1000 attract 5% GST, while others are taxed at 18%. This regressive slab structure penalizes quality-conscious consumers and creates a market where cheap, poorly made products dominate due to their lower tax liability, pushing families toward low-durability, unsafe, or environmentally harmful goods.

Household items—buckets, kitchen tools, storage containers, cleaning products, light bulbs, and furniture—also carry GST between 12% and 28%, depending on their material and branding. Even stainless-steel utensils, which are widely used in Indian kitchens for their safety and durability, are taxed despite their necessity. This taxation model does not distinguish between need and luxury. A pressure cooker and a dishwasher are both taxed, even though their social utility and affordability are worlds apart. The policy framework seems to treat all purchases as voluntary indulgences rather than survival-driven expenditures.

This blanket approach to taxation is where the injustice becomes institutionalized. It imposes the same percentage burden on a struggling labourer and a corporate executive buying the same soap or rice packet. It does not factor in income inequality or household budgets. GST, which was designed as a consumption tax, ends up becoming a regressive tool when applied to essential commodities. The more you consume just to live decently, the more you are punished. And since prices include tax, people rarely understand how much of their money is going to the government. There is no tax invoice in a retail store or small shop—just a total price that hides the state's share behind it.

Corporate sellers often pass on input taxes to the consumer while enjoying input tax credit mechanisms that small vendors don't have access to. This means that your purchase from a supermarket contributes to corporate balance sheets while simultaneously making you the last payer in a long chain of tax recoveries. This silent transfer of tax liability from big businesses to end consumers goes unchallenged due to the invisibility of the process. The entire structure is designed to exploit scale and automation—where systems benefit the organized sector while extracting maximum compliance from ordinary buyers through pricing.

Beyond the financial toll, there's a deeper philosophical violation here. A democracy must ensure that access to food, clothing, and essential goods is treated as a right, not a taxable transaction. When a woman pays tax on sanitary pads or a child's raincoat, it's not just money—it's a quiet signal that even her dignity and health are considered revenue sources. This dehumanizing view of citizens as perpetual taxpayers, rather than people with fundamental needs, reflects a system that has lost touch with its ethical obligations. The state's urge to generate income, no matter how, has overridden its responsibility to make life affordable and dignified for its people.

Even seasonal demands are not spared. During festivals or school reopening seasons, prices for sweets, uniforms, and related goods skyrocket—not only due to demand but also due to embedded taxes. Yet, no one questions it because it has become normal. The normalization of taxation on survival needs is perhaps the most dangerous outcome of this system. When people stop noticing or questioning what they're paying for, the state gains absolute power. It no longer needs to justify anything. It simply sits behind the price tag, quietly collecting money as citizens unknowingly surrender parts of their livelihood in every transaction.

4.8 Tax on Education

Education, long considered a noble pathway to empowerment and national progress, is increasingly being reshaped in India as a commercial commodity subject to systemic extraction. Under the current tax regime, while preschool, primary, and secondary schooling remain exempt from GST, nearly every other form of knowledge delivery—be it higher education, vocational training, professional courses, or e-learning platforms—carries an 18% GST burden. This policy reflects a deeper malaise: the commodification of learning and the transformation of education into a lucrative revenue stream for the state. In a country where access to quality education already remains unequal, such a taxation structure effectively punishes aspiration and reinforces the class divide between the privileged and the striving majority.

Take the case of private universities and deemed institutions offering graduate and postgraduate programs. These institutions are often not classified under the "education institution" bracket that qualifies for tax exemption. As a result, the services they procure—ranging from software tools and online infrastructure to faculty consultations and guest lectures—are all taxed at 18%, and this cost trickles down to students through bloated tuition fees. The GST mechanism doesn't differentiate between an elite business school and a small-town coaching center trying to prepare students for a government exam. In both cases, the learner is penalized for seeking advancement. Unlike many essential services that the government supports through subsidies or exemptions, education is increasingly treated as a voluntary luxury—a stance that is not only unethical but also short-sighted in a country with a massive youth population.

The rise of e-learning, especially post-pandemic, has introduced a new frontier for educational taxation. Platforms offering coding bootcamps, online certifications, competitive exam prep, language training, and professional development courses are all categorized under the standard 18% GST slab. What this means is that students paying for an online UPSC course or a digital marketing certificate from a reputed platform are paying nearly one-fifth of their course fee directly to the government. This is despite the fact that these platforms fill a critical void in public education infrastructure. When state colleges are underfunded and government coaching centers scarce or absent, online learning emerges not as an option but as a necessity. Taxing it heavily punishes self-driven learning while letting the government avoid responsibility for formal education reform.

Vocational training—meant to uplift blue-collar laborers, artisans, and rural youth—is another victim of this taxation strategy. While a few government-certified programs are GST-exempt, the vast majority of practical skill-based courses offered by private institutes are taxed. A course in welding, tailoring, computer hardware repair, or nursing assistant training can attract 18% GST even though these are meant to generate employability among the economically disadvantaged. This effectively raises the entry barrier for those who need it most. Unlike affluent students who can afford costly coaching or degrees abroad, these learners are priced out of opportunity in their own country. The taxation here is not just economic—it is ideological. It suggests that only the elite deserve to learn without penalty, while the rest must pay for every step they take towards dignity.

Adding to this structural inequity is the ambiguity in classification. Many institutions and course providers struggle with the confusion around whether they qualify for tax exemptions. A university-affiliated distance education provider might be GST-exempt while an identical private course with better content and delivery is taxed. This inconsistency not only complicates compliance but also encourages loopholes and legal battles. The government, instead of simplifying the framework to prioritize learning, has turned the tax maze into a revenue collection instrument. The very idea that education can be interpreted as a "service" subject to commercial tax rules reflects a systemic disregard for the transformative role of knowledge in nation-building.

What deepens the irony is the lavish exemptions given to industries that are far less critical than education. Religious pilgrimages, political event organizing, and even gambling-related services in some cases enjoy lighter scrutiny or categorization benefits. Meanwhile, a student learning Python online or a teacher offering remote classes is viewed through the same taxation lens as a corporate vendor. This flattening of categories betrays the intellectual blindness of the tax architecture. It does not value learning as sacred or strategic—it sees it merely as a transactional exchange. This is a dangerous precedent in a country that claims to aspire toward global knowledge leadership.

One must also examine the mental toll this taxation system takes on parents and students. With job markets becoming more competitive and the demand for higher credentials rising, families invest heavily in education—often taking loans or spending their savings. The inclusion of GST inflates the burden silently, as it's rarely itemized separately in course pricing. This silent erosion of educational affordability forces many to abandon quality courses, settle for substandard options, or worse, drop out entirely. When the choice is between daily survival and taxed learning, survival wins—and the nation loses a future skilled contributor. The government may celebrate rising enrolment statistics, but they mask a growing dropout rate among those pushed out by cost, not capacity.

In the larger scheme of things, taxing education also contradicts the spirit of constitutional mandates and national goals. India's New Education Policy envisions an inclusive, tech-enabled, and lifelong learning culture. But how can this be achieved when every technological touchpoint in education is taxed? A professional seeking mid-career upskilling through a ₹10,000 course pays ₹1,800 in GST. A teenager learning coding via an app pays the same rate as a company buying luxury software. The policy is tone-deaf to the very objectives it claims to support. Education cannot flourish in an environment where taxation outpaces facilitation.

Finally, there is the philosophical question: Should knowledge ever be taxed? In ancient Indian tradition, education was seen as a sacred exchange between guru and shishya—never monetized, let alone taxed. Today, that sacredness has been replaced by financial extraction. The state, rather than being a facilitator of enlightenment, has become a toll collector on the road to personal growth. By taxing those who seek to rise through learning, it ensures that the ladder of education is not extended but shortened, accessible only to those who can afford the price of aspiration.

4.9 You Pay More Than You Realize

The Indian citizen today lives in a landscape of taxation so deeply embedded and disguised that most people have no idea how much of their money is actually going to the government. What looks like a normal price tag is often a cleverly wrapped final figure that includes several layers of direct and indirect taxes. The problem is not just that these taxes exist, but that they are intentionally hidden from the common man, making it nearly impossible to distinguish between the actual cost of a product or service and the state's share in it. This invisibility is not a flaw—it's a design. A system that collects without accountability thrives best when its methods are invisible, and this is exactly what modern taxation has become.

Take, for example, your monthly electricity bill. It doesn't just include the energy charges; it often hides surcharges, fuel adjustment costs, and state-imposed levies. A ₹1000 bill may include ₹200–₹300 of government-imposed extras. Water supply, considered a basic human right, is subject to local taxes and infrastructure cess. Mobile phone recharges, DTH services, and internet packages all carry GST in the 18% slab, which means nearly one-fifth of what you pay is a tax—yet it's rarely felt because the charge is integrated into the total. When you eat out at a restaurant, GST of 5% or more is charged directly on the bill, but you also indirectly pay taxes on each ingredient that went into that food, thanks to the input tax system. You're essentially being taxed on taxed goods.

This cascading taxation—though technically addressed under the GST regime—still lives on in new forms. Import duties on raw materials, fuel surcharges, cess on fuel, and environmental levies on industries all add layers to the cost of producing goods. Companies pass on these costs to the end-user. You, as a consumer, become the final sponge soaking up every layer of tax that the chain accumulates. There's no escaping it. Every shampoo bottle, pair of shoes, t-shirt, packet of bread, and even a school notebook contains not just the price of the product but an invisible government premium baked into it. If you try to calculate how much tax you pay annually, you'll be shocked to realize that your income tax is just a small part of the burden—the real weight lies in your consumption.

The illusion of affordability is maintained by slicing the truth into small, digestible lies. A biscuit pack that costs ₹10 doesn't feel like a burden, but it hides GST, transport fuel taxes, packaging taxes, warehouse charges, and more. Multiply this by the hundreds of items you buy every month, and the total becomes staggering. The government's revenue increases quietly, while your savings quietly vanish. The structure is so well-oiled that you will never receive a cumulative annual tax statement detailing what you paid across all forms of taxation. And because it's hidden behind routine purchases, there's no revolt—just acceptance. It's a trap where the victim doesn't even realize they've been caught.

This also distorts the perception of government generosity. Politicians boast of subsidies and schemes for the poor, but these are often funded by the very people they pretend to help. When a ₹500 LPG subsidy is handed out, the government has often already earned more than that through taxes on refills, transportation, and oil imports. When free food grains are distributed, the funding often comes from GST collected on other essentials like kitchen gas, salt, or hygiene items. This circular model is never explained to the public, because it would expose the truth—that the state takes from your right hand and gives to your left, calling it welfare. The net result? You always pay more than you realize, and the illusion of help becomes a tool to silence dissatisfaction.

In urban areas, where consumption is higher and brand dependency is unavoidable, the tax burden is even more brutal. Branded rice, milk, and pulses carry taxes, while their unbranded counterparts may be exempt—but safety concerns, shelf life, and health consciousness force city dwellers to stick with the branded versions. Similarly, fast-moving consumer goods—detergents, soaps, packaged food, cosmetics—are heavily taxed, even though they're considered daily necessities. This disproportionate impact of hidden taxes on urban middle-class households goes unaddressed in policy debates because their pain is subtle and silent. They don't qualify as poor, and they are not rich enough to evade the cost.

Moreover, there is no opt-out mechanism. Whether you are jobless or a millionaire, as long as you buy something, you're contributing to government revenue. There's no rebate for the unemployed, no exemption for students, no refund for the elderly. Even those below the income tax threshold are involuntary taxpayers through consumption. You can live without an income, but you cannot live without spending. This universal compulsion is what makes indirect taxation the most powerful and least debated financial control tool available to any regime.

This system also undermines real economic awareness. Most Indians believe they pay little to no tax if their income is below the exemption limit. They fail to recognize that their daily tea, bus ride, phone call, and electricity usage are all tax-enabled. This ignorance suits the state perfectly—it allows for control without protest, funding without transparency. The less people know about the total cost of their citizenship, the easier it is to rule over them while pretending to serve them.

The final blow comes when governments use this hidden tax revenue not for real development but for populist optics—large statues, ad campaigns, mega events, and temporary giveaways before elections. The funds you unknowingly surrendered through hidden taxes are often recycled into spectacles meant to distract you from the very structure that keeps you poor. It's not just economic exploitation—it's psychological manipulation.

The silent weight of hidden and everyday taxes is perhaps the most cunning form of economic control in modern India. Unlike direct taxes that announce themselves openly, these levies are embedded in the everyday rhythm of life—tucked inside fuel costs, tucked under your mobile plan, curled into your electricity bill, and stitched into your grocery bag. They don't need your consent, and they don't offer clarity. They are built on your ignorance, running on autopilot while you work harder and save less. This isn't just taxation—it's a quiet siphoning of your freedom, masked as normal life. And unless you see through the illusion, you will continue paying for your own chains, one small purchase at a time.

Chapter 5
Poor Pay the Most – The Silent Victims

In a country where economic disparity has long been normalized, the tax system subtly sharpens its blades against those least capable of resistance—the poor. While public discourse revolves around income tax slabs and corporate loopholes, the real burden creeps silently into the lives of daily wage workers, laborers, and informal sector earners through a web of indirect taxes and inflated costs. These citizens, who barely earn enough to survive, end up funding a disproportionately high share of national revenue without ever realizing it. From overpriced food to overtaxed utilities, their every basic need becomes a taxable event. The very mechanisms designed to protect and uplift them often reinforce their vulnerability, trapping them in a cycle of contribution without recognition. There is no tax rebate for hunger, no deduction for living in slums, and no credit for resilience under hardship. They are the anonymous financiers of a nation that rarely acknowledges their sacrifice, and when policies are designed, their lived reality seldom enters the equation. This chapter exposes how the architecture of taxation is skewed against the poor, not just through policy but through deliberate ignorance of their existence.

5.1 GST Makes Daily Items Costlier

The implementation of Goods and Services Tax (GST) in India was initially marketed as a game-changer that would reduce prices, simplify the tax system, and encourage economic growth. However, for many ordinary citizens, especially in the lower and middle-income groups, it has had the opposite effect, making daily essentials significantly costlier. When GST came into effect, the government's promise of reduced tax burden on everyday items seemed promising. The idea was to create a uniform tax structure, which would reduce the cascading effect of multiple taxes and, theoretically, lower costs for the average consumer. But in reality, while some goods were brought under lower tax brackets, others saw a sharp rise in their prices due to the new tax regime. Items that were once considered affordable for the average household have now become more expensive, leading to frustration and resentment among consumers. The most immediate and noticeable impact of GST on daily life has been in the increase in the prices of food, fuel, medicines, and household goods. For instance, basic food items like milk, wheat flour, and rice saw a rise in prices due to the imposition of GST at rates that were previously not applicable under the old system. These are items that form the backbone of every household's expenditure, and when their prices rise, it impacts the entire family's budget. For low-income households, who rely on these staples, the increase in cost directly hits their already stretched budgets.

The effect of GST on the cost of living is felt particularly hard by the urban and rural poor. While urban areas have better access to a variety of goods and services, the rural poor often rely heavily on local markets for their basic needs. With GST raising the cost of essentials, it becomes even more difficult for them to make ends meet. The government's argument for a single tax rate, which is meant to simplify the system, seems to have overlooked the varying economic conditions across different regions and income groups. As a result, the ones who end up paying the highest price are those who can least afford it. The increase in the cost of daily essentials is not just an issue for the low-income households, but for the entire middle class as well. For people living in cities, even a marginal increase in the cost of goods can lead to significant changes in their overall expenses. This is particularly true for families that are already struggling with rising housing costs, transportation expenses, and school fees. The combined pressure from all these fronts has made it increasingly difficult for the middle class to maintain their standard of living.

While the government has made efforts to promote GST as a reform aimed at benefiting the economy as a whole, the benefits have not been clearly visible to the majority of consumers. The idea that the price of goods would decrease due to the unification of taxes has not been fully realized. In fact, the reverse has happened for many products. The argument that GST would reduce the hidden tax burdens of the past is also undercut by the fact that many goods and services, which were previously untaxed or taxed at lower rates, now fall under the GST regime at higher rates. This creates a situation where consumers are paying higher prices for items they use every day, while the promise of simplification and lower taxes remains unfulfilled. For the ordinary citizen, this is an unfair burden that adds to their financial stress and affects their purchasing power.

With the price hikes on essentials like food and fuel, many households are forced to cut back on other discretionary spending to make up for the increased cost of living. These sacrifices may not be immediately apparent, but over time, they lead to a decline in overall well-being. The extra expenditure on GST-laden goods means that families have less money to spend on things like entertainment, leisure, or saving for the future. In addition, the increase in prices has disproportionately affected vulnerable groups in society, such as the elderly, the disabled, and those on fixed incomes. These groups are particularly sensitive to price increases and are often forced to go without basic necessities due to the higher costs associated with GST.

What adds to the confusion is the inconsistent application of GST rates across various sectors. The prices of certain goods fluctuate depending on their classification under the tax structure. For instance, the GST rates on luxury goods and non-essential items may remain high, but the prices of everyday household items, which should ideally have lower rates, have seen an increase. The discontent surrounding these price hikes has led many to question the true intent behind the GST reform. Was it really designed to benefit the common man, or has it only served the interests of large businesses and multinational corporations? The public's perception of GST as a burdensome tax that increases the cost of living seems to be growing stronger, and it is unlikely to subside until tangible benefits are seen at the consumer level.

In the end, the most significant challenge with GST's implementation is its failure to reduce the financial burden on the people who need it the most. Instead of seeing lower prices for their daily needs, the average citizen is grappling with increased costs that push them further away from economic stability. The expectation of a simplified, fairer tax structure has been marred by the reality of higher living costs, and until this issue is addressed, the promise of GST remains far from being fully realized.

5.2 No Tax Benefits for the Poor

In the Indian tax system, a glaring and deeply unjust reality remains largely unspoken—the poor, who are the most financially vulnerable, receive no meaningful tax benefits or targeted relief, despite bearing a disproportionately heavy indirect tax burden. While the narrative of progressive taxation is repeatedly cited in political discourse, in practical application, the system is skewed in favour of those with structured incomes, documented financial activity, and access to tax planning resources. For the poor, who mostly work in the informal sector, earn irregular incomes, and consume essential goods and services disproportionately taxed through GST, there are neither exemptions nor rebates to lighten their load. The result is a system that rewards privilege and punishes subsistence.

India's direct tax exemptions, such as those under Section 80C or deductions for health insurance, home loans, or investments, are tailored to benefit those who have stable incomes and financial literacy. These schemes mean nothing to a daily wage labourer, a rickshaw puller, a street vendor, or a domestic worker whose income is not even taxed directly. For them, the only tax they ever pay is embedded invisibly in the cost of every good and service—bread, soap, oil, transport, school notebooks, electricity recharge, second-hand clothes, mobile top-ups. The tax system does not recognize these payments because they occur silently and continuously, without billing records or itemized invoices. Yet, they contribute to state revenue with the same percentage as any middle-class or upper-class consumer, making their burden grossly regressive.

Take the case of a family earning ₹10,000–₹15,000 per month in a city. Every item they purchase—cooking gas, groceries, school stationery, basic medicines, public transport, or even shared housing utilities—comes embedded with GST. Unlike salaried individuals who get tax deductions, this family has no way to claim back anything they pay, no matter how much they struggle. For every ₹100 they spend, up to ₹18 may be collected as GST on various goods and services, depending on the slab. There is no mechanism for a reverse benefit, a rebate, or a credit. There is no concept of "poor citizen tax protection" in the current architecture. The policy assumption seems to be that those outside the income tax net require no support—when in truth, they deserve the most protection from indirect taxation.

Worse still, the official economic philosophy equates taxation with citizenship participation. That logic collapses when applied to the poor. The average urban poor pays more in proportion to their income through indirect taxes than any upper-class citizen. Their contribution is made even more unfair because the goods they consume form a larger share of their total income. For a middle-class person, a ₹50 GST on restaurant food is a negligible blip. For a construction worker, an 18% GST on a pressure cooker or LPG refill is a cruel dent in the monthly budget. And yet, at no point is this imbalance corrected by state policy. There's no GST refund mechanism for poor households, no vouchers, and no monthly subsidy accounts that neutralize what is being extracted daily through consumption.

Adding insult to injury, government welfare schemes that should ideally function as redistributive tools are themselves diluted by embedded tax mechanisms. Many subsidized products still contain GST, just at a lower rate. Affordable housing schemes involve stamp duties and registration charges that eat into the savings of the buyer. Public distribution system (PDS) items are narrowly limited and often fail to meet a family's monthly needs. What they must buy from the open market comes with full GST. Even health services, if taken from private providers due to failure of public infrastructure, come with tax-loaded diagnostics, medicines, and hospitalization bills. There is no insulation or shielding. The poor live in an economic battlefield without armor, exposed to every fiscal weapon used by the state.

Contrast this with the middle and upper classes, who not only have access to tax-saving instruments, but also benefit from structured exemptions and professional advice. The Income Tax Act is replete with provisions that allow housing loan deductions, education loan interest write-offs, investments in ELSS, medical insurance deductions under 80D, and more. A salaried individual with a ₹10 lakh annual income might end up paying less tax than a poor family pays cumulatively in GST and duties over a year, simply because the system allows that person to optimize liability. In effect, the tax regime treats the ability to navigate bureaucracy as a precondition for relief. That leaves the poor—disorganized, informal, and voiceless—entirely outside its concern.

Another layer of injustice lies in the complete absence of tax representation for the poor. The GST Council, the Income Tax Board, and other policy-making bodies are populated by bureaucrats, economists, and political appointees. None of them represent the lived experience of the unbanked, the uninsured, the undocumented working class. Policy continues to be drafted from the top down, with no grassroots audit of its real-world impact on subsistence livelihoods. Data-driven decisions often use consumption indices, but they fail to reflect the hidden sacrifices made by the poor. For example, a decline in rural FMCG sales might be seen as market fluctuation, when in fact it's an outcome of tax-embedded inflation forcing people to choose between food and soap.

The notion of universal taxation often used to justify GST assumes all citizens are equal contributors, but that's a lie cloaked in policy language. When a wealthy family spends ₹1 lakh on a vacation and pays 18% GST, they do so voluntarily and often receive air miles or credit card perks. When a poor woman buys a sanitary pad taxed at 12% (earlier rate), it comes at the cost of something else in her monthly basket—often milk or rice. These are not just economic transactions; they are brutal choices dictated by a blind tax regime. The state appears more interested in appearing efficient than in being fair, more focused on simplifying compliance than on alleviating suffering.

In this system, the poor are punished not because they avoid taxes, but because they cannot navigate the ones they already pay. Their taxes are invisible to policy, undocumented in ledgers, and uncounted in recognition—yet they are very real, cutting into their dignity day after day. Until that structural bias is addressed, any talk of inclusive development remains a hollow slogan echoing through corridors of privilege.

5.3 Inflation – The Hidden Killer Tax

Inflation, though rarely described as a tax, operates with surgical precision as one of the most oppressive fiscal tools that affect the poor more than any other class. While governments and economists debate macroeconomic indicators and monetary policies, the ground reality is that inflation silently erodes the purchasing power of the poorest citizens with ruthless consistency. Unlike income tax, which is direct and visible, inflation extracts value from every rupee a poor person earns without ever declaring itself. It punishes saving, rewards debt, and destabilizes even the most disciplined households. For the poor, it is a shadow tax — unacknowledged, unrecorded, yet omnipresent and devastating.

The destructive nature of inflation on lower-income groups is rooted in how their consumption pattern is structured. A large portion of a poor family's income goes towards essential commodities — food, fuel, transport, housing, and utilities. When inflation strikes, it disproportionately targets these sectors first. The price of rice, wheat, vegetables, pulses, and cooking oil typically climbs at a rate that far outpaces any nominal increase in daily wages or casual labour rates. Unlike the middle class, who can shift budgets, reduce discretionary spending, or absorb the shock temporarily, the poor face a direct assault on survival. What they could afford yesterday becomes unreachable today, and tomorrow forces compromise — less food, fewer medicines, and no safety net.

Inflation in India is particularly harsh because it combines with indirect taxation like GST, which adds a layer of artificial pricing. For example, if wholesale vegetable prices increase due to fuel costs or seasonal shortage, the retail price doesn't just reflect that increase. It also includes transport tax, fuel GST, retail vendor margin, and sometimes even packaging and logistics GST. Each layer adds weight, and the burden rests on the shoulders of the end consumer. The poor don't pay inflation through numbers on a spreadsheet — they pay it with hunger, stress, and deeper debt.

There is also a dangerous psychological effect of inflation that economic models rarely capture. When prices rise consistently, hope begins to shrink. A daily wage worker who could save ₹500 a month in 2015 finds in 2025 that the same expenses now cost him ₹700 more. That erodes his ability to plan, to dream, or to invest in education or healthcare. Inflation becomes a chronic stressor, an invisible presence that stalks every financial decision. For people on the margins, it creates an unending race against time — the longer they wait to buy something, the more expensive it gets. So, urgency replaces logic, and survival replaces aspiration.

While policymakers frame inflation as a consequence of global commodity trends or necessary monetary tightening, these explanations mean nothing to those who queue for ration rice or compromise on their children's nutrition. The Reserve Bank may hike interest rates to control inflation, but such measures rarely touch the informal markets where the poor operate. Interest rate hikes, in fact, make small loans more expensive, pushing poor borrowers further into informal moneylending systems with exploitative rates. Meanwhile, corporates shift pricing upwards to maintain margins, creating a cascade where every product and service — from bus tickets to biscuits — becomes a bit more expensive every few months. The cumulative effect is not just economic decline, but a systemic push into chronic poverty.

The state's indifference to this hidden tax is best seen in how inflation is measured and addressed. The Consumer Price Index (CPI), the most widely cited inflation measure, includes a basket of goods that may not fully represent the rural or urban poor's consumption pattern. Also, averages conceal more than they reveal. A CPI of 6% may hide the fact that food inflation is actually 14% for a poor household, while rent and fuel have risen by 18%. These numbers are filtered through national averages and policy interpretations, never reflecting the true cost of living for a street vendor in Mumbai or a brick kiln worker in Bihar. The official inflation narrative remains sanitized, detached from street-level suffering.

Welfare programs, meant to be buffers against such inflationary shocks, often lag behind the pace of real price rise. By the time Minimum Support Prices (MSP) are revised or MGNREGA wages are adjusted, inflation has already extracted its toll. There is also no automatic inflation-indexed support system for the poor — no food subsidy linked to real-time market prices, no rent control subsidies that adjust monthly, no price capping mechanism that secures essential goods from profiteering during inflationary periods. What the poor get instead are sporadic relief announcements or symbolic gestures that rarely change their lived economic pressure.

There's also a cultural normalization of inflation, which makes it even more dangerous. People grow accustomed to paying more, expecting less, and shrinking their ambitions. The elderly cut medicines in half to stretch prescriptions. Children skip protein-rich meals. Families stop saving entirely, knowing that saved money loses value faster than it grows. Inflation erodes not just wealth but the idea of economic dignity. It turns budgeting into an exercise of desperation and converts households into silent victims of a system that extracts without accounting.

Moreover, inflation benefits the state. It allows the government to reduce real debt burdens, inflate away deficits, and increase tax revenues through nominal growth in prices. As prices rise, the GST collected on goods increases, creating an illusion of revenue growth without actual productivity growth. Inflation, then, becomes a silent accomplice of the government — extracting more from the poor while returning nothing extra. It acts like an invisible tax collector with no accountability and no legal check. The very people who contribute the most proportionally, suffer the most, and gain the least.

Inflation is not just an economic phenomenon — it is a political decision made visible through fiscal choices. When the state spends lavishly on infrastructure and cuts fuel subsidies, when it deregulates essential commodities while keeping GST high, it is choosing to let inflation rise on the backs of the weakest. This is not an accidental outcome — it is a conscious redistribution of economic pain away from boardrooms and into the lanes of slums and villages. Until inflation is treated not as a number but as a lived tax on the poor, it will continue to serve as the most brutal and least acknowledged weapon of financial extraction.

5.4 Even Subsidies Come with Taxes

In India, the idea of subsidies has always been sold as a token of relief for the economically disadvantaged. It is marketed as a protective shield offered by the government to the poor, a gesture of inclusivity in a country marked by deep economic divides. However, this narrative often fails to account for the fact that these subsidies come laced with indirect taxes, service charges, and embedded costs that are invisibly pushed back onto the very citizens they claim to help. What seems like a concession on paper transforms into a sophisticated cycle of give-and-take where the state returns a portion of its collection, only after extracting it through hidden channels. Subsidies, in practice, become instruments of illusion—temporary discounts that are quietly counterbalanced by the invisible tax machinery operating behind the scenes.

Take the example of LPG cylinders, which are often showcased as one of the most direct subsidy benefits received by low-income families. The government offers subsidies on the basic cost of the cylinder, but that doesn't exempt the consumer from paying the Goods and Services Tax. The GST is calculated on the full price of the cylinder, not the subsidized amount, which means the poor still end up paying tax on a benefit that is supposed to support them. For a household surviving on daily wages, this hidden cost, though numerically small, becomes a recurring burden. In this setup, the poor effectively finance their own subsidies, as the state takes with one hand what it seemingly gives with the other.

Public Distribution System (PDS) ration schemes offer another layer to this complex structure. Food grains like wheat and rice are sold at heavily discounted prices, but the journey of these commodities from the procurement centers to the ration shops involves multiple tax incidences. From packaging materials and transportation fuel to storage facility equipment, every step is taxed under GST. These taxes are not visible on the final bill issued to the ration cardholder, but they have already been absorbed into the logistics and infrastructure, which in turn are sustained by public funds drawn from general taxation. As a result, even the poorest consumers using ration cards are indirectly paying back the subsidy costs, not through direct bills but through broader fiscal policies that draw from tax collections affecting the entire consumer economy.

Affordable housing is another domain where subsidies meet indirect taxation. Government housing schemes promise low-cost homes to economically weaker sections, but the structure of such schemes involves statutory fees, service taxes, GST on construction materials, and registration charges. Cement, bricks, iron rods, and electrical wiring are all taxed under GST. Though the end-user may believe they are receiving a subsidized home, what they are actually buying is a product inflated by the cost of multiple taxed inputs. In the long run, their home may cost significantly more than what the initial announcement suggests. This is not only a financial burden but also a psychological betrayal where the most vulnerable sections of society are led to believe they are being uplifted, when in truth they are being rotated through another cycle of extraction.

Electricity subsidies follow a similar template. While subsidized units of electricity may reduce the immediate burden on the consumer's bill, the infrastructure that supports electrification is built on taxed components. From transformers to cables and meters, all electrical goods involved in rural electrification projects attract GST. The public utility services, though government-run, recover these costs through service charges and general budget allocations sourced from tax revenues. As electrification expands to rural and economically backward regions, the actual cost of electricity remains high due to these layered taxes. Villagers who were previously in darkness are now paying for light, not just through monthly bills but also by shouldering the hidden cost of infrastructure.

Healthcare is not exempt from this invisible burden. Public health schemes like Ayushman Bharat offer free treatments and services to below-poverty-line families, but the infrastructure running these hospitals and health centers is built on taxed machinery and equipment. Hospital beds, scanners, x-ray machines, surgical tools, medicines, and ambulances all attract GST. These costs are reimbursed by the government using the same tax money it collects from the public, including the poor. Even when services are declared 'free,' the poor have indirectly contributed to the cost through the taxes embedded in daily transactions, be it on food, fuel, mobile recharge, or bus fares.

E-learning subsidies and vocational skill training programs promoted under various national missions also come with underlying tax complications. Digital tablets, laptops, smart classroom tools, and educational software used in government-funded schemes are procured at market prices with GST included. Students from poor backgrounds receiving free digital access are not spared from this cycle. The funds used to subsidize these digital tools are pooled from the very tax base that taxes basic goods they consume every day. What appears as empowerment is thus offset by an ecosystem that ensures nothing is truly given without a return route.

Transportation subsidies such as concessional railway tickets or bus passes for students, senior citizens, and low-income travellers also rely on infrastructure and fuel that are taxed heavily. Railway engines, spare parts, diesel, and even uniforms for staff attract various taxes. These are not visible on a passenger's ticket, but are factored into the budgeting of government departments and public sector undertakings. So, the discount on the ticket price is only the tip of an iceberg built on invisible levies paid across other economic sectors. This integrated structure ensures that the poor pay not only in money but also through a layered system of indirect contribution to the welfare projects they are meant to benefit from.

By weaving taxation into the very fabric of subsidy distribution, the Indian system turns every act of welfare into a disguised transaction. The poor are never truly recipients; they are consistent contributors, caught in a loop where relief and recovery occur simultaneously through different fiscal channels. Whether they understand it or not, they live in an economy where even generosity has a tax rate.

5.5. Farmers and Workers Not Really Exempt

In India, it is widely believed that farmers and workers—especially in the unorganized sector—are largely exempt from taxes. This belief is used by governments and media as a soft justification for the lack of direct welfare support, as if tax exemption automatically ensures economic comfort. But this is a myth. The truth is that even though these groups may not pay income tax, they are deeply entangled in a web of indirect taxes, inflated costs, and systemic financial pressures that quietly extract money from their limited earnings. The illusion of exemption masks a cruel reality: the poorest laborers and cultivators are paying taxes embedded in everything they consume, use, or depend on, without receiving proportionate benefits or representation in policymaking.

Farmers in particular are often presented as beneficiaries of a benevolent system. There is no income tax levied on agricultural income, which sounds like a fair policy considering their fluctuating and uncertain earnings. However, the inputs required to produce food—such as fertilizers, pesticides, tractor parts, diesel, irrigation equipment, and even plastic sheeting for greenhouses—are all taxed under GST. None of these costs are subsidized in a way that offsets the taxation fully. Fertilizers attract 5% GST, pesticides 18%, and diesel, which is a critical input, is not under GST but is heavily taxed by both state and central governments. When the cost of production is inflated through these taxes, farmers end up earning less per yield while paying more to simply keep farming. They are not taxed on output, but the system punishes them on every input.

Even the seeds that small farmers buy—unless they're traditional and saved from previous harvests—are often genetically modified or hybrid seeds purchased from corporates. These are bundled with taxes and marketed as high-efficiency solutions, but they trap farmers into cycles of dependency. Once used, hybrid seeds can't be reused, forcing the farmer to repurchase them every season, each time with added GST. The promise of modern agriculture turns into a treadmill of recurring expenses, all of which include hidden levies. Despite being "exempt" from tax, the farmer is cornered into paying through every stage of the production cycle.

The situation of rural and urban workers in the informal sector is no better. These workers might be street vendors, construction laborers, domestic helpers, tailors, barbers, and small shop assistants—none of whom are enrolled in income tax systems. Yet they are taxed daily, passively, and invisibly. Every time they recharge a mobile phone, buy soap, board a bus, or drink tea, they pay GST. Their housing rents are inflated because construction materials are taxed. Their food is more expensive because of the layered taxes on transport and logistics. Their tools—be it a sewing machine, a spade, or even a bicycle—carry GST. Their lives are structured around the consumption of basic items taxed at rates they do not understand but must pay nonetheless. This indirect tax structure hits them harder than the rich, because it reduces their already meagre disposable income.

Even government welfare schemes like MNREGA (Mahatma Gandhi National Rural Employment Guarantee Act) have hidden tax implications. A labourer under MNREGA is paid from government funds, which are generated through nationwide tax collection. The tools used in the scheme—shovels, pipes, bricks—are purchased with tax-paid money. Food distributed during the project is taxed. Transportation of laborers to the site may include taxed fuel. In essence, the money circulates back to the system through indirect channels, leaving the worker barely ahead. The economic value of a day's wage is reduced not by direct deductions but by an ecosystem that ensures every rupee earned is immediately subject to multiple drains.

Most informal workers are not covered under formal labour laws. They don't get health insurance, paid leave, pensions, or maternity benefits. But when they go to government hospitals, they pay for medicines that carry GST. If they try to educate their children, they buy notebooks, pens, uniforms, and schoolbags that are all taxed. Even if tuition is waived, the hidden costs persist. When they send money home using banking services or mobile wallets, transaction charges apply. Every layer of economic activity they engage in—no matter how small—is taxed in some form. Their contributions to the economy are not recognized, but their role as taxpayers is silently assumed.

Farmers, similarly, are not given priority access to healthcare, education, or legal support. Their suicides are often blamed on weather or debt, but few mention the heavy cost of farming under a taxed input system. For those who manage to sell their crops in open markets, the prices are volatile, controlled by middlemen, and barely cover expenses. Government procurement schemes offer Minimum Support Prices, but access to these schemes is limited, bureaucratic, and often rigged by corruption. Most marginal farmers end up selling in local mandis where commissions and market fees again chip away at their earnings. These market fees are a form of localized tax that adds no value to the farmer's life but ensures a functioning administrative layer that survives on their transactions.

Even cooperative societies, which were once a lifeline for collective farming and savings, are now subject to taxation, regulatory filing costs, and administrative compliance. Setting up or running a farmer producer organization (FPO) involves accounting services, software, internet, and office rent—all of which come with embedded taxes. These costs are transferred back to the farmers in the form of fees or reduced margins. With such systemic pressures, the idea of tax exemption becomes a mocking joke. The farmer may not file returns, but he pays daily. The worker may not be registered, but he contributes endlessly.

This reality turns the idea of tax exemption into a technical gimmick rather than a lived truth. The poor, unorganized, and agrarian segments of the population bear a disproportionate share of the tax load through consumption and compliance that isn't visibly named as "tax," yet functions exactly like one. Their tax is paid through survival itself.

5.6 Less Income, More Burden

In a taxation system where contribution is supposedly based on capacity to pay, India's tax structure offers a baffling contradiction—those with less income often bear a disproportionately higher burden. The irony deepens when we examine how indirect taxes like GST, fuel levies, and surcharges are structured. Unlike direct taxes that can be graded based on income brackets, indirect taxes are uniform, meaning everyone pays the same rate on goods and services regardless of their economic status. A multi-millionaire and a daily wage labourer both pay the same 18% GST on basic household items like soaps, toiletries, mobile bills, and even train tickets in some cases. This flat-rate taxation ignores financial disparities and ends up penalizing the poor for consuming the same essentials as the rich.

For those in lower income brackets, every rupee counts. When a person earning ₹10,000 a month pays ₹1,800 in indirect taxes due to GST and other charges, it constitutes nearly 18% of their total income. For someone earning₹1,00,000, this percentage drops significantly in relation to their income. This disproportionality is a hidden regressive mechanism within the tax system. While the government claims to offer subsidies and support schemes for the poor, it is simultaneously extracting a significant share of their spending power through indirect taxes. This contradictory cycle traps the economically weak in a loop where they struggle to meet daily needs and pay hidden taxes that silently erode their limited earnings.

Even the exemptions that exist in the tax structure often bypass the real necessities of the poor. For example, unbranded food grains or milk might be exempted from GST, but processed foods, basic health items, footwear, and clothing beyond ₹1,000 are taxed. A daily wage worker may avoid buying branded rice, but cannot escape paying taxes on packaged salt, cooking oil, or basic medicines, which are essential for survival. The more they try to uplift their lifestyle slightly—by purchasing slightly better goods or accessing improved services—the more taxes they end up paying, reducing their incentive and ability to upgrade their standard of living.

Transportation, a daily necessity for workers and small vendors, is another example of this silent burden. Bus fares, auto rides, and even railways include multiple hidden taxes in fuel and service categories. The poor who travel long distances for work every day end up surrendering a portion of their income to the tax net disguised within ticket prices. They don't realize that a share of their already meagre earnings goes to the government even before they earn a fair wage. This is not a system of fair contribution, but one of institutional extraction designed without empathy for the financially vulnerable.

Another major area of indirect taxation hits the poor through telecom, internet, and digital services. As digital transactions and Aadhaar-linked services become compulsory, even the poorest are forced into using smartphones and mobile data plans, all taxed at 18%. The state, while pushing for digital inclusion, has failed to offer these services at tax-free or subsidized rates to the economically disadvantaged. The very tools that could empower the poor are taxed heavily, turning what should be gateways to opportunity into sources of exploitation.

Even employment and entrepreneurial opportunities come taxed. Small vendors trying to grow by accepting digital payments or setting up small e-commerce storefronts face compliance requirements and platform fees that include service taxes. Informal labourers, gig workers, and part-time earners are subtly pushed into economic ecosystems where their tiny incomes are chipped away by invisible tax claws. For example, a delivery person earning ₹15 per delivery loses a part of their pay when platforms apply GST on commissions. The earnings are already low, and taxation without direct notice adds insult to injury.

There is also a psychological toll on the poor. Every price hike justified by

"GST revision" or "tax adjustment" is a silent reminder that the system is not designed for them. The constant budgeting, the compromise on quantity or quality of essential goods, and the inability to save a rupee without worrying about tomorrow's price hikes—all create a mental cage of poverty reinforced by policy choices. The idea of tax justice disappears in such a context, and instead, taxation becomes an unavoidable punishment for being poor in a growing economy.

While the wealthy enjoy deductions, exemptions, and tax-saving instruments, the poor get none. They don't have financial planners or the luxury to invest in insurance or long-term schemes to save tax. Their incomes are too low to fall under income tax brackets, but that doesn't shield them. They pay tax every time they eat, drink, travel, or communicate. And what do they receive in return? Minimal access to healthcare, poor-quality education, decaying infrastructure, and unreliable public services—none of which reflect the scale of their contribution.

This silent imbalance—the poor paying more relative to their means while receiving less—represents a structural failure of tax design. A system that doesn't recognize economic disparity in its architecture cannot claim fairness. When the gap between income and burden widens, hope diminishes. The real tragedy is not just in rupees lost, but in the opportunities denied, in the dreams deferred, and in the quiet despair of millions who work hard, pay their share, and still remain trapped.

5.7 No Service is Free – You Pay Like a Customer

In a nation where the government projects itself as a provider and protector, the illusion of "free services" has become one of the most widespread deceptions. For the poor and working-class citizens, public services such as healthcare, education, transportation, and even safety are often advertised as rights or social welfare provisions. However, in practice, these services operate under a cost-recovery model that treats every citizen, regardless of economic background, as a paying customer. From token charges at government hospitals to user fees at ration shops, from stamp duties in welfare-related documentation to taxes embedded in every government-issued utility bill, nothing comes without a price. The idea of "free" services vanishes the moment one closely examines the layered structure of embedded costs.

Start with healthcare. Government hospitals may waive the consultation fee or provide subsidized medicines, but the patient is still paying indirectly. Taxes on life-saving medicines, hospital equipment, diagnostic services, and transport to the hospital are all transferred to the end-user in some form. Even government ambulance services often charge per kilometer after a certain limit, and blood tests in "free" diagnostic camps are usually outsourced to private labs that embed taxes into service charges. A poor individual facing an emergency ends up paying not only from their pocket but also through the indirect tax channels baked into the system. They don't just suffer from disease—they suffer from systemic insensitivity disguised as policy efficiency.

Public transport, another supposed lifeline for the poor, is no different. Whether it's a state-run bus, a train, or metro service, the ticket cost includes components of service tax, fuel surcharge, and maintenance levy—all passed on to the traveller. What was once envisioned as an affordable and accessible mode of transport for workers and daily-wage earners now functions like a commercial service provider. The poor, who rely on public transport for survival, bear a greater burden in proportion to their earnings, as these costs consume a significant share of their daily income. Even student passes and subsidized schemes are limited, and accessing them often involves bureaucratic hurdles and token payments that negate their purpose.

The situation is even more troubling in education. Government schools, often highlighted as free, demand payments in various hidden forms—exam fees, uniform costs, notebooks, school maintenance charges, and parent-teacher committee funds. In higher education, as previously discussed, an 18% GST applies to online courses, vocational training, and professional education. Even certification programs under government-sponsored skill initiatives may involve indirect taxes or service fees for certification, assessment, or placement services. Poor students, already burdened with social and economic disadvantages, are taxed on their attempts to break free from their condition.

Another area is documentation and legal compliance. Ration cards, Aadhaar updates, voter IDs, caste certificates, and income certificates often require either official fees or unofficial payments. While the services are mandated to be free, the reality includes travel costs, documentation charges, and often the need to pay intermediaries—whose services are taxed. When poor families need to establish their identity to access welfare, they must navigate a system that bleeds them with invisible costs under the guise of administrative expenses.

Utility services—water, electricity, and sanitation—are perhaps the most glaring examples of taxation disguised as service. Poor households often reside in areas with erratic supply and poor infrastructure, yet their bills include various surcharges, electricity duties, fuel adjustments, and GST on private providers. Even subsidized connections are subject to conditions, and arrears or late fees hit hardest when incomes are unstable. The poor don't just pay with their money, but also with their time, dignity, and emotional resilience as they chase officials to correct bills or restore interrupted services.

What makes this structure especially cruel is its silent normalcy. No receipts clearly list these hidden taxes. No government form acknowledges that a part of every transaction is being siphoned off through a policy that targets the weakest. The messaging remains: these are free or subsidized services for the underprivileged. The reality is far from it. This gap between political narrative and practical experience erodes trust and reinforces the perception that poverty is punished, not alleviated, in modern India.

Even funeral services for the poor, which should be a dignified closure, are often chargeable. Crematoriums may levy service charges, wood or gas may be taxed, and if the family cannot afford the rituals, they're left with stripped-down processes devoid of dignity. The idea that a citizen can die without being taxed becomes laughable when the final rites themselves are monetized under some revenue model.

To compound matters, private services entering welfare domains make things worse. Whether it's private garbage collection, tanker water supply, mobile health vans, or educational NGOs, their services are taxed, and the costs passed on. Government failure creates space for privatized welfare, and the poor pay more for the same service they were once promised for free. Their silence becomes the cost of survival.

This section reveals a truth that many in power refuse to acknowledge: the poor in India are not passive beneficiaries but active payers in a rigged system. They are customers to a government that sells them their own rights and taxes their struggle. No slogan, no manifesto, no welfare scheme can change the fact that they are being charged, at every step, for being born without privilege.

5.8 Poor Die Paying, Get Nothing Back

The notion of "paying your dues" is ingrained deeply into society's understanding of taxation, where it is expected that individuals who contribute to the economy through taxes will, in turn, receive something in return—whether it is social benefits, infrastructure development, or quality services. But for the poor, this system operates differently. They live a reality where, despite contributing disproportionately through taxes in every form, they receive very little in return. Instead, their existence is marked by a relentless cycle of payment and deprivation, where they die still owing, without ever receiving their due.

Every transaction, no matter how small, is burdened with hidden taxes. From the basic necessities like food and water to healthcare and transportation, the poor pay taxes on almost every part of their daily existence. Yet, when it comes to receiving adequate government support, public services, or social security, they are often left wanting. Government-run hospitals are overwhelmed and underfunded, and what little relief is available is often plagued by inefficiency, corruption, and a lack of basic infrastructure. While the middle class and wealthy can afford private healthcare or insurance, the poor are left to bear the brunt of an overburdened, underfunded system. What's worse is that these services, if they are available, are not truly free—there are always hidden charges, fees, and taxes, either directly through user fees or indirectly through the high cost of living.

This paradox is especially evident when looking at the state of public education and social welfare. While education is supposedly a right, the hidden costs of uniforms, books, transportation, and even administrative fees add up to a sum that is simply unaffordable for the poor. Scholarships and free education schemes are either non-existent or severely limited. Similarly, welfare programs like food security or housing subsidies are riddled with delays, corruption, and bureaucratic red tape. The poor, who rely on these programs to survive, end up trapped in a cycle where they pay through indirect taxes on their income and consumption, but never see the promised benefits materialize in their daily lives.

Even in death, the poor continue to pay. Funerals, which should be a time for closure, are monetized to an extent where the poorest cannot even afford a dignified final rite. From the costs of funeral ceremonies to the taxes levied on essential goods for burial or cremation, the poor are again hit hardest. At the same time, the very services that could alleviate their plight—like pension funds, life insurance, and healthcare benefits—are either inaccessible or completely inadequate.

The greatest tragedy lies in the fact that the poor, despite paying into the system their entire lives, do not receive the social safety net that they so desperately need. They die still in debt to a system that profits from their labour and taxes but offers them nothing in return. Their labour, their contributions, and their very existence are commodified for the benefit of others, yet in the end, they remain excluded from the benefits that should rightfully be theirs.

This system is not just exploitative; it is a cycle of denial that stretches across generations. The poor, often born into poverty, are forced to remain in this perpetual state of indebtedness, paying taxes they can never escape, contributing to a system that benefits only the already privileged. The state, which should be their protector, instead turns a blind eye to their suffering. This relentless taxation is not only a financial burden but a spiritual and emotional one as well, as the poor see no tangible results of their contributions—no improvement in healthcare, no better roads, no quality education, no safety net in times of crisis. Instead, they die paying, and their deaths go unnoticed by the very system they sustained.

In a system that promises equal rights and justice, this is the ultimate betrayal: the poor give their lives to a system that takes without giving back, leaving them with nothing but empty promises and a never-ending cycle of taxation that they can never break free from. They are not simply the victims of a flawed policy—they are the invisible casualties of a system that has failed to deliver on its most basic promises of equity and social justice.

5.9 Local Products Suffer Due to Import Pricing

The notion that imported goods are a luxury reserved for the elite is outdated in today's Indian market. Surprisingly, products imported from other countries often land on Indian shelves cheaper than locally produced equivalents. This anomaly stems from a tax framework that favours global supply chains over domestic artisans, farmers, and small manufacturers. For the economically disadvantaged, this imbalance affects not just their purchasing choices but also the livelihood options available to them. Local products, which should ideally be the backbone of rural and semi-urban employment, struggle to compete—not because of quality, but because of how tax structures silently penalize them.

When a product is imported, it typically benefits from a well-oiled system of bulk production, logistics optimization, and in some cases, free trade agreements that reduce duties. In contrast, local producers face a layered maze of taxation: GST on raw materials, manufacturing, packaging, transport, and even marketplace commissions. At every stage, the tax burden accumulates—without offsetting subsidies or policy support—pushing up the final retail price. A handmade cotton kurta from a rural cooperative may cost more than a factory-made, mass-imported T-shirt from Southeast Asia, not because the latter is inherently cheaper to produce, but because the former is weighed down by a disproportionately heavy tax chain.

The problem magnifies in sectors like agriculture and handicrafts. For example, locally produced pulses or spices may pass through multiple intermediaries before reaching the consumer. Each intermediary pays GST on services like transport, warehousing, and packaging, inflating the price of the final product. Meanwhile, imported packaged food items often arrive pre-processed, are sold in large volumes, and attract lower effective tax rates due to strategic classification. Even electronics assembled in India with imported parts often cost more than ready-to-use imported devices because of the layered taxation during each phase of the supply and manufacturing chain.

For the poor, this tax-driven price gap between imported and local products has far-reaching implications. It reduces their ability to support local markets—not because they prefer foreign brands, but because affordability forces their hand. When an imported non-stick pan is cheaper than a locally-made iron skillet, the choice isn't one of loyalty or patriotism; it's one of survival. Similarly, low-income consumers often end up choosing chemically treated, imported food products over organic local produce simply because of the lower shelf price. Inadvertently, they fund international industries while their own community's producers remain unsold, unrecognized, and eventually unemployed.

On the production side, this tax structure is a slow poison for small-scale industries. Local weavers, potters, farmers, and other micro-producers are priced out of their own domestic markets. With high input costs, inadequate GST credits, and minimal government incentives, they can't scale up or even break even. The bureaucratic burden of tax compliance—complicated returns, e-invoicing, and frequent notices—adds a layer of psychological taxation that deters many from entering the formal economy altogether. Those who do are barely surviving, constantly undercut by mass-produced imports that arrive tax-efficient and policy-favoured.

This scenario creates a dangerous precedent where self-reliance becomes a slogan rather than a policy reality. 'Vocal for Local' campaigns sound noble, but the silent tax war being waged against local goods ensures that consumers and producers alike are pushed toward foreign-made alternatives. The poor bear the brunt—either by paying more for local goods or sacrificing quality and sustainability for cheaper imports. It's a lose-lose situation in which national productivity suffers, local skills decay, and cultural heritage is commodified out of existence.

In the grand narrative of taxation, this invisible gap is rarely acknowledged. But for India's poor and lower-middle class, it is an everyday reality. Their purchases are political acts shaped by tax codes they never consented to and policies they can't influence. They are forced to watch their communities deteriorate while multinational brands flood their neighbourhoods, not because they're better, but because they're less taxed. This is not just a market failure—it is a systemic injustice, quietly endorsed by the very structures meant to uplift the nation's most vulnerable.

5.10 Work till Death, Gain Nothing – The Big Illusion

In a nation where the average citizen spends the better part of life working relentlessly, one would assume that this hard-earned labour results in some measure of stability, comfort, or return. Yet for India's poor and lower-middle-class population, this belief is nothing more than a manufactured illusion. The reality is brutal—despite decades of backbreaking work, the poor retire with little to nothing. From cradle to grave, they are squeezed by a system that rewards consumption over contribution and taxes survival more than luxury. This endless cycle of effort without reward is not a misfortune but a deliberate design of an economic framework that thrives on their perpetual labour without ever ensuring meaningful upliftment.

Daily wage workers, contractual laborers, small farmers, and informal sector employees form the backbone of India's economy. They work without job security, pensions, healthcare, or any real safety net. Still, they contribute directly and indirectly to the nation's tax revenues. Every time they buy a matchbox, a sachet of shampoo, a bus ticket, or mobile data, they pay embedded taxes. But what do they get in return? Public hospitals are underfunded, education quality in government schools remains questionable, and employment guarantee schemes are inadequate and inconsistent. Despite being the most compliant class—contributing a significant portion of indirect taxes—they are the least prioritized in policymaking.

This economic structure keeps them on a treadmill—always running but going nowhere. They pay GST on almost everything they consume, service charges on utilities, fuel taxes to get to work, and education taxes if their children aspire to break free from the poverty trap. Yet when they grow old, there's no financial cushion. Provident fund benefits are largely out of reach for informal workers. Pension schemes either don't reach them or provide a meagre amount that doesn't even cover basic monthly needs. The myth that "hard work pays off" becomes a cruel joke when one realizes that a lifetime of labour often results in old age spent in debt, dependence, or destitution.

The illusion is further sustained by token schemes and one-time subsidies that provide temporary relief but no structural change. An occasional LPG subsidy or a free ration during elections does not compensate for decades of tax extraction through everyday essentials. These superficial benefits are then paraded as evidence of a benevolent system, while in truth, they merely mask the deeper failure of redistribution. Government welfare, rather than being a right of the citizen, is offered as charity—while the real cost of living remains beyond reach due to indirect taxation on every stage of consumption.

There is also a psychological taxation involved—the loss of hope. For many poor Indians, dreams of a better life are replaced by a resigned acceptance of survival. They see their hard work feeding a system that enriches those at the top while they continue to borrow to pay hospital bills, sacrifice meals for children's tuition, or delay retirement indefinitely. Their identity becomes reduced to that of a voter, a consumer, and a labourer—never as a citizen with equal rights and dignified expectations. The burden of lifelong work becomes not a pathway to liberation, but a permanent form of economic imprisonment.

Meanwhile, corporate entities and high-income groups navigate the tax maze with professional help, exploiting loopholes and benefiting from policies tailor-made to encourage wealth accumulation. They invest, get returns, claim rebates, and use strategic philanthropy for image polishing. In stark contrast, the poor can neither invest nor save, let alone dream of legacy-building. Their only inheritance to the next generation is survival skills in a rigged economy. The idea that taxation fuels national development collapses when development consistently bypasses those who contribute most passively and suffer most visibly.

This broken promise of reward for labour turns India's economic engine into a machine of quiet cruelty. The dignity of work is stripped away when it fails to offer dignity in life. The poor do not resent hard work—they've never known anything else. What they resent, often silently, is the lie that their efforts matter equally. They may not have a voice in elite policy circles, but their silent sacrifice speaks volumes. They are the invisible taxpayers, the unacknowledged nation-builders, and the true sufferers of a system that works them to the bone and gives them nothing in return but illusion.

The Indian tax system doesn't just overlook the poor—it quietly exploits them. From the daily cup of tea to the final rites of death, the underprivileged pay at every step, often without realizing how deeply the system extracts from their lives. They receive no proportional relief, no visible return, and no meaningful change that honours their lifelong contribution. Instead, they are trapped in a relentless loop of labour, inflation, and invisibility. The cost of poverty is not just having less—it is paying the highest price for the smallest share of national progress. This isn't merely tax injustice; it is the silent foundation on which an unequal economy stands.

Chapter 6
Fear, Confusion, and Forced Compliance

The Indian tax system is not just a network of financial obligations—it is a psychological structure built to instil fear, foster confusion, and extract submission. From the outside, it may appear to be a set of well-organized laws designed to collect revenue for the nation. But for the average citizen navigating this labyrinth, it feels more like a hostile battlefield where the weapons are ambiguity, arbitrary deadlines, complicated terminology, and the ever-looming threat of penalties or prosecution. The ordinary Indian does not merely comply with tax rules; they surrender to them, often without understanding what they are complying with. The very design of the system seems to discourage clarity and self-sufficiency. Instead, it cultivates dependency—on tax consultants, on interpretations, on approvals—and punishes even unintentional errors with disproportionate severity. In this chapter, we explore how the tax structure goes beyond monetary transactions and acts as a psychological cage, forcing citizens to live in a constant state of stress, vigilance, and confusion.

6.1 Complicated Rules Made on Purpose

The Indian tax system thrives on complexity, not clarity. Laws are written in a language that seems intentionally convoluted, filled with technical jargon, circular references, and footnotes that redirect readers to other equally obscure documents. This is not an accidental by-product of an evolving legal structure; it is a strategic design. By ensuring that the average citizen cannot make sense of the rules without external help, the system creates an artificial dependence on professionals who make a living decoding the bureaucratic mess. The complexity also works as a convenient defence for the state. When citizens make mistakes, the government can claim it was their responsibility to understand the law. When officials overreach or misuse their power, they can hide behind the ambiguity of poorly framed clauses. This shield of legal obscurity benefits the state and its enforcers, while the public, especially small earners and the self-employed, are left in a state of perpetual anxiety.

Even the most basic terms are often poorly defined or interpreted in conflicting ways by different departments. For instance, the criteria that determine whether an individual is a salaried employee or an independent professional may vary across tax forms, leading to discrepancies that can trigger scrutiny or penalties. Similarly, the definition of "income" may seem straightforward, but in practice, it involves layers of calculation, inclusion, and exclusion that often contradict each other depending on which act, rule, or circular is cited. This legal vagueness ensures that no citizen ever feels completely safe or confident about their compliance. There is always a lingering doubt: "Did I do this right?" The fear of having misinterpreted a clause or missed a mandatory declaration is constant. It forces individuals into a state of over-cautiousness, where avoiding risk becomes more important than understanding rights.

The tax codes are also bloated with frequent amendments. Every year, during the Union Budget, the finance minister announces changes—some small, others sweeping—that modify deduction limits, redefine categories, or shift filing procedures. These changes are often announced with patriotic rhetoric, implying simplification or taxpayer relief. In reality, they add new layers of exceptions, qualifications, and conditions. Instead of replacing outdated provisions, new ones are simply stacked on top, creating a monstrous legal entity that few can navigate without specialized training. Taxpayers are then expected to stay up to date with every new clause, or risk falling into non-compliance unknowingly. This constant evolution ensures that the goalpost is always moving. There is no solid ground to stand on, no stable ruleset to learn once and follow for a lifetime.

This complexity isn't just about difficult language or shifting definitions. It extends to forms, portals, and procedures. Income tax returns involve not just basic income and expenditure figures but various schedules, annexures, and verification processes that differ based on profession, income bracket, and even geographical region. GST return filing is another nightmare. With multiple forms like GSTR-1, GSTR-3B, and annual returns, each with separate due dates and intricate input tax credit rules, even small businesses require full-time attention to just stay compliant. One missed field, one incorrect figure, or one delayed submission can lead to system lockouts, penalties, or cancellation of registration. The digital systems, rather than simplifying things, have become electronic gatekeepers of an already twisted domain.

The deliberate complexity also serves to intimidate. It sends a subtle message: "You are not smart enough to understand this on your own." That message, repeated year after year, fosters a culture of silence and obedience. Citizens become afraid to question officials, fearing that doing so will expose them to closer scrutiny. They stop trying to understand the rules and instead just ask others to do it for them—for a fee. It is a vicious loop: the more confusing the system, the more people rely on paid intermediaries, and the less empowered they feel. Even students graduating with commerce degrees often struggle to decipher the actual implementation of the tax code. The tax system is not merely a legal framework—it is a psychological tool that normalizes complexity to such an extent that most Indians have internalized the idea that taxation must always be confusing.

This complexity also plays a defensive role for the state during legal disputes. When citizens challenge unjust tax demands or procedural lapses, authorities often produce circulars, notifications, or retrospective clarifications that reinterpret the law conveniently in their favour. Many of these instruments are not even debated in Parliament. They are issued quietly, sometimes as press releases or departmental memos, but they carry enough force to affect real outcomes. For example, a sudden clarification by the Central Board of Direct Taxes (CBDT) can redefine what counts as tax-exempt, nullifying court judgments or rendering taxpayer arguments moot. The rulebook is constantly edited in the shadows, making it nearly impossible for the average citizen to ever catch up. The strategic layering of laws, sub-laws, and interpretive tools ensures that the state never loses the upper hand.

In essence, the tax system is built not just to extract money, but to dominate the mental space of the taxpayer. Confusion becomes compliance. Fear becomes routine. Complexity becomes the norm. Those who control the rulebook also control the fate of every honest citizen trying to survive in a nation where ignorance of the law is not just an excuse—it is a manufactured condition.

6.2 Fear of Government Makes People Obey Silently

In India, the relationship between the citizen and the state is deeply influenced by fear, particularly in matters related to taxation. While democratic principles preach that the government serves the people, the reality often reverses that relationship when it comes to taxes. The average taxpayer does not experience the tax department as a helpful institution facilitating national development. Instead, they perceive it as an unpredictable and punitive authority always watching, always ready to strike. This underlying fear is not limited to those evading taxes or hiding income. Even those who are honest, compliant, and transparent feel it. The fear is institutionalized, psychological, and cultural. It stems from stories of midnight raids, notices for minor errors, and lifelong battles in courts over mere procedural lapses. The fear ensures silent obedience. People do not question tax deductions they don't understand. They do not ask why the rates are so high or why certain exemptions are so hard to access. They simply comply, often without knowing what exactly they are complying with.

This culture of silence is reinforced by the sheer imbalance of power between the individual and the tax authorities. A single notice from the Income Tax Department can turn a person's life upside down. The language used in such notices is often intimidating—dense with legal threats and vague accusations that make even the most innocent taxpayer feel guilty. For someone unfamiliar with legalese or without immediate access to professional advice, this can be mentally devastating. There is no hotline that reassures you. No counsellor to guide you. The message is clear: you are on your own. This isolation heightens fear and reduces resistance. Many people, even when wrongly charged or incorrectly assessed, prefer to pay up rather than engage in a protracted and costly appeal process. The cost of proving innocence often outweighs the cost of paying up quietly.

This fear is passed down through generations. Children grow up watching their parents nervously gather documents at the end of each financial year, panic at the sight of tax notices, or spend entire evenings waiting outside the office of a chartered accountant. For salaried individuals, the arrival of Form 16 or the annual TDS summary can trigger anxiety rather than clarity. Business owners live in fear of GST audits and revenue intelligence summons. Even well-off individuals with strong documentation fear being picked randomly for scrutiny. This is not how a healthy tax system function. When fear becomes the dominant force driving compliance, it's no longer taxation—it is psychological coercion masked as civic duty.

The government, knowingly or unknowingly, uses this fear as a tool of control. Rather than simplifying procedures and educating the public, the state often chooses to amplify the fear narrative. Campaigns that highlight severe punishments for tax evasion, the glorification of raids, and the repeated warnings about linking PAN with Aadhaar or meeting e-verification deadlines are all instruments to reinforce the idea that the government is always watching. In some cases, high-profile raids on celebrities or business magnates are used as symbols, sending the message that if even the rich and powerful can be brought down, ordinary citizens should not even dream of defiance. The result is a mass psychology of submission where people internalize the belief that questioning the system is dangerous and noncompliance—intentional or accidental—will lead to harsh consequences.

At the grassroots level, fear is even more evident. Street vendors, small shopkeepers, and gig workers often have no clue about their tax liabilities. Many live in constant fear of being penalized for not registering under GST, even when they are technically below the threshold. This fear is exploited by local officials or so-called tax agents, who charge money to "protect" them from imagined or exaggerated risks. The government rarely steps in to clarify or educate these vulnerable segments, and the fear remains a profitable ecosystem for intermediaries. In some cases, people are tricked into paying taxes or registration fees they were never obligated to pay in the first place. The silence of the exploited is not a sign of approval—it is a symptom of fear too deep to be expressed.

Even the digital infrastructure amplifies fear. The online portals, with their deadlines, warning messages, OTP verifications, and system-generated notices, add an impersonal and mechanical layer to an already stressful process. If a person misses a return deadline by a day or fails to e-verify a form within a specified window, the system responds with automated penalties and restrictive consequences, sometimes without giving any meaningful explanation. There's no human face to appeal to—just a rigid system that assumes guilt before innocence. This lack of empathetic engagement further entrenches fear. Most citizens do not even realize they have rights in such situations. The assumption is always that the government cannot be wrong, and the citizen must bear the burden of fixing the problem, even if it was a glitch or a miscommunication.

What makes this fear more dangerous is that it normalizes passivity. When people become used to a system where fear is the main motivator, they stop thinking critically about how that system should work. They stop asking for transparency, fairness, or simplification. They stop demanding accountability from the government and start blaming themselves for not understanding the rules. This internalization of fear is the ultimate victory for any oppressive system—it doesn't need to physically punish every individual; it only needs to create a climate where everyone believes they could be punished at any moment. That possibility is enough to ensure obedience. And in such an environment, taxation ceases to be a civic obligation. It becomes a ritual of surrender.

6.3 Mistakes Cost Big – Huge Fines

In the Indian tax system, mistakes are treated not as human errors but as criminal offenses. Even the smallest miscalculation, delay, or misreporting can lead to penalties that far exceed the original tax amount. This creates a high-risk environment where citizens, especially those without formal education in finance, live under the constant threat of disproportionate punishment. The system is built in such a way that it assumes guilt before innocence, and it operates on the premise that the taxpayer is either lying, hiding, or cheating. What gets overlooked is the fact that most of these so-called "mistakes" are not attempts to evade tax but genuine errors due to lack of understanding, confusing forms, ever-changing rules, or technological glitches. But in this system, there's little tolerance for confusion—errors are punished severely, and mercy is rare.

The range of fines and penalties can be astonishing. A minor delay in filing income tax returns can cost ₹5,000 to ₹10,000, which is a massive blow to someone earning the minimum wage or running a small business. The irony is that the same government that boasts of financial inclusion and digital literacy punishes its own citizens for not mastering complex legal and fiscal frameworks. Suppose a rural businessman fails to file GST returns on time due to internet outages or simply forgetting the exact due date. In that case, he may face a late fee for each day of delay, interest on unpaid taxes, and even the threat of license suspension. These are not empty threats. They have been enforced, leaving thousands in financial ruin not because they defrauded the government, but because they misunderstood a form or missed a deadline.

Worse still, these fines are not always transparent. Many citizens are not informed clearly about the nature of their mistake or how the penalty has been calculated. A notice arrives, filled with codes and sections from obscure tax laws, demanding payment without explanation. Even if the taxpayer believes they've done everything right, the burden of proof lies entirely on them. They must then navigate the legal labyrinth of appeals, hearings, and paperwork, usually by hiring expensive tax consultants or lawyers. The punishment begins not with the fine, but with the fear and confusion triggered by such notices. People often pay just to escape the ordeal, even if they're not at fault. This turns the tax system into a kind of psychological warfare, where errors—accidental or not—can cost months of peace and hard-earned savings.

A particularly painful example is the treatment of TDS mismatches. Imagine an employee whose employer deducts tax at source but fails to report it correctly to the government. The employee, unaware of the back-end error, files their return in good faith. Later, a mismatch notice is issued, and the employee is asked to pay tax again or prove that it was already deducted. This verification process is not user-friendly and often drags on for months, during which the person might face penalties, interest, or even restrictions on future filings. The fact that the mistake was not theirs becomes irrelevant. The system, once triggered, shows no flexibility. The person is penalized simply because the machinery of compliance did not function as expected. The emotional and financial toll of such events can be devastating.

Another area where mistakes are heavily punished is in the realm of GST. The rules change frequently, portals often lag or crash near filing deadlines, and the compliance requirements are extremely high. A simple error in input tax credit claim can lead to reversed credits, additional tax demands, and interest on the wrongly claimed amount—even if it was claimed in good faith. For many businesses, especially those in manufacturing and retail, where margins are thin, such adjustments can push them into loss. Worse, repeated minor mistakes—even if unintentional—can trigger audits or surveillance flags, branding the business as "risky." Once you get that label, even vendors and clients hesitate to deal with you, fearing their own compliance risks. Thus, a small error in one column of a return can snowball into loss of reputation, business, and peace of mind.

It doesn't end there. There are hidden fines in various corners of the tax system—penalties for not linking PAN with Aadhaar, for non-compliance with tax audit requirements, for incorrect disclosure of foreign assets, and for not maintaining books of accounts beyond a certain income level. Most citizens don't even know these requirements exist until a fine is imposed. This is the hallmark of an unjust system: rules that are difficult to find, harder to interpret, and lethal when broken. The lack of clarity and accessibility ensures that mistakes will happen. And when they do, the penalties are not corrective—they are punitive. They do not teach or help; they punish and shame.

This approach betrays a fundamental lack of trust in citizens. Instead of designing a system that assumes goodwill and educates people to comply better, the state has built a surveillance and punishment machine. It is as if the government expects every taxpayer to act with the precision of a chartered accountant and the discipline of a corporate CFO. This is not a reasonable expectation in a country where financial literacy is still low, where tax rules are dense and jargon-filled, and where digital access remains limited. Yet the cost of falling short is massive. Penalties are not proportional to income or intent. A poor man pays the same late fee as a millionaire. This flat and unfeeling punishment structure ensures that the most vulnerable suffer the most.

In such an environment, people stop taking risks. They avoid legitimate deductions for fear of making a mistake. They under-report income or overpay taxes just to stay safe. They avoid registering new businesses or expanding existing ones because the compliance burden feels like a trap. This loss of entrepreneurial confidence is invisible in tax reports but deeply real in the economy. A system that punishes mistakes with ruthless fines does not build a responsible tax culture—it builds a culture of fear, hesitation, and silent resignation.

6.4 Harassment by Tax Officials

In the everyday life of many Indian citizens, the looming presence of tax officials is not just a symbol of law enforcement but a source of deep psychological pressure. The idea that a government officer can question, summon, or penalize an individual at will—based on mere suspicion or procedural interpretation—has created a culture where fear is more powerful than justice. Harassment by tax officials is not a myth or an exaggeration; it is an experience shared by small business owners, salaried employees, professionals, and even retired pensioners. The system is designed in such a way that it gives disproportionate powers to officials without ensuring an equally strong mechanism of accountability. This imbalance becomes the breeding ground for intimidation, bribery, and mental distress that often goes unreported, undocumented, and unresolved.

One of the most common tools used for harassment is the issuance of notices—cryptic, ambiguous, and often sent without warning. These notices can be for reassessment, mismatch, non-disclosure, or suspected evasion, and they arrive wrapped in legal language that most ordinary people can't decipher. For the average citizen, receiving a notice is like receiving a threat letter. It forces them into a position of defence even before knowing what the accusation is. Many spend sleepless nights fearing raids, frozen accounts, or permanent black marks on their financial records. Even if the notice later turns out to be routine or wrongly sent, the emotional damage and expense caused during the interim are irreversible. This misuse of official authority as a psychological weapon makes the relationship between taxpayer and tax officer one of master and servant rather than citizen and state.

Raids and surveys, which are supposed to be tools of last resort, are often used as instruments of power display. The sudden appearance of tax officials at business premises or homes can damage reputations, paralyze operations, and cause massive loss of trust among customers and partners. The idea behind a raid is to uncover large-scale fraud, but it is increasingly used against small traders, doctors, jewellers, and other middle-class earners. The pretext is always suspicion, but the real purpose is often extortion. The presence of these officials, backed by vague laws and unchecked powers, pushes citizens into compromise. They settle matters unofficially, pay bribes, or surrender rights, just to avoid prolonged harassment. The system, rather than offering recourse, rewards silence and compliance with unjust demands.

Tax officials also harass through endless document requests, repeated inspections, and arbitrary deadlines. Even after full compliance, new queries are raised to keep the case open. This forces people to repeatedly take time off work, engage chartered accountants, and attend hearings. The financial and time cost of simply responding to these never-ending queries becomes higher than the alleged tax dues. Many times, the documents asked for are already submitted or available in government systems, but the burden of providing them again and again lies on the citizen. This unnecessary duplication and obstruction are deliberate. They are used to create pressure, and often, to extract informal payments in return for closing the case or providing a favourable assessment.

Another subtle but dangerous form of harassment lies in the discretionary power tax officers wield over refunds. Many taxpayers—especially small businesses and exporters—complain that their refunds are held up for minor technicalities or vague doubts raised during scrutiny. This delay, often stretching into months or years, causes acute cash flow problems and even bankruptcy. While the government earns interest on holding that money, the taxpayer earns nothing and is expected to wait patiently or beg for what is rightfully theirs. In some cases, refunds are released only after paying an "unofficial fee" through mediators or agents who operate as the hidden bridge between the citizen and the tax office. This institutionalized extortion has become part of the compliance ecosystem, accepted as the cost of doing business in India.

The harassment does not end at the individual level. Entire communities and castes—especially those historically engaged in small trades or informal economy—face targeted scrutiny. Because they operate without heavy paperwork or formal systems, they are presumed to be suspicious. Tax officials, in their hunt for quick targets, focus more on the visible poor than the hidden rich. A small trader in a market is easier to corner than a digital scammer or a corporate manipulator. This results in biased enforcement where vulnerable groups face the full brunt of state machinery while large players escape through legal teams, lobbying, and complex loopholes. Such selective enforcement delegitimizes the tax system and destroys the idea of equal justice under law.

What makes this harassment worse is the lack of accountability for tax officials. If an officer makes a false charge, delays a refund without reason, or issues a notice purely to pressure someone, there is no quick or effective penalty. Internal reviews and departmental complaints rarely result in action. Most officers continue their careers untouched, and in many cases, are rewarded for aggressive tax recovery targets irrespective of the methods used. The absence of a strong taxpayer grievance mechanism ensures that citizens have no real option but to submit. In such a system, power becomes its own justification. The line between enforcement and extortion becomes blurred, and harassment becomes institutionalized.

The true cost of this harassment is not just financial. It erodes the citizen's trust in governance. It creates a mindset of defensiveness where people start seeing the government not as a partner in progress but as a predator waiting for the next slip-up. Instead of fostering voluntary compliance, this atmosphere cultivates fear, secrecy, and resentment. People begin to find ways to hide income, forge records, or stay outside the formal economy—just to avoid the trauma of facing tax officials. This is the paradox of the Indian tax system: in its aggressive attempt to enforce compliance, it often ends up pushing honest people toward evasion, not because they want to cheat, but because they want to survive.

6.5 Online Filing is Hard for the Common Man

The digital shift in India's tax administration was introduced with promises of transparency, simplicity, and ease of access. Yet, for the average Indian citizen, particularly those outside metropolitan areas, online tax filing remains a complex and intimidating ordeal. While the government promotes digital India campaigns with pride, the reality on the ground is vastly different. A major chunk of the population, including small business owners, farmers, senior citizens, daily wage workers, and informal sector participants, struggle not only with digital infrastructure but also with basic digital literacy. The systems in place are not designed with their realities in mind, but with the convenience of the bureaucracy and urban elite at heart. As a result, online tax filing has evolved into a modern-day gatekeeping mechanism that filters access based on technological proficiency, pushing those less digitally aware into helplessness or dependency.

One of the core issues lies in the assumption that all citizens have reliable internet connectivity and the tools to navigate complex government portals. In rural and semi-urban India, internet speeds are often erratic, power outages are frequent, and cyber cafes have become rare. Even if someone manages to find access to a device, the Income Tax portal itself is riddled with bugs, frequent downtime, and confusing interfaces. Numerous citizens have reported system crashes during filing, OTPs that never arrive, PAN-Aadhaar mismatches despite correct data, and repeated logouts that reset all progress. This frustrates even experienced users, let alone someone trying to file their taxes for the first time without professional help. Instead of enabling self-reliance, the system ends up reinforcing helplessness.

Language also becomes a formidable barrier in digital tax filing. Although India has over twenty-two official languages and hundreds of regional dialects, the income tax portal predominantly operates in English, with limited support in Hindi and almost negligible usability in other languages. For millions of Indians who are not fluent in English or lack formal education, this acts as a silent exclusion. A farmer in Tamil Nadu, a small trader in Assam, or a pensioner in Odisha has no meaningful access to the tax filing system unless they seek help from intermediaries. This digital divide is not just a technological gap—it's a linguistic and cultural marginalization that effectively renders a large part of the population invisible in the e-governance landscape.

Even for those who manage to access the portal, the filing process is anything but intuitive. The forms are packed with jargon that mirrors the language of bureaucratic documents rather than plain communication. Sections like 80C, 80D, or 44ADA are not self-explanatory. Terms like "advance tax liability," "self-assessment tax," "TDS mismatch," and "form 26AS reconciliation" may as well be in a foreign language to an average filer. There is no simple walk-through, no built-in guidance tailored to different income categories, and no real-time assistance embedded into the portal. The FAQs are often generic, outdated, or buried under layers of links. Even the AI chatbots, where available, respond with templated messages that hardly resolve real-world problems. What was supposed to be a digital assistant ends up being an impersonal wall.

The system's over-reliance on linking different government databases also makes things unnecessarily complex. A minor mismatch between bank records, Aadhaar data, PAN details, or mobile numbers can derail the entire filing process. In many cases, citizens don't even know where the error is, and the portal won't explicitly tell them. They are left jumping between different platforms—NSDL, UIDAI, bank portals, GSTN—trying to make corrections that often require long waiting periods or physical verification. This scattered architecture goes against the promise of digital convenience. Instead of centralizing services, it disperses them in a confusing maze that deters rather than empowers.

Moreover, frequent updates and changes in the filing rules or software itself make it almost impossible for a layperson to keep up. Every year, new tax slabs, new forms, revised deadlines, or compliance requirements are introduced. The government's assumption is that people are constantly following these changes via websites or news channels, which is a luxury most don't have. There's no effective mass-level awareness campaign in vernacular languages, no targeted training for vulnerable groups, and no practical education at the school level on how to file taxes digitally. As a result, the system continues to favour the informed and disadvantage the uninformed.

This growing digital dependence has opened a new market of middlemen and tax filing consultants who charge fees even for the simplest filings. What should have been a self-service system now forces people to outsource tasks they could have done themselves if the platform was truly user-friendly. For many, this is a recurring annual expense they cannot afford. The digital model was meant to reduce corruption and remove intermediaries, but ironically, it has created new forms of dependency that are exploitative in nature. The government absolves itself of responsibility by claiming that digital access is universal, while in truth, millions are priced out of their own participation.

The ultimate irony is that those who manage to cross all hurdles and file successfully are still not guaranteed peace. They remain vulnerable to system glitches, miscalculations in auto-filled data, or post-filing discrepancies flagged by automated risk engines. A digitally filed return is no protection against future harassment if some obscure checkbox was left unticked or a decimal point misplaced. The system is unforgiving to human error, even when that error is caused by its own complexity. For the common man, this doesn't feel like digital progress—it feels like digital punishment.

In the grand narrative of India's march toward a digital economy, online tax filing has been painted as a symbol of modernization. But beneath the surface, it tells a different story—a story of alienation, exclusion, and forced adaptation. Until the system is redesigned from the citizen's point of view—with empathy, simplicity, and multilingual inclusivity—it will continue to be a fortress, not a gateway. And the common man, left standing outside that gate, will see technology not as an ally but as yet another silent oppressor in the name of compliance.

6.6 Have to Pay Consultants for Basic Things

In an ideal democratic tax system, a citizen should be able to understand and comply with their tax obligations without having to seek professional help for basic matters. However, in India's current tax structure, what should be simple has been deliberately complicated to such a degree that ordinary people are forced to rely on paid consultants to carry out even the most basic procedures. This dependency has become a deeply entrenched norm, silently siphoning money from taxpayers and reinforcing a system where understanding the law is a privilege, not a right. The need to hire chartered accountants, tax return preparers, or agency intermediaries just to decode standard compliance steps like income declarations, GST filings, or refund claims is not a sign of citizen incompetence—but a glaring indictment of how confusing and inaccessible the system has become.

At the root of this problem is the excessive technicality of tax regulations. From the structure of tax slabs to the requirements for deductions and exemptions, the law is saturated with fine print that constantly changes. The common man is expected to be aware of various sections—like 80C, 80D, 24(b), 10(14), and others—that are rarely explained in simple language. Each new Finance Act or budget update introduces fresh interpretations, exemptions, and compliance windows. Yet, the government provides no consistent, vernacular, citizen-friendly education around these changes. The result is a growing knowledge vacuum that only consultants and chartered professionals are equipped to fill—often at high and recurring costs to the taxpayer.

For salaried individuals, the problem begins with Form 16 itself, a document that's supposed to simplify filing but is filled with confusing rows of data, partial disclosures, and assumptions that require verification. If an employee switches jobs mid-year, the complications multiply. Many are unaware of how to handle double taxation, advance tax, or the need to reconcile Form 26AS. A small misstep in choosing the right ITR form or missing a deadline can trigger notices, penalties, or audits. Instead of empowering people to correct these themselves, the system intimidates them into hiring help. What should be an annual civic duty has turned into a professional dependency enforced by fear.

In the GST regime, the situation is worse. Small business owners, freelancers, and shopkeepers must navigate an exhausting cycle of monthly filings, reconciliation between GSTR-1 and GSTR-3B, e-way bills, and frequent changes to invoice rules. Despite the introduction of QRMP (Quarterly Return Monthly Payment) schemes and e-invoicing systems, the majority still depend on GST practitioners just to maintain compliance. Every minor deviation—from wrongly classified HSN codes to late filing of NIL returns—can attract fines or freeze access to ITC (Input Tax Credit). This has created an environment where consultants are no longer optional but essential for survival.

Even schemes that claim to simplify compliance, like the faceless assessment or pre-filled returns, often require review and correction. In faceless systems, taxpayers cannot directly communicate with officers, and any submission must be legally precise to avoid misinterpretation. This procedural rigidity makes professional representation almost mandatory. Middle-class individuals who once managed to file on their own are now pushed to seek consultants just to navigate the faceless maze. And these consultants, often unregulated, charge widely varying fees depending on the complexity involved—even for basic clarifications.

The dependency doesn't end at return filing. Responding to scrutiny notices, rectification requests, TDS mismatches, refund delays, or defective return notices involves technical knowledge of income tax laws and online procedures. Even seasoned professionals admit that the system lacks consistency in behaviour. One year, a particular method might be accepted without issue; the next, it might trigger a warning or penalty. This lack of predictability drives even cautious, honest taxpayers into consultants' offices, fearing they may accidentally attract scrutiny despite best efforts.

What's deeply troubling is the way this system fuels a new informal industry where consultants act as gatekeepers. From small towns to major cities, unlicensed agents now operate tax filing centers that prey on digital illiteracy and regulatory complexity. Often, they offer low-cost services without full transparency, occasionally making errors that later fall back on the citizen. Yet, people flock to them not by choice but by necessity, because the official system does not provide a truly accessible or guided route for independent navigation. The government turns a blind eye to this rising shadow market, even though it exists only because of the system's built-in opacity.

There is also a psychological toll in constantly needing someone to interpret your relationship with the state. The idea that a citizen needs a middleman to fulfil their basic legal duty distorts the very notion of democratic governance. It breaks the sense of trust and clarity that should define interactions with the law. Instead of feeling like active participants, taxpayers feel like passive victims of a system whose language they do not speak and whose mechanisms they do not understand. This dependency becomes generational—where younger family members automatically assume their parents' consultant will take care of filings, without ever learning how the system works.

In the long run, this creates two classes of taxpayers—those who can afford personalized professional help and stay compliant without stress, and those who cannot, and live in constant fear of making costly mistakes. A democratic tax system should not require expert interpretation at every step. Until the architecture of compliance is rebuilt to be human-centric, multilingual, and intuitive, the common man will continue to pay an unofficial "consultancy tax" year after year—not to the government, but to the growing army of intermediaries the system has indirectly created. And in doing so, the state will have failed in its most basic promise—to make civic participation equal, transparent, and accessible to all.

6.7 Legal Maze: Tribunal Delays, Appeals, and No Quick Justice

For an average Indian citizen caught in a dispute with the tax department, the pursuit of justice becomes a soul-draining odyssey through a legal system that is both overburdened and opaque. Whether it is a wrongful demand, a misinterpretation of deductions, or a dispute over refund eligibility, seeking redress means navigating an elaborate maze of tribunals, appellate bodies, and judicial forums that are plagued by procedural complexity and endless delays. The citizen, already financially stressed, is left feeling powerless in front of an unyielding state machinery that appears more focused on defending its stance than delivering timely justice. The idea of "innocent until proven guilty" fades into the background, replaced by a default suspicion that forces the taxpayer to prove their honesty at every step while the system drags its feet on verdicts.

When a taxpayer receives a disputed tax demand or a penalty, the first formal redressal begins with the Commissioner of Income Tax (Appeals), commonly referred to as CIT(A). While this forum is supposed to act as a fair appellate body, in reality, decisions are often delayed for months or even years. The pendency at this level is massive, owing to inadequate staffing and the routine practice of adjournments. Many appeals are dismissed on technical grounds—like improper format, minor documentation gaps, or filing delays—which further discourages genuine grievances from being heard on merit. Even when the appeal is heard, there's no guarantee of impartiality. Since CIT(A) officials are still under the broader umbrella of the Income Tax Department, the perception of bias naturally persists in the minds of appellants.

If the taxpayer is dissatisfied with the CIT(A)'s decision, the next recourse is the Income Tax Appellate Tribunal (ITAT), an independent quasi-judicial body. While ITAT benches are known to function more professionally than lower appellate bodies, the process of getting there is not only time-consuming but also financially draining. Filing an appeal to the ITAT requires professional legal representation, which adds to the already mounting costs of compliance and defence. Additionally, ITAT benches are not uniformly spread across the country. In smaller towns or cities, taxpayers must travel to metro centers where benches are located, which creates logistical hurdles. Even then, the backlog of cases ensures that final verdicts take years to arrive—by which time, the disputed amount may have already been forcefully recovered by the tax department through bank account attachment or refund adjustment.

Should the ITAT ruling go against the citizen or if further redressal is needed, the case may proceed to the High Court and eventually the Supreme Court. At this stage, the entire process enters the realm of full-scale litigation, where the legal language becomes arcane, and timelines stretch into decades. Most individuals give up before this point, simply because the cost of pursuing justice—court fees, advocate charges, documentation, time off work—is greater than the disputed tax amount itself. For a system that claims to uphold fairness and equity, this is a bitter contradiction. Only corporations or high-net-worth individuals with deep legal pockets can afford to sustain the battle; the average taxpayer is bullied into silence or submission.

Even when judgments favour the taxpayer, implementation is another nightmare. The department often appeals against orders that go against it, using taxpayer money to fund its legal resistance. This creates a vicious cycle where the system keeps challenging the very people who fund it, delaying the finality of justice and creating an adversarial relationship between the state and its citizens. Refunds resulting from favourable verdicts can take years to process. And in some instances, officials continue to harass the taxpayer despite court rulings, using loopholes to reopen old assessments under new pretences.

The other critical issue is the inconsistency in rulings. Due to the fragmented and overburdened nature of the tribunal and court system, different benches often interpret the same law differently. What is accepted in one region is rejected in another, leading to a lack of standardization. This inconsistency forces taxpayers and professionals into a constant state of doubt—never sure whether their compliance will be accepted or questioned based on shifting interpretations. The department rarely issues clarifications or binding circulars to resolve such conflicts. This legal ambiguity becomes yet another tool of indirect coercion, where the threat of dispute is used to keep taxpayers submissive.

Compounding all of this is the mental and emotional exhaustion of dealing with an adversarial legal system. Taxpayers—many of whom are law-abiding citizens—report feeling criminalized simply for defending their interpretation of the law. The constant barrage of notices, the need to present themselves at hearings, the burden of collecting and preserving years of documentation, and the anxiety of potential financial seizure take a heavy psychological toll. Many individuals decide to accept unjust tax demands just to avoid this ordeal, sacrificing their rights for the sake of peace.

What emerges is a scenario where the pursuit of justice becomes a punishment in itself. The legal infrastructure—far from being a support system—acts like a slow, grinding wheel that wears down the very people it is supposed to protect. When ordinary citizens begin to view justice as inaccessible or futile, the social contract between the state and its people breaks down. Compliance is no longer based on trust or mutual respect but on fear and survival instinct. This silent erosion of legal faith has deep consequences, not just for taxation but for democracy itself. And until the tax dispute resolution mechanism is overhauled to become fast, citizen-friendly, and truly independent, the average Indian will continue to feel like a lone voice fighting a faceless giant in a courtroom that rarely listens.

6.8 Following Rules Feels Like a Full-Time Job

In the present-day tax system, where the rules are intricate, ever-changing, and often contradictory, adhering to them has become an exhausting and overwhelming responsibility that consumes far more time and energy than should be necessary. Taxpayers are no longer merely fulfilling an obligation—they are constantly engaged in a battle to keep up with regulations that seem designed to trip them up rather than guide them. What was once a straightforward task of paying taxes has evolved into a multi-layered process that feels like a full-time job. The mental and emotional drain of trying to stay compliant while juggling work, family, and personal commitments has become a significant burden for millions of people.

The tax system's sheer complexity requires taxpayers to constantly monitor updates, amendments, and notifications. Every year, the budget brings new tax provisions and modifications to existing laws, along with confusing technical jargon and policy nuances. For instance, tax slabs may shift, deductions may change, new reporting requirements might be introduced, or entire sections of the Income Tax Act could undergo revisions. Keeping track of these modifications, especially for those who are not tax professionals, becomes a constant cycle of confusion. People find themselves spending hours reading through tax-related notices, updates from the government, and sometimes even blogs or news articles just to understand how these changes affect their filings. The effort to keep pace with these updates is not just a minor inconvenience—it often feels like a second job, requiring taxpayers to educate themselves about complex and technical issues that most are not trained to understand.

Moreover, the online filing system has become a confusing labyrinth in itself. Each year, the e-filing portal undergoes modifications, sometimes with new fields to fill, new documents to upload, and new verification processes to complete. Even with pre-filled forms, taxpayers must verify and update information to avoid errors, which often require a deep understanding of tax laws. The need for constant vigilance is overwhelming. A seemingly innocent oversight—such as neglecting to update a bank account number or forgetting to declare an additional source of income—could lead to penalties, audits, or a rejection of returns. For the average person, this constant attention to detail consumes hours of their time, which could have been spent on more productive or fulfilling activities.

Taxpayers also face the constant fear of receiving notices. These notices are often ambiguous, giving little clarity on why they have been issued or what needs to be rectified. The dread of receiving such notices forces individuals to keep meticulous records, fearing that any mistake could result in long legal battles or financial penalties. This vigilance extends to ensuring that every receipt, transaction, and form is accurately documented—adding to the administrative burden that already takes a significant toll on their personal and professional life. Many individuals even hire personal assistants or use specialized software to track their finances and stay on top of deadlines, all because the burden of compliance is too great to handle alone.

The time commitment doesn't end with filing. The process often involves addressing disputes, following up on refunds, answering department queries, or appealing unfair assessments. Each of these tasks requires a considerable amount of attention and effort. Once a taxpayer submits their return, they must monitor its status regularly to ensure that there are no pending issues. This means checking the portal, waiting for acknowledgment, reviewing any discrepancies, and sometimes re-submitting documents. Even once the return is processed, taxpayers can find themselves in prolonged follow-up situations regarding refunds or requests for additional documentation. In many cases, individuals are compelled to revisit the tax portal to track their refund status or respond to additional queries, leading to a sense of constant engagement with the system.

The most unfortunate part of this entire process is the lack of clarity regarding the purpose of such an overwhelming system. Instead of simplifying compliance and making the process more transparent, the government's approach has turned tax adherence into an exhausting, perpetual chore. This relentless focus on compliance over clarity leaves citizens feeling that they are in a perpetual state of vigilance—constantly working to avoid errors, meet deadlines, and prevent any slip-ups that might trigger penalties or audits. In the end, following the rules becomes less about fulfilling a civic duty and more about surviving a gauntlet.

For most people, it would be unimaginable to spend hours each week, or even each month, navigating these complexities. But that is the reality in today's tax environment. For small businesses, freelancers, and self-employed individuals, the cost of non-compliance is even higher, often resulting in the need to hire consultants or professionals who can handle the intricacies of tax laws. These professionals are not just tax preparers; they become advisors, coaches, and guides who help individuals navigate a system that is designed to be difficult to navigate in the first place.

What emerges from this situation is a deep sense of frustration and burnout. People no longer feel like active participants in the democratic process—they feel like they are constantly running a marathon, only to be told they missed a step and must start over. The idea of tax compliance, which should be an orderly and efficient process, has become a source of daily anxiety, confusion, and exhaustion. The very citizens who fund the state's machinery are, ironically, the ones whose time is wasted and whose mental health is strained by the complexity of a system designed to serve them. The government's failure to make this system straightforward and accessible not only damages trust in the system but also reinforces the notion that the rules are there to trap and exhaust the common person—rather than to foster equity, fairness, and transparency.

The intricate web of regulations, the constant fear of mistakes, and the unrelenting burden of compliance have transformed what should be a simple civic duty into a full-time job for ordinary citizens. Rather than empowering the taxpayer, the system has instead created an environment where fear and confusion dominate, driving many to comply out of sheer exhaustion rather than understanding. As the complexity deepens and the government's response remains slow and impersonal, taxpayers are left feeling alienated and disillusioned. What was once meant to be a framework for societal contribution has now become a complex maze that citizens must navigate just to avoid penalties, audits, and harassment. The relationship between the taxpayer and the state has deteriorated, not just because of unfair practices but because the system itself is built to overwhelm. This chapter has explored the insidious nature of this fear-driven compliance culture, but the question remains: How long can the system continue to demand so much from its citizens before the cracks begin to show, and before those who once complied are left questioning the very fairness of it all?

Chapter 7
Where Does the Money Go?

The issue of accountability in government spending has been a long-standing concern that affects the very fabric of society. While taxpayers diligently fulfil their obligations, they often wonder where their hard-earned money truly goes. Despite hearing about lofty budgets, ambitious plans, and progressive policies, the reality on the ground tells a different story. In this chapter, we examine the crisis of accountability in India's financial system, where public funds are mismanaged, siphoned off through corruption, and wasted on non-essential projects. The failure to effectively allocate resources leads to a deep sense of disillusionment among citizens who are left questioning the priorities of their government. The disconnect between the promises of politicians and the lived experience of the people is more glaring than ever, raising questions about the true purpose of taxation and how the nation's wealth is being used—or misused.

7.1 Budget Sounds Good, Ground Reality is Bad

Every year, citizens are presented with the government's budget, a grand declaration of the state's fiscal priorities. The budget sounds promising—goals for infrastructure development, schemes for welfare, investments in healthcare and education, and various initiatives aimed at uplifting the poorest sections of society. Politicians deliver their speeches with confidence, boasting of plans that seem to promise a better future. However, when one steps outside the confines of the parliament and looks at the ground reality, the picture is far less rosy. The lofty claims made during budget presentations are often met with disappointment as people see little tangible impact in their daily lives. The disconnect between the budget's promises and the actual execution of these plans is stark and raises a fundamental question: Where does the money really go?

The budget, in theory, is a detailed document that outlines how the government intends to spend taxpayers' money for the year ahead. In it, various sectors are allocated specific amounts based on their importance to national progress. The finance minister may promise improvements in public health, education, and infrastructure, while also allocating funds to government welfare schemes aimed at helping the economically disadvantaged. However, when examining these allocations closely, many find that the actual expenditure is nowhere near what was promised. Funds often get stuck in bureaucratic red tape, siphoned off by corruption, or simply misallocated due to inefficiencies within the system.

Take, for instance, the allocation for infrastructure development. While the budget may promise significant investments in roads, bridges, and urban planning, the reality on the ground is that these projects are often delayed, over-budget, or plagued by quality issues. Roads are left incomplete for years, infrastructure projects face continual cost overruns, and citizens are left with half-built constructions that do little to improve their daily lives. This is not due to a lack of funds but due to poor planning, lack of accountability, and the inefficient management of resources.

Similarly, welfare schemes that are designed to uplift the marginalized sections of society are often mired in inefficiencies. The amount allocated for these programs is rarely fully utilized, and the benefits fail to reach the intended recipients due to corrupt practices and bureaucratic hurdles. For example, government subsidies for food and healthcare may sound beneficial on paper, but corruption at the local level and the mismanagement of resources prevent these programs from having the desired impact. The funds allocated for such schemes are diverted before they can reach the people who need them the most.

In many cases, the funds earmarked for crucial areas such as education and healthcare are not utilized effectively. Teachers may still lack proper resources in classrooms, hospitals may still be understaffed and underfunded, and citizens are left waiting for services that should be readily available. The problem is not that the government is not spending money—it is that it is spending it in ways that do not benefit the people who are the true stakeholders. These discrepancies highlight a failure in governance and a lack of accountability, which leads to a deepening sense of distrust among the public.

The budget often fails to address the root causes of systemic inefficiencies. Political priorities, not public needs, dictate spending patterns. A large portion of the funds allocated for infrastructure development, for instance, may end up in the pockets of contractors with political connections, leaving taxpayers with substandard roads and bridges. Similarly, welfare programs may be manipulated to serve political agendas rather than the intended beneficiaries, further alienating the common people. This cycle of misallocation and mismanagement continues year after year, creating a widening gap between the promises made in the budget and the reality experienced by the citizens.

As these discrepancies become more evident, the question arises: If the government's promises are not reflected in the actual spending, where is the money going? The absence of transparency in the allocation and distribution of funds leaves citizens in the dark. The public is left to wonder how much of their tax money is actually reaching its intended purpose, and how much is being lost in the labyrinth of corruption and inefficiency. This disconnection between the budget's promises and the ground reality is a primary cause of public frustration and growing disillusionment with the government's handling of public funds. As the years go by, the gap between the two only widens, leaving citizens questioning whether the government's promises are ever meant to be fulfilled—or if they are just empty words designed to appease the masses.

7.2 Corruption Eats Up Public Funds

Corruption has long plagued India's public sector, eroding the financial integrity of governance. A large chunk of public funds, raised through taxpayer contributions and meant for welfare and infrastructure, often vanishes into private pockets. Whether it's bribes to expedite permits or large-scale embezzlement through fake contracts, corruption diminishes the value of every rupee collected. More disturbing than isolated cases is the normalization of corrupt practices—a culture deeply rooted in the administrative machinery, where exploitation has become routine. This culture ensures that while taxpayers fund the system in good faith, those in power exploit it for personal enrichment.

The government allocates massive budgets for public development—highways, schools, hospitals, and welfare schemes—but a shocking share of these funds never reach their intended purpose. Billions are siphoned off by officials, contractors, and politicians working in unholy alliances. These funds could have transformed lives, but instead, they fuel luxury lifestyles for a few and deepen hardship for the masses. At the project initiation stage itself, the rot sets in. Large infrastructure contracts often go to companies with political backing rather than capability. Once in control, these contractors cut corners—using substandard materials, employing fewer workers, or leaving projects incomplete—while billing the full amount to the government. The public ends up with potholed roads, unsafe bridges, and unusable public buildings—all at full price.

Welfare schemes are no exception. Programs designed to provide food, healthcare, or financial aid to the poor are routinely manipulated. Corrupt officials inflate beneficiary lists or demand bribes to issue benefits. The truly needy are left out, while the rich and politically connected manage to milk the system. In numerous villages, people must pay bribes just to be included in government relief lists. What reaches the grassroots is often a fraction of what was sanctioned. The gap between policy and delivery is filled with theft, favouritism, and bureaucracy. This corruption is not only rampant but also protected. Whistle-blowers face retaliation—transfers, demotions, or worse. Even when scandals come to light, investigations are slow, and convictions are rare. The judiciary, itself plagued with delays, rarely ensures justice in corruption cases. Media exposés make headlines for a day before disappearing into obscurity. A cycle is maintained where corruption breeds more corruption, and no one is truly held accountable. The taxpayer, meanwhile, continues funding this failed system, seeing no improvements in public services.

Even anti-corruption measures, when introduced, tend to be superficial. New policies are diluted by political pressure or legal loopholes. Committees set up to oversee corruption are often filled with insiders or those lacking independence. These institutions protect interests rather than challenge them. Public outrage is pacified with token arrests, but structural reform is never on the table. The end result is that corruption becomes institutionalized—accepted as an unavoidable part of governance.

The real impact of corruption extends beyond financial loss. It destroys public trust in the system. Citizens see broken roads, overcrowded hospitals, and failing schools and know that their tax money is being stolen. The poorest suffer the most, relying on government programs that often exist only on paper. Inefficiency and theft deepen inequality, making the rich richer while the majority are left with nothing but promises. Basic services, such as clean drinking water, electricity, and housing, remain out of reach for millions, not due to a lack of resources, but because those resources have been looted. This betrayal is emotional as well. People lose faith not just in government, but in the idea of fairness. Honest taxpayers begin to feel like fools for playing by the rules while watching the corrupt flourish. Over time, cynicism replaces civic duty. Why participate in a system that rewards crime and punishes honesty? Why obey when disobedience yields rewards? This psychological toll is harder to measure but no less damaging than financial loss.

Corruption also sustains inequality at a structural level. The rich and powerful manipulate laws, influence regulators, and evade scrutiny. They use stolen wealth to build influence, fund political campaigns, and secure more contracts. It's a feedback loop where corruption ensures more power, and power ensures more corruption. Meanwhile, taxpayers fund this machinery that operates against them. The government's budget announcements—grand on paper—are often just camouflage to distract the public from the vast theft occurring behind the scenes.

Until there is systemic reform that prioritizes transparency, accountability, and punishment for the guilty, this cycle will not break. Cosmetic changes won't help; what's needed is a complete overhaul of how public funds are tracked and protected. Without such change, the public will continue to pay into a system that robs them—and the future will be no different from the present: a nation where the honest fund the dishonest, and hope is the greatest casualty.

7.3 Wasting Money on Useless Projects

Every year, the government announces ambitious projects to enhance infrastructure, improve quality of life, or boost economic growth. These initiatives are marketed as transformative, targeting roads, health, urban development, and more. Yet, a significant number of them end up as colossal failures, draining public funds without delivering real benefits. Public money is often mismanaged, diverted, or wasted entirely, leaving citizens—who fund these projects through taxes—with little to show in return.

Large-scale infrastructure undertakings exemplify this waste. Roads, bridges, and airports are frequently built at massive expense but fail to address actual public needs. A city might receive a new flyover while basic road networks crumble, or an airport may be constructed in a region with minimal traffic demand. These projects, while visually impressive, rarely contribute to functional progress. The absence of integrated planning leads to disconnected infrastructure that serves more as a political showpiece than a public utility. This inefficiency stems from a lack of vision and planning. Funds are often funneled into symbolic constructions rather than critical areas like healthcare, education, or sanitation. Projects become political tools, designed to showcase a politician's legacy rather than address the population's pressing concerns. Such ventures are frequently launched ahead of elections, with the intention of wooing voters instead of serving them. What results is a pattern of prioritizing electoral optics over real developmental needs.

Compounding the issue is the endemic lack of accountability. Once budgets are sanctioned, they pass through layers of bureaucracy, contractors, and political interests. Contracts are often awarded without transparent bidding, favouring firms with political ties. These firms deliver substandard work using inferior materials, leading to rapid degradation and increased long-term maintenance costs. Corruption, in the form of kickbacks and inflated billing, thrives unchecked within this opaque system. This problem extends beyond roads and bridges. Welfare schemes—whether focused on poverty alleviation, health, or rural development—also suffer from chronic inefficiency. Funds intended for struggling farmers or marginalized communities often end up in the hands of intermediaries or large corporate entities. The programs, which should uplift millions, turn into opportunities for exploitation, benefiting those who need them least while excluding those who need them most.

Transparency is severely lacking. When inquiries are made, officials rely on vague figures and incomplete reports to justify expenditure. Detailed breakdowns of spending are either unavailable or deliberately obscured by bureaucracy. Without proper auditing or consequences for failure, failed projects are quickly forgotten, and the cycle of waste continues. Contractors with poor records are re-hired, and officials responsible for mismanagement are seldom held to account. As this cycle repeats, public trust erodes. Citizens grow disillusioned with a system that seems incapable of using tax revenues wisely. The frustration stems not just from visible corruption, but from the lost opportunities—schools, hospitals, clean water systems, or rural roads that could have transformed lives. Instead, billions are funneled into vanity projects that serve the few while the majority continue to wait for basic necessities. Unless serious reforms prioritize efficiency, transparency, and real needs over political theatrics, the burden of this waste will remain squarely on the shoulders of the people.

7.4 Pay for Roads Twice – Tax and Toll

In a country where road infrastructure remains a pressing concern, one of the most exasperating realities for citizens is the dual financial burden they bear for the same service. The average Indian is compelled to pay for roads not once, but twice—first through an elaborate taxation system and again through tolls imposed on highways and expressways. This practice doesn't merely extract more money from citizens; it exposes deep structural inefficiencies in public finance management. Roads, by definition, are public goods meant to foster connectivity, facilitate commerce, and support daily life. Yet, the way this infrastructure is funded reveals a pattern of policy failures and misplaced priorities that shifts the responsibility onto the public without offering corresponding benefits.

The first payment happens indirectly through taxes. Indian taxpayers contribute significant revenue to the government through various means—income tax, fuel surcharges, excise duties, GST, and more. A portion of this money is theoretically earmarked for infrastructure development, including roads. Citizens naturally expect that these taxes will cover the creation and maintenance of public roads, ensuring they are safe, durable, and efficient. Unfortunately, the reality is far from this ideal. Funds meant for infrastructure are often rerouted to other budgetary needs or disappear into administrative inefficiencies. The consequence is that roads continue to degrade, potholes remain unaddressed, and the promise of reliable connectivity is perpetually deferred. Taxpayers, therefore, find themselves in a cycle of frustration, contributing to a system that yields diminishing returns.

The second payment arises when tolls are collected on these very roads, often without clarity or justification. In the name of maintaining roads or recovering investment, tolls are charged even on stretches already built using public funds. This results in a scenario where the taxpayer, who has already financed the road's construction through taxes, is now forced to pay again for its use. It is not merely a matter of paying for premium services—it is the normalization of a double payment system that disproportionately affects the everyday commuter. What should be a one-time public investment becomes a recurring private expense, without transparency or accountability.

This issue is compounded by the opaque handling of toll revenue. In most cases, there is scant information about how toll collections are utilized. Are the funds reinvested into maintaining the road, or do they vanish into general government expenditure? Often, there is no publicly available audit or breakdown. Meanwhile, toll charges continue to rise year after year, justified by inflation or vague policy objectives, without any noticeable improvement in road quality or user experience. Adding to the injustice, toll booths frequently remain in operation long after the projected cost recovery period has elapsed. The public is left to wonder why tolls are still being charged on roads that have already "paid for themselves" many times over.

Toll charges are also implemented inconsistently, with no uniform policy across regions. In some states, rates are calculated based on distance, while in others, a flat fee applies. A person traveling across state boundaries often encounters dramatically different toll systems, creating confusion and unpredictability in commute planning. The absence of a standardized national toll framework makes it difficult for citizens to understand what they are paying for or to hold anyone accountable for excessive charges. The result is an arbitrary and scattered fee structure that feels less like a policy tool and more like a cash-grab mechanism.

The double payment model hits the lower and middle-income groups the hardest. Individuals from suburban or rural areas who rely on highways for daily commutes to cities for work, healthcare, or education, feel the pinch with every toll gate. For them, tolls are not optional conveniences but compulsory expenditures that erode their monthly budget. These are the same people who are contributing to infrastructure through direct and indirect taxes, yet they see little relief or return on their payments. Each toll payment is a reminder that the system is skewed against those who cannot afford to navigate it comfortably.

Conversely, the affluent segment of the population often escapes the brunt of this burden. Wealthier individuals may choose alternative routes or have the financial resilience to absorb toll costs without stress. In some cases, they benefit from exclusive infrastructure developments—high-speed expressways or premium corridors—funded partly by the general public and maintained through high tolls that price out average users. This leads to a lopsided infrastructure model, where the best facilities are accessible only to those with means, while the majority continue to pay without proportionate benefits.

In a disturbing trend, many toll-funded projects seem to serve specific commercial interests rather than public need. Roads developed for industrial corridors, luxury residential zones, or special economic areas often come with hefty tolls that subsidize elite mobility. Yet, the general populace contributes indirectly by paying taxes that partially fund these projects in the first place. This cross-subsidization deepens the socio-economic divide and reveals a system where the poor unknowingly bankroll conveniences for the rich. It reaffirms the perception that infrastructure in India increasingly serves capital more than it serves citizens.

The imposition of tolls on roads already financed by public money underscores a deeper flaw in the government's funding logic. Instead of maximizing the utility of collected taxes, the state has resorted to repetitive monetization of basic services. Until there is a systemic shift—either through abolishing tolls on publicly funded roads or ensuring tax revenues are used transparently and efficiently—the citizen will continue to pay twice for the same road, locked in a cycle of financial extraction that benefits a select few while draining the rest.

7.5 Big Companies Get Loans Forgiven

In the realm of taxation and government spending, there is a bitter truth that many taxpayers find hard to digest: the preferential treatment extended to large corporations, especially concerning loans and debts. While ordinary citizens are pressured to pay taxes on time without respite, big corporations often enjoy privileges like loan forgiveness, creating a two-tiered system where the wealthiest are shielded from financial consequences, while the middle and lower classes absorb the full impact of rigid tax policies.

One glaring example is how massive corporations manage to escape accountability for unpaid loans. When such entities default or fail to meet financial obligations, they are frequently granted leniency unthinkable for a common citizen or small business. Rather than being penalized, these companies are offered renegotiated terms, extended deadlines, or outright loan forgiveness. This is often justified with the argument that these corporations are essential to the national economy and their collapse could lead to job losses, economic slowdown, or tax revenue dips. But this overlooks a critical fact—these corporations often have vast resources and financial buffers that small businesses and individuals lack, making their claims for financial relief more strategic than essential.

What makes this practice particularly unjust is the staggering amounts involved. In numerous high-profile cases, large corporations have been allowed to walk away from millions—or even billions—of rupees in debt. All the while, the average taxpayer continues to contribute toward government expenditures, indirectly footing the bill for these corporate failures. This dynamic reveals a harsh inequality, where the public bears the financial weight of mismanaged corporations while receiving no similar mercy if they were to default on a loan, delay taxes, or fall behind on EMIs.

The absence of transparency in these corporate bailouts deepens public frustration. Often, deals involving massive debt write-offs happen behind closed doors. The public remains unaware of the justifications, the negotiations, or even the total amount forgiven. Media access is restricted, official statements are vague, and scrutiny is minimal. This secrecy robs taxpayers of their right to hold institutions accountable and feeds the perception that powerful interests operate in a parallel system immune from consequences.

Loan forgiveness is merely one element of a much broader structure of corporate favouritism. These companies also enjoy tax breaks, massive subsidies, and government-backed loans, all of which create unfair advantages over smaller businesses. Equipped with superior lobbying power and political connections, these corporations often manipulate policy frameworks to their benefit. The result is a concentration of wealth and economic influence that reinforces inequality across society.

The culture of crony capitalism further entrenches this imbalance. Many top corporations maintain close financial or personal ties with political figures, creating a toxic mix of influence and favouritism. This nexus ensures that tax reforms, fiscal relief measures, and even regulatory changes disproportionately favour large corporations. For instance, while small businesses are taxed heavily and subjected to stringent compliance standards, bigger companies use loopholes and political access to escape or reduce their tax liabilities.

Often, the justification provided for such corporate relief is that it safeguards the economy and employment. But this logic collapses when the same corporations, after receiving massive financial support, continue to lay off workers, offshore operations, or report record profits without contributing proportionately to the public welfare. The narrative that big companies must be preserved at any cost conveniently ignores their failures, unethical practices, and disproportionate consumption of public resources. This culture of corporate immunity distorts the economy at its core. It signals that failure, if committed by the powerful, will be rewarded or ignored. Such a message breeds moral hazard—where companies are emboldened to take reckless financial risks knowing the government will cushion their fall. This safety net, paid for by public taxes, undermines the spirit of accountability and hard work, encouraging a cycle where the corporate elite play high-stakes games with public money while remaining insulated from consequences.

Meanwhile, citizens receive no such luxury. A delay in paying a bank loan or income tax can result in penalties, asset seizure, or a ruined credit record. The contrast is stark—while commoners are penalized instantly, corporations are forgiven silently. The legal and institutional system, which should be impartial and just, instead becomes a fortress protecting the rich from the same laws it imposes on the poor.

Ultimately, this points to a systemic flaw in how tax and financial policies are framed and implemented. The apparatus is structured not to protect the average citizen, but to safeguard the interests of those at the top. As long as this disparity continues, public resentment will grow, and trust in institutions will deteriorate. Loan forgiveness for big corporations is not just an economic issue—it is a moral one. It symbolizes how deeply rigged the system is in favour of the powerful, and how far it has strayed from the ideals of fairness, equality, and justice.

7.6 No One Knows How the Money is Spent

One of the most glaring issues citizens faces is the opacity surrounding government spending. Although taxes are collected from every working citizen, there is a troubling lack of transparency regarding how this money is used. Public funds, supposedly gathered to serve the greater good, often disappear into a bureaucratic void with little clear information on the outcomes they are meant to achieve. For the average taxpayer, this creates deep frustration and disillusionment, as tracing how their hard-earned money is spent becomes nearly impossible. This begins with the government's budgetary process. While it seems the government provides detailed budget documents each year, these are frequently written in dense jargon and technical language that the public cannot easily interpret. The breakdown of spending is often so convoluted that even experts struggle to make sense of it. Instead of promoting transparency, these documents serve more as tools of obfuscation than efforts to inform the citizenry.

Beyond complicated budget reports lies a deeper problem: the implementation of these spending plans. Even when funds are allocated, there's little oversight or timely reporting on how effectively the money is used. Public projects may appear on paper, but completion is often delayed, over budget, or substandard. Yet there is rarely any accountability. Citizens are left wondering if their taxes are being funneled into ineffective or corrupt ventures masked as developmental projects or political favours.

The decision-making process regarding fund allocation is equally opaque. When governments direct money to certain sectors or regions, the rationale is rarely clear. Who decides where the money goes? What criteria are used? Often, these decisions are politically motivated. Infrastructure projects may be announced in regions with electoral significance rather than in areas with genuine need. The result is the emergence of "ghost projects" — initiatives that exist only in documents but have no real-world impact.

Audits, which should offer independent evaluations of public spending, often lack both rigor and independence. Reports are delayed, diluted, or disregarded, making it hard to hold leaders accountable for financial mismanagement. When audits do occur, they tend to spotlight minor procedural faults while ignoring larger systemic issues. This weakens institutional checks and allows inefficiencies and corruption to persist unchecked.

The absence of transparency is a fertile ground for corruption. Without oversight, public money becomes a target for embezzlement and kickbacks. Bribery and fraudulent contracting often go unnoticed due to the lack of scrutiny. In such an environment, corruption thrives while citizens are deprived of the infrastructure and services their taxes are supposed to fund. For the ordinary taxpayer, this is a double injustice: they are forced to contribute but have no control or clarity over how their contributions are misused.

This situation not only breeds corruption but also obstructs effective governance. Without visibility into how funds are allocated to sectors like healthcare, education, or welfare, citizens cannot judge whether these areas are being adequately supported. As a result, critical public services remain underfunded while superfluous or politically motivated projects continue draining resources. The lack of public feedback worsens this cycle of misallocation and inefficiency.

Worse, the lack of transparency leaves citizens feeling powerless. Without clear knowledge of how public funds are spent, how can people demand better services or challenge mismanagement? The result is disengagement. When the system appears opaque and indifferent, people lose trust in it. The government's failure to be transparent alienates its citizens, undermining public faith in democracy itself. This is not a theoretical concern — it has real, daily consequences. When people can't see where their money is going, they can't participate meaningfully in governance. They can't advocate for change or push for better policies. Democracy requires informed participation, but that becomes impossible when financial dealings are hidden behind layers of bureaucracy and silence.

Ultimately, the crisis of transparency in government spending points to the need for structural reform. To rebuild trust and ensure that taxes are used responsibly, governments must commit to openness and accountability. Clear, comprehensible budget reports must be made available to all citizens. Oversight mechanisms must be strengthened and enforced. Audit systems should be independent, timely, and comprehensive. Only then can citizens begin to believe that their tax contributions are genuinely serving the public interest. Until that happens, the cycle of secrecy, corruption, and waste will continue — and people will keep asking the same question: where did our money go?

7.7 No Help for Honest Taxpayers

One of the most disheartening realities for honest taxpayers is the overwhelming lack of support they receive from the government. While taxes are collected with the promise of improving public services and infrastructure, the individual taxpayer is often left alone to navigate the complexities of the system. Those who diligently pay their dues and contribute to the economy are met with indifference—or even hostility. The entire burden of compliance rests on their shoulders, with little assistance or guidance. This starkly contrasts with how large corporations and wealthy individuals are treated, often enjoying tax breaks, exemptions, or opportunities to manipulate the system in their favour.

For the average citizen, filing taxes is a daunting task. From convoluted forms to ever-changing regulations, staying compliant is like a second job. Yet, there's no accessible government support system to help navigate these intricacies. Those with wealth can afford accountants and consultants; the common taxpayer cannot. Even when they seek help, the bureaucracy ensures that answers are slow, vague, or simply unhelpful. Confusion mounts, and what should be a straightforward civic duty becomes a stressful ordeal.

When issues arise—such as filing mistakes or confusion over deductions—taxpayers rarely receive proactive support. Instead of offering solutions, the tax department is quick to issue penalties or demand corrections without aiding the taxpayer in understanding what went wrong. The system seems designed not to prevent errors, but to punish them. This punitive approach worsens the overall experience, discouraging even the most well-intentioned citizens from maintaining voluntary compliance. This neglect feels particularly unjust to those trying to do the right thing. Honest taxpayers who make an effort to obey the rules end up feeling penalized, while tax evaders and opportunists often escape serious consequences. The system, instead of supporting integrity, appears to reward manipulation. This imbalance generates widespread resentment. People who fulfil their obligations get entangled in red tape, while those who exploit loopholes live comfortably without scrutiny.

What emerges is a deeper systemic inequality. The rich and powerful have access to elite tax strategists who ensure they minimize liabilities legally. Meanwhile, ordinary citizens—especially those with limited financial literacy—are left defenceless. They cannot maximize deductions or manoeuvre through exceptions simply because they don't understand how. This disparity turns the tax code into a tool that reinforces class divides rather than ensuring fair contribution.

Even worse, when taxpayers reach out with legitimate questions or concerns, they're often met with silence or bureaucratic dismissal. Emails go unanswered. Calls are passed between departments. Queries are buried under layers of administrative process. This cultivates a sense of alienation and helplessness. The unspoken message is clear: the tax system is not built to assist you—it is built to extract from you. The taxpayer becomes a target, not a stakeholder.

In a healthy democracy, government institutions should support those who fund them. There should be user-friendly guides, responsive helplines, streamlined procedures, and genuine customer service. Yet, these supports are either absent or woefully inadequate. The message this sends to honest taxpayers is that their contributions are taken for granted. They're expected to give, but should not expect anything in return—not even clarity or fairness.

The psychological toll of this neglect is substantial. Taxpayers feel abandoned, demoralized, and disrespected. They're aware that their money is essential to national functioning, yet they receive no help navigating the very system they sustain. This erodes trust not only in the tax administration but in the government itself. People begin to question whether compliance is worth the effort when those who don't comply seem to suffer less. The failure to support honest taxpayers isn't a minor oversight—it's a structural flaw that requires urgent attention. A truly just tax system must begin with the premise that those who willingly comply deserve assistance, clarity, and respect. This means simplifying tax procedures, offering real-time help, creating accountability in communication, and ensuring that penalties are applied with fairness and empathy.

Until such reforms are implemented, the average taxpayer will continue to bear the brunt of a system that is unnecessarily complex and fundamentally unsympathetic. The irony is painful: the government demands obedience from its taxpayers, but provides little in return beyond threats of fines and penalties. In this imbalance, trust breaks down, and civic engagement weakens.

A nation cannot expect loyal compliance while refusing to support its citizens. The current system, by neglecting the very people it depends upon, undermines its own foundation. Real reform begins not just with legal amendments but with a shift in attitude—a recognition that honest taxpayers are the backbone of the country and deserve better than indifference.

7.8 Asking Questions is Seen as Crime

In any functioning democracy, the act of questioning is not only a right but a responsibility. Citizens should have the freedom to ask about the use of their taxes, the policies that govern their lives, and the overall functioning of the government. However, in the Indian tax system, this right often leads to severe consequences. Simply asking questions or seeking clarity about tax policies can quickly escalate into a perceived challenge to authority. Taxpayers who question the government about how their money is being spent, or who seek explanations for confusing tax laws, are often met with disdain or labelled as troublemakers. The atmosphere surrounding the tax system discourages inquiry, as citizens are made to feel that asking questions is a threat to the established order.

The fear of reprisal is a powerful deterrent. Taxpayers, especially those without the resources to fight back, are often afraid to ask for clarity on policies or seek information on how taxes are spent. The government's response to such inquiries is rarely to provide clear answers; instead, it often results in an attempt to shut down the conversation, sometimes through bureaucratic delays, vague responses, or outright refusal to address concerns. This discourages people from engaging with the system at all, leaving them to navigate the complexities of tax laws alone, often with little understanding of their own rights. This silence, enforced by fear, stifles the accountability that any government should uphold. The tax authorities, instead of being approachable or transparent, create an atmosphere where questions are seen as acts of defiance. This makes it difficult for citizens to hold their government to account. Those who question are often treated as adversaries rather than contributors to a constructive dialogue. The broader public is left with the impression that the government is not interested in hearing their concerns, as any challenge is met with resistance or punishment.

The power dynamics at play in the tax system are also telling. While large corporations and wealthy individuals can hire experts to navigate the complexities of the tax system, the average taxpayer has no such luxury. They are forced to deal with an opaque system that is difficult to understand. When they attempt to ask questions, they often face the risk of being penalized or scrutinized for even the smallest discrepancy. This environment is particularly harmful because it undermines trust in the system. If the government is unwilling to engage openly with the people, how can it expect to maintain legitimacy in the eyes of the public? This oppressive environment fosters a culture of compliance through fear, rather than one of civic engagement and accountability. Asking questions becomes an act of rebellion, and taxpayers are expected to remain passive recipients of whatever the government decides to impose. The relationship between the citizen and the state becomes one of distrust and suspicion, rather than cooperation and mutual respect. In a system where questioning is seen as a threat, citizens are discouraged from seeking improvements or reforms that could benefit the system as a whole.

The discouragement of questions leads to a breakdown in the democratic principles that should underpin the functioning of the state. When citizens no longer feel empowered to engage with their government, the system becomes less responsive to their needs. It also creates a public that is less informed, less able to challenge injustices, and less likely to demand changes that could improve the system. The failure of the government to address legitimate concerns only deepens the divide between the rulers and the ruled, creating an environment where the truth is obscured and the taxpayer is left in the dark.

The real harm of treating questions as crimes is that it destroys trust in the system. It makes citizens feel like their voices do not matter, that their questions will be ignored or punished. This results in a situation where the tax system becomes more of a burden than a service, where the taxpayer is just a passive source of revenue, rather than an active participant in a democratic society. Until the government changes its approach and recognizes that questions are vital to a healthy system, the tax system will remain a tool for suppression rather than one for service.

7.9 Lifelong Taxes, But No Free Services

The concept of paying taxes is based on the premise that individuals contribute to the system for the greater good, and in return, they should have access to services that improve their quality of life. Ideally, tax revenue should be used to fund public services such as healthcare, education, infrastructure, and social welfare programs. However, in India, despite citizens paying taxes throughout their lives, many essential services remain either inaccessible, subpar, or far too expensive for the average taxpayer. This stark contradiction creates a feeling of frustration and betrayal among the public. The expectation that taxes should yield tangible benefits for all is not met, leaving people questioning the fairness of the system.

For many, the taxes they pay seem to vanish into a black hole, with little to show in terms of personal or collective improvements. While taxes are levied relentlessly, the average citizen often struggles to access basic services such as quality healthcare or education without paying exorbitant additional fees. The notion that tax payments should result in free or at least subsidized services is continually undermined. Instead, citizens are forced to rely on private alternatives that many cannot afford, exacerbating existing inequalities. As a result, while the government collects taxes, it fails to provide even the most basic rights that citizens expect in return for their contributions.

The issue becomes even more concerning when you consider that many essential services—like healthcare, which should be a fundamental right—are not available to those who need them the most. A significant portion of the population still has to pay out-of-pocket for medical expenses, despite contributing heavily through taxes. The same is true for education. Government schools and colleges, despite being funded by taxpayer money, are often in disrepair, underfunded, or unable to provide the quality of education that students deserve. Private institutions, which offer better facilities and services, are often out of reach for the majority due to the high fees they charge, leaving those who cannot afford them in a precarious position.

Meanwhile, the infrastructure that is funded by taxes—roads, public transportation, sanitation—remains inadequate in many parts of the country. While there are some high-profile projects and areas that do benefit from tax-funded development, for many, the public infrastructure is either outdated, poorly maintained, or simply non-existent. People are left to deal with the consequences of this underfunded infrastructure every day, paying taxes all the while, but receiving little in return. Even basic needs like clean drinking water and reliable electricity remain inconsistent in many parts of India, despite the continuous flow of tax revenue into the system.

The lack of free services, or services that are at least accessible without crippling costs, leads to a fundamental disconnect between the government and its citizens. People see their tax contributions as something that should guarantee them a certain level of service. When that expectation is not met, they begin to feel as though their taxes are being wasted or misused. This disillusionment fuels resentment towards the government and undermines any trust in the system.

The government's failure to provide free services disproportionately affects the poor and marginalized. While wealthier individuals can afford to bypass the inadequacies of the public system by paying for private services, the majority of the population is left with no choice but to accept whatever meagre services the government provides. This perpetuates a cycle of inequality, where those with more financial resources can buy access to better services, while those without must make do with subpar alternatives. The tax system, rather than acting as a tool for equity, becomes another means of entrenching the divide between the rich and the poor.

The very idea of lifelong taxes without corresponding services also contributes to the feeling of being trapped. Taxpayers are burdened with the idea that they are paying into a system that offers them little in return. Over the course of a lifetime, people contribute to the system with the understanding that, at the very least, they should be entitled to basic services and a safety net. Yet, this is not the case, and this creates a sense of injustice that runs deep within society. The system becomes one where citizens feel they are simply contributing to a never-ending cycle of taxation without ever reaping the benefits.

The lack of accountability for the mismanagement or underuse of tax revenue adds to this frustration. While the government continues to collect taxes, it often fails to provide transparency about how those funds are spent or why certain services are so underfunded. In some cases, the government even justifies its failure to provide adequate services by claiming a lack of funds, despite the continuous stream of revenue from taxes. This creates a sense of inequity and highlights the systemic failures that make it impossible for many people to get the services they rightfully deserve.

Ultimately, the idea that citizens must pay taxes throughout their lives yet receive nothing in return in terms of free services is one of the most glaring issues with the current system. While the government continues to levy taxes, it fails to meet its most basic responsibilities, leaving taxpayers with the crushing realization that their hard-earned money is not being put to use in a way that benefits them or society as a whole. This disparity between what people pay and what they receive leads to growing discontent and a loss of trust in the system, which ultimately weakens the social contract between the government and its citizens.

7.10 GDP Grows, Citizen's Life Doesn't – No Policy for Real Progress

India's GDP growth is often hailed as a sign of economic progress, with rising figures held up as evidence of the country's development. The government regularly showcases this growth in economic reports, making it appear as though the nation is on a path of prosperity. However, the reality for most citizens tells a different story. While the economy grows on paper, the average citizen's quality of life remains largely stagnant, or in some cases, deteriorates. The disconnect between GDP growth and personal progress is a stark reminder that economic indicators do not always reflect the lived experiences of the population.

The lack of direct benefits from GDP growth is particularly evident in sectors that impact ordinary citizens, such as healthcare, education, and infrastructure. Despite the continuous increase in GDP, these basic services are either underfunded, inefficient, or inaccessible to a significant portion of the population. The promise of economic growth should ideally translate into better public services, improved living standards, and greater opportunities for individuals. Instead, many citizens find themselves grappling with the same issues they faced years ago, with little hope of meaningful improvement.

One key reason for this gap is the absence of policies that prioritize real progress for the population over abstract economic growth figures. While the GDP might rise, it does not necessarily indicate that wealth is being distributed equitably or that the benefits are reaching the most vulnerable in society. Instead, the fruits of growth often go to the already privileged—large corporations, wealthy elites, and foreign investors—while the working class and marginalized communities see little to no improvement in their everyday lives. The gap between the rich and the poor continues to widen, and the promise of "economic progress" becomes a hollow slogan.

Even as India's economy expands, the average citizen is burdened with rising living costs. Inflation outpaces wage growth, and basic necessities like food, fuel, and housing become increasingly unaffordable for many. This discrepancy highlights the failure of economic policies to address the real needs of citizens. The government's focus on macroeconomic growth often overlooks the need for policies that directly improve the lives of ordinary people. The increase in GDP does not necessarily mean that individuals are better off or that they have access to the services they need to thrive.

The rapid pace of economic growth has led to environmental degradation, job insecurity, and rising inequality, all of which further detract from any meaningful progress for the average citizen. The pursuit of GDP growth has often come at the cost of long-term sustainability, with little consideration given to the welfare of the people or the environment. Economic development that disregards the health of the environment or the well-being of workers is not truly progress. In fact, it often perpetuates cycles of poverty and exploitation, undermining the very idea of a fair and prosperous society.

While the government often points to GDP growth as evidence of success, it fails to recognize that the true measure of a nation's prosperity is not just in its economic output but in the well-being of its people. Economic growth that does not improve the lives of the citizens it is meant to benefit is ultimately meaningless. The lack of focus on social welfare, equitable distribution of wealth, and access to essential services undermines the potential of GDP growth to create real, tangible progress. Citizens remain trapped in a system where the economy grows, but their lives stagnate, leaving them questioning the value of the economic growth that they are told to celebrate.

In the absence of policies that genuinely address the needs of the people, GDP growth becomes nothing more than an abstract figure, disconnected from the realities of life for the average citizen. The government's inability or unwillingness to craft policies that ensure growth translates into tangible improvements for the population is a glaring failure of governance. Until economic policies shift focus from superficial growth figures to real, inclusive progress, the average citizen will continue to experience stagnation, while the country's GDP continues to rise, leaving millions behind in the pursuit of an unattainable, hollow prosperity.

As we reach the end of this exploration into the complexities and injustices of the tax system, it becomes clear that the burdens placed on the average citizen are vast, while the benefits often remain elusive. From the convoluted rules and oppressive compliance demands to the lack of accountability and transparency in the system, taxpayers are left to shoulder an unfair load. The promise of a fair and just tax system that benefits all citizens has yet to be realized, leaving many to question the true purpose of their contributions. Until there is a shift towards a more equitable and transparent system, where citizens see tangible returns on their hard-earned money, the current system will continue to foster resentment, inequality, and a growing sense of disenfranchisement. The journey towards real change will require not just policy reforms but a fundamental rethinking of the relationship between the government and the citizens it serves. Only then can we begin to build a system that truly reflects the ideals of fairness, justice, and shared prosperity.

Chapter 8
A System Built to Trap You

From the moment a citizen enters the tax net, it becomes clear that the system is not merely about collecting revenue—it is about control. What appears to be a civic duty is actually a complex labyrinth designed with one purpose: to make escape impossible and obedience inevitable. Layers of rules, yearly amendments, selective enforcement, and power imbalances don't just extract money—they shape behaviour, suppress dissent, and lock citizens into a perpetual cycle of financial and psychological submission. This chapter exposes the tax regime not as a neutral structure, but as a deeply engineered trap that benefits the architects of power while silently chaining the average individual.

8.1 Made Complicated So You Can't Escape

The Indian tax system has been deliberately structured with excessive complexity, creating a fortress of financial jargon and procedural ambiguity that the average citizen cannot penetrate without expert help. This complexity is not a coincidence—it is the cornerstone of a system designed to keep people confused, dependent, and obedient. From the moment a person begins to earn, they are bombarded with an alphabet soup of terms: GST, TDS, PAN, HSN codes, ITC, Form 16, Form 26AS, and more. Each carries its own set of interpretations, calculations, deadlines, and risks of penalties if misunderstood or misfiled. While the government claims these mechanisms are for streamlined governance, the result is a highly stratified system where only the educated elite or high-income individuals can afford professional advisors to stay compliant. Everyone else remains in a vulnerable position, one misstep away from notices, fines, or prosecution. This isn't governance—it's entrapment.

Even for those who attempt to stay informed, the legal language used in tax regulations is not designed for public comprehension. Statutory provisions are couched in layers of legalese, referencing subsections and clauses that only trained professionals can decipher. A single filing error can lead to months of back-and-forth with authorities, often involving multiple agencies and ambiguous responses. The maze of tax return filing platforms, digital verification processes, input-output reconciliation, and quarterly compliance obligations keeps small business owners, freelancers, and salaried employees in a constant state of anxiety. For them, staying compliant feels like a second full-time job. And this is not by accident—it is by design. A complicated system ensures the citizen is too busy surviving within the rules to ever question the rules themselves.

This deliberate confusion serves another important purpose: it breeds fear. When tax rules are so complicated that even experts occasionally disagree on interpretations, it becomes easy for authorities to penalize ordinary citizens selectively. This selective enforcement creates an environment of psychological submission. The fear of being picked for scrutiny or audit—even when you've tried to follow every rule—discourages resistance and encourages silent compliance. Citizens begin to internalize guilt, believing that any mistake is their own fault, rather than recognizing that the system itself is constructed to be a trap. In such a state of mental uncertainty, people are less likely to protest, ask questions, or seek reform. Instead, they prioritize survival within a framework they don't understand and cannot challenge.

The complexity also provides a convenient smokescreen for corruption and favouritism. When laws are difficult to interpret, those in power have greater discretion over how and when to enforce them. This leads to arbitrary interpretations, backdated notices, and sudden changes in procedural expectations. Small-scale entrepreneurs and middle-class taxpayers often fall victim to this flexible enforcement. Meanwhile, larger corporations with access to top legal counsel navigate the same laws effortlessly, exploiting loopholes and receiving favourable treatment. This duality strengthens the power hierarchy—one set of rules for the wealthy, another for the rest. Complexity becomes a weapon to protect privilege and punish vulnerability.

Digitalization, often hailed as a step toward transparency, has paradoxically intensified this complexity for the average person. Online portals for income tax, GST, and other compliances are rarely user-friendly. They require not just a working knowledge of taxation but also proficiency in digital operations, documentation, and platform updates. Errors made during digital filing can be extremely hard to reverse, often requiring professional intervention. The illusion of accessibility masks a deeper inaccessibility—what was once a paper-based complexity is now buried beneath an electronic shell that most cannot penetrate without help. For the digitally illiterate or older generations, this becomes an insurmountable hurdle.

This engineered complexity results in economic behaviour that serves the state, not the citizen. People begin to tailor their investments, expenditures, and even professional choices around tax implications rather than genuine personal or societal benefit. Investment decisions are not made based on value or growth but on tax-saving potential. Career shifts are delayed or avoided due to the compliance burden involved. Business ideas are shelved because the bureaucratic maze is too risky to navigate. Thus, instead of empowering economic freedom, the tax system restricts it. Citizens live with the constant burden of compliance hanging over their heads, like an invisible leash keeping them from running too far off the path laid out by the state.

What makes this trap even more insidious is how it's rationalized. The complexity is justified as a necessity for preventing fraud, broadening the tax base, or improving national infrastructure. But in practice, this structure has yielded little in terms of reducing evasion among the powerful or ensuring tax justice. The burden still falls disproportionately on those who are easiest to track—salaried individuals and small business owners—while the truly wealthy manipulate the same laws to escape scrutiny. Each year, despite promises of simplification, new rules are introduced, exemptions modified, and compliance thresholds adjusted, adding more layers to the already unmanageable pile. The net effect is stifling, not empowering.

8.2 Rules Change Every Year

One of the most frustrating and destabilizing aspects of the Indian tax system is the way its rules and regulations seem to shift every single year. Whether it's during the Union Budget or through mid-year notifications and circulars, the rules governing your financial obligations are rarely constant for more than a few months. For the average citizen, this creates a permanent sense of uncertainty. Imagine trying to plan your finances, investments, or business decisions when the very ground beneath your feet keeps moving. This instability is not just inconvenient—it's a deliberate strategy of control. When citizens are forced to constantly relearn the rules, they spend their energy reacting instead of questioning. The perpetual changes disorient people, leaving them reliant on experts and trapped in a cycle of compliance that never ends.

Take, for example, the frequent changes in tax slabs, exemption limits, surcharge rates, or deductions allowed under various sections of the Income Tax Act. Just when a person thinks they've understood how to plan for deductions under Sections 80C or 80D, the conditions change—either the limits are adjusted, the eligibility criteria are tweaked, or an entirely new scheme is introduced. For small business owners, sudden tweaks in GST return formats, compliance timelines, or e-invoicing thresholds can lead to chaos in operations. Compliance becomes a moving target. It's not just about following the law—it's about guessing what new version of the law will apply next quarter or next year. That kind of constant legal instability discourages innovation and punishes the financially disciplined.

What this also does is kill trust. A responsible citizen who followed every rule last year might find themselves penalized this year because a clause was quietly changed. These changes are often buried in long documents, legal bulletins, or departmental notifications that rarely reach public awareness in time. Unlike in more citizen-friendly tax systems, where major changes are accompanied by public education campaigns or grace periods, in India the burden of knowledge is placed entirely on the citizen. They're expected to be perpetually up-to-date with every technical and procedural alteration. It creates an environment where ignorance—no matter how unintentional—is punishable. And when laws change faster than citizens can adapt, the law itself becomes a trap.

Even for tax professionals and Chartered Accountants, keeping up with the changes has become a full-time struggle. Circulars and notifications from the Central Board of Direct Taxes (CBDT) or the GST Council often contradict earlier guidelines or come with ambiguous phrasing that leads to multiple interpretations. As a result, even among professionals, there's confusion, debate, and hesitation. When the experts themselves are unsure, what chance does a common citizen have? This quarterly or annual mutation of rules leads to a bizarre reality where one can never say with certainty whether they are fully compliant or not. It's like driving on a road where traffic signals change colour randomly without warning, and then being fined for crossing a red you never saw turn. This shifting legal terrain serves the state in multiple ways. First, it ensures that any citizen can be declared non-compliant at any time, simply because the rules changed without their knowledge. Second, it makes resistance futile. When the rules are in constant flux, any attempt to question or challenge a tax demand can be easily deflected with technicalities.

"The rule changed," becomes the all-powerful response that shuts down protest. This legal shape-shifting creates a kind of bureaucratic gaslighting, where citizens are made to feel incompetent or guilty—not because they've cheated, but because they failed to keep up with a game designed to be untrackable. In this way, unpredictability becomes a form of silent coercion, psychologically conditioning citizens to submit without question.

For the salaried middle class, the constant tinkering with rules affects their savings and retirement planning. Tax exemptions on provident funds, National Pension Scheme (NPS) contributions, or standard deductions are revised so frequently that long-term financial stability becomes a gamble. Just when a financial product gains traction among the masses, the government tweaks the tax benefits attached to it, reducing the incentive and forcing people to rework their strategies. It's a cycle that never stabilizes. The message it sends is clear: don't get comfortable. Don't assume security. Stay alert. Stay submissive.

In a society where the majority of people are already struggling to cope with inflation, job insecurity, and lack of social safety nets, this kind of legal instability adds a crushing mental burden. Tax should ideally be a predictable, stable contract between the citizen and the state. In India, it feels more like a roulette wheel, where the rules are rewritten even as the wheel spins. And because every new rule is justified in the name of progress or reform, citizens feel pressured to applaud the changes even when they are unfair. The yearly ritual of the Union Budget has become less about fiscal planning and more about watching your fate change at the hands of a few in power. You don't participate—you spectate and comply. This constant alteration of rules is not a mere inefficiency or administrative oversight—it is a deliberate method of social and economic control. It ensures that people never develop financial sovereignty or confidence. It trains them to wait for instructions instead of taking initiative. It keeps them occupied with compliance instead of resistance. And above all, it enforces the unspoken rule of modern taxation in India: adapt, obey, and don't ask too many questions. Because in a system where the rules never stay still, questioning the system itself becomes the most dangerous act of all.

8.3 Tax Laws Used to Target Citizens

In a democracy that claims to uphold equality and justice, tax laws are expected to function as neutral instruments of economic governance. However, in India, these laws are often weaponized to exert control, suppress dissent, and maintain state dominance. Far from merely collecting revenue, tax laws have morphed into surveillance tools—designed to monitor behaviour, punish deviations, and instil fear. Through audits, retroactive penalties, and vague legal language, the tax system becomes a silent instrument of oppression.

Consider how income tax raids and notices are used. These aren't confined to the corrupt or criminal. Activists, journalists, small business owners, and outspoken citizens often find themselves at the receiving end. When a voice becomes too loud, a tax notice arrives. An old compliance slip-up is suddenly revived and exaggerated. These notices are deliberately written in opaque legal jargon, aimed less at clarification and more at psychological intimidation. While censorship is constitutionally barred, tax investigations are perfectly legal—offering the state a loophole to penalize critics without overtly violating rights. What appears as lawful enforcement is often political coercion in disguise. This misuse is facilitated by the extraordinary discretionary powers given to tax officials. Unlike in advanced economies where audits are algorithm-driven and transparent, Indian officials often act on vague criteria. Terms like "undisclosed income" or "unexplained expenditure" are broad enough to allow near-unlimited interpretation. A citizen might be honest, but if they fail to justify a transaction to an officer's subjective satisfaction, they may still be branded a tax evader. The ambiguity of the law becomes a trap; enforcement turns into exploitation.

This selective aggression isn't randomly applied—it is structural. While billion-dollar corporations often escape with settlements or protracted litigation, the small trader or middle-class professional faces instant penalties, reputational damage, and even financial ruin for minor errors. A trader might be penalized for an honest mistake in accounting, while a conglomerate shifting profits offshore through shell entities is barely touched. The system protects the powerful while punishing the vulnerable. The law, applied inconsistently, serves to reassure the elite and terrorize the rest.

The complexity of Indian tax law only compounds the issue. Legal provisions like Section 234F (late filing fee) or 44ADA (presumptive taxation) are filled with exceptions and nested conditions. A minor error—like picking the wrong ITR form or overlooking a checkbox—can attract heavy penalties. These are not fraudulent actions; they're predictable consequences of a system deliberately designed to confuse. But instead of guiding citizens, the authorities often respond with punitive action. Ignorance becomes a liability, confusion becomes guilt. Complexity is not a flaw—it's a feature used to justify punishment. This climate of fear is worsened by the erosion of financial privacy. The linking of PAN, Aadhaar, bank accounts, UPI IDs, and digital wallets means your financial life is constantly exposed. Deviations from normal transaction behaviour—like a sudden deposit or a foreign payment—can trigger scrutiny. Even if legitimate, such actions may demand immediate documentation. The burden of proof is on the citizen, and failure to justify a transaction can bring legal threats. Financial freedom becomes illusionary; every rupee earned, saved, or spent could turn into a legal risk.

Such hyper-surveillance doesn't only control money—it controls people. Citizens become wary not just about finances, but about speech and expression. If participating in protests or criticizing government policy risks inviting tax scrutiny, many choose silence. This creates a society of self-censorship, not through bans or police brutality, but through bureaucratic intimidation. Taxation, in this sense, is psychological conditioning. The state doesn't need to imprison dissidents—it can simply entangle them in legal complications, draining their time, money, and will to resist.

The effects ripple beyond individuals. Entrepreneurs may hesitate to expand or innovate if the cost of failure includes legal scrutiny. NGOs may avoid bold causes fearing their donations will be flagged. Citizens may avoid legitimate income streams—like freelance gigs or crypto—because reporting them accurately is too risky or complex. In this way, tax law shapes behaviour not just through regulation, but through deterrence. People learn to avoid the state's radar at the cost of ambition, honesty, or activism.

While tax compliance is essential for a functioning state, the current model turns this civic duty into a minefield. It's no longer about what you owe, but about how vulnerable you are. When honesty offers no protection and silence becomes a strategy, something is deeply broken. A tax regime should reflect fairness, clarity, and trust. Yet in India, it operates like a tool of fear—shaping society not through justice, but through the calculated use of legal ambiguity and institutional might.

By transforming taxation into a selective, punitive, and manipulative apparatus, the state ensures that even law-abiding citizens live with a lingering sense of threat. It is no longer a question of innocence—it is a question of exposure. And in a system designed for control, every citizen is exposed by default.

8.4 No Say in How Tax Rules are Made

In any true democracy, the creation of laws—especially those that impact every working citizen financially—should be transparent, participatory, and representative of the people's voice. But in India, tax rules are crafted behind closed doors by bureaucrats and political elites with little to no involvement from the common taxpayer. This top-down approach to policymaking effectively side-lines the very people who bear the brunt of the system. You pay the tax, you suffer the penalties, you comply with the rules—but you have absolutely no role in shaping them. Year after year, governments introduce changes through opaque budget declarations, surprise amendments, and retrospective laws, leaving citizens to decipher and obey them without question. This isn't just exclusion; it's systemic alienation dressed as governance.

The Indian taxpayer is not consulted, polled, or surveyed before new tax regulations are implemented. Instead, Finance Bills are tabled with little public debate, and crucial changes are buried in long documents filled with technical jargon. For instance, sudden changes in income tax slabs, imposition of cess, or new mandatory disclosures are often revealed in the annual budget speech—a political spectacle more focused on optics than on engaging citizen feedback. There is no open call for public input, no referendum, and no real mechanism through which ordinary people can contest or influence these decisions. In a nation where over 60 million individuals file returns, it is staggering how few voices are ever heard in the formation of the very laws that dictate their financial fate.

The complexity of this issue is compounded by the fact that tax laws are increasingly becoming instruments of political convenience. New rules are often introduced to serve short-term electoral gains, accommodate influential lobbyists, or retaliate against political rivals. Consider the sudden imposition of retrospective taxation in high-profile international corporate cases—it wasn't about justice; it was about exerting sovereign authority and saving political face. Similarly, digital taxation rules, capital gains modifications, and GST compliance shifts are often executed without giving small traders or professionals time to adapt. These are not policy evolutions born from public need—they are shockwaves fired from ivory towers that hit the ground with destructive impact.

Citizens often find themselves navigating an ever-shifting maze of rules, with no prior knowledge of why these changes were introduced or who demanded them. A change in TDS rates, a revision in tax return formats, or an introduction of new compliance portals—none of these come from grassroots consultation. They're pushed top-down, wrapped in bureaucratic language, and marketed as reforms for efficiency or transparency. Yet, those most affected—the salaried class, freelancers, shopkeepers, and small entrepreneurs—remain voiceless. Their lived experiences, day-to-day challenges, and financial struggles are invisible to the rule makers. The laws are built for theoretical models, not for practical reality.

Even more alarming is the absence of institutional mechanisms that allow citizens to question, appeal, or amend tax rules through democratic processes. Tax Tribunals exist only for individual case redressal, not for policy shaping. Parliament's role in debating tax changes is minimal at best, with many key decisions made by executive orders or under the garb of administrative efficiency. Unlike some developed nations where taxpayer advocacy bodies exist as intermediaries between the public and the state, India has no such channel. The relationship is unidirectional: the government dictates, and the public obeys. The illusion of democracy is maintained, but the substance of participation is absent. This disconnect creates a dangerous culture of compliance without consent. Citizens do not feel ownership of the system; they fear it. They do not trust that the rules are designed in their interest; they accept them as inevitable burdens. This breeds a form of silent rebellion—where evasion, underreporting, or disinterest in taxation become acts of self-defence. It's not just about saving money; it's about resisting a structure that treats them like subjects, not stakeholders. When people begin to perceive tax laws as tools of oppression rather than instruments of collective progress, the moral legitimacy of the state begins to erode.

The irony is thick: in the world's largest democracy, the most vital economic rules are made by a few, imposed on many, and questioned by none. The lack of citizen agency in tax policymaking reveals a deeper flaw in our governance model—one that treats the public not as co-creators of the system, but as data points to be managed. This is not just a technical failure;

it is a democratic crisis. Without inclusion in rulemaking, there can be no ownership. Without ownership, there can be no accountability. And without accountability, taxation transforms from a civic duty into a form of financial subjugation.

In the end, what we are left with is a nation where citizens fund a system that refuses to hear them. They pay for a structure that excludes them from its core decisions. They comply with laws they had no hand in crafting. This is not how democracy is supposed to function. This is how a trap is built—one that locks you in obligation while denying you participation. The chains are legal, but the bondage is real.

8.5 Laws Protect the Rich, Not You

The Indian tax system, though framed in the language of fairness and equity, is fundamentally structured to favour the rich. Beneath the democratic veneer lies a framework engineered to shield wealth, reward financial leverage, and insulate the elite from the burdens imposed on the working and middle classes. Laws that come down harshly on salaried workers and small entrepreneurs are riddled with loopholes when applied to corporations, billionaires, and politically connected entities. This disparity is not accidental—it is strategic and cloaked in rhetoric like "growth" and "investment climate." The outcome is a legal machine that extracts relentlessly from the poor while legally empowering the rich to preserve, expand, and perpetuate their wealth.

One of the clearest examples is the disparity in exemptions, deductions, and tax treatments available to high-net-worth individuals and large businesses. A salaried person has limited options to reduce taxable income—mainly standard deductions and savings-related exemptions. In contrast, corporate entities manipulate depreciation, capitalize expenses, or relocate to Special Economic Zones (SEZs) to enjoy tax holidays. These are justified as development incentives but often serve as legalized avenues for tax avoidance. The wealthier you are, the more tools you have to shrink your tax burden. The average citizen has no offshore accounts, luxury loopholes, or elite tax advisors—only fear of penalties and notices.

Even the judiciary, expected to act as a balancing force, often aligns with entrenched privilege. Tax disputes involving powerful players are handled with caution, and delayed justice serves them well. In contrast, small-time defaulters face swift prosecution. When was the last time a billionaire went to jail for tax evasion in India? Compare that with the countless small traders and middle-class citizens receiving threatening notices over minor discrepancies. The law behaves differently depending on your capacity to fight it. For the rich, it becomes a shield; for the rest, a sword.

Tax amnesty schemes further expose this bias. Periodic "voluntary disclosure" programs allow large defaulters to settle dues by paying reduced penalties, erasing their past misdeeds. This not only mocks honest taxpayers but incentivizes large-scale evasion. The state essentially tells citizens: if you cheat big, we'll negotiate; if you earn modestly and follow rules, we'll scrutinize every rupee. Such policies don't just favour the elite—they foster public cynicism and disillusionment. Why should the honest taxpayer feel moral duty when dishonesty gets rewarded?

Policy design is subtly but consistently aligned with elite interests. Corporate tax cuts, the absence of a wealth tax, and silence on the misuse of agricultural income exemptions reveal where real influence lies. Even indirect taxes like GST, praised as progressive, hit the poor harder. Basic goods and services become costlier while luxury consumption is shielded through sophisticated structures. The rich consume via entities that soften tax impact; the poor pay the full cost plus tax.

Media narratives reinforce this imbalance. Tax raids on billionaires are rarely covered, and when they are, language is cautious and judgment-free. Meanwhile, minor defaulters are publicly shamed. This selective portrayal fosters the illusion that the system monitors everyone equally. In truth, it targets where resistance is weak and enforcement is easiest. It's simpler to terrify a shopkeeper than pursue a conglomerate defended by elite accountants and lawyers.

The very language of tax laws deepens the divide. The Income Tax Act is written to allow wide interpretation, which only the affluent can afford to navigate. A salaried individual can't risk legal gray areas, but a corporation can hire teams to exploit them. Ambiguity becomes a strategic asset for the wealthy. Identical actions—like underreporting or expense misclassification—lead to vastly different outcomes depending on one's status. The poor receive notices. The rich get loopholes. All of this unfolds under a state narrative that frames tax compliance as a moral duty. Citizens are told to "do their part," contribute to nation-building, and shoulder the fiscal weight of the country. But what morality remains when the system itself behaves without it? When fairness is absent and justice is uneven, what incentive does an honest taxpayer have to remain loyal?

What we face is not a neutral legal system but a calculated architecture that protects wealth while punishing labour. This isn't the taxation model of a just society—it's the economic skeleton of a financial caste hierarchy. The rich are shielded by the very laws that discipline the rest. The same statute that fences off their fortunes is the lash that strikes your income. You are not merely overlooked; you are actively targeted by a system that presents inequality as order and exploitation as progress.

8.6 No Real Reform Ever Happens

Every few years, a new government promises sweeping reforms to the tax system, claiming that the outdated, exploitative, and convoluted structures will finally be dismantled in favour of simplicity, fairness, and transparency. These assurances are sold to the public with glossy slogans, expertly drafted press releases, and staged interviews with economists. But once the dust settles, nothing truly changes. The real face of the Indian tax system remains the same—designed not to liberate but to ensnare. What appears as change is often just a reshuffling of language, a redirection of the same burdens under new labels, or worse, a deepening of the very inequalities that reform was supposed to correct.

The core issue lies in the nature of how reforms are conceived—not from the ground up, with citizen welfare in mind, but from the top down, tailored to favour institutional power brokers, corporate lobbyists, and entrenched bureaucracies. Even the much-hyped Goods and Services Tax (GST), which was marketed as a "revolutionary simplification," ended up becoming a Kafkaesque maze of rates, slabs, and rules. For small businesses, traders, and common consumers, GST did not represent liberation from the previous tax mess—it added a new layer of confusion and control. Compliance costs went up, not down. Harassment from authorities increased. And the flexibility to manage cash flow diminished severely for the informal sector.

When governments speak of "reforms," what they really mean is realignment of the status quo without disrupting the power structure. Cosmetic changes like altering filing deadlines, digitizing platforms, or rewording tax provisions are sold as progress, but they do not touch the heart of the problem—the asymmetry in burden between classes, the inaccessibility of legal remedies for the poor, and the institutional corruption that breeds in complexity. These "reforms" are never people-centric; they are policy tools wrapped in illusion, implemented not to empower but to pacify.

A crucial reason genuine reform never takes root is that the very beneficiaries of the existing system are the ones tasked with redesigning it. Bureaucrats, who enjoy near-absolute power in interpretation and enforcement of tax laws, have no incentive to simplify the system in a way that reduces their discretionary authority. Politicians, who fund their campaigns through deals with business elites, are unlikely to push for structural reforms that would curtail the privileges of the super-rich. The result is a mockery of transformation—one where slogans change but control mechanisms stay intact.

Even well-intentioned reform proposals are eventually watered down in parliamentary committees, diluted by special interest groups, or completely derailed through bureaucratic resistance. The moment a tax change begins to threaten elite interests—be it inheritance taxes, wealth taxes, or closing corporate loopholes—it is quickly branded as "anti-growth" or "populist," and is shelved indefinitely. What passes through instead are reforms that shift burdens onto the shoulders of the many—raising indirect taxes, increasing user fees, or reducing public services to create fiscal room without touching the affluent.

The refusal to undertake real reform also stems from how tax ideology is shaped in the country. The discourse is intentionally muddled. Taxation is not discussed as a tool for equity or justice; it's sold as a civic responsibility. But this "responsibility" disproportionately weighs down on the powerless, while the powerful are allowed to carry far less, or even none at all, using legitimate legal mechanisms and underhanded manipulation. As long as the narrative frames tax reform as a matter of efficiency rather than justice, the deeper sickness in the system remains undiagnosed.

One of the most perverse features of this non-reforming tax regime is the enforcement machinery. Tax officials are rarely trained to serve or support citizens—they are conditioned to extract, penalize, and intimidate. Genuine reform would involve a cultural overhaul of these institutions, turning them from revenue hunters into facilitators of financial citizenship. But that would mean giving power back to the people—something the state machinery instinctively resists. It is easier to maintain a culture of fear and ambiguity, where people comply not out of pride but out of terror of reprisal.

Reforms in India are always reactive, not visionary. They are triggered by crises—economic slowdowns, international pressure, or electoral compulsions. Even then, the changes are often tokenistic. A new tax form, a digital app, or a one-time rebate is rolled out and paraded as reform. But the deeper issues of structural injustice, regressive taxation, and bureaucratic overreach are never addressed. This reveals a tragic reality: reform, in its truest sense, is not part of the state's agenda. It is a myth sustained to keep hope alive in the minds of an overburdened citizenry.

The irony is that India has no shortage of minds capable of designing a truly fair and transformative tax regime. Economists, policy thinkers, and civil society activists have repeatedly laid out blueprints for participatory, progressive, and citizen-oriented tax models. But these rarely see the light of day, because implementation is in the hands of those who benefit from inaction. Real reform would mean shaking the very foundations of power. And so, reforms are kept shallow—just deep enough to look real, but never deep enough to change anything.

In this endless theatre of change-without-change, citizens are left exhausted and disillusioned. Every budget season reignites hope, only to crush it under the weight of small print and hidden clauses. People adjust, adapt, and continue bearing the yoke of a system that promises transformation but thrives on stagnation. The reform story in India is not one of evolution—it is one of strategic evasion, where the system transforms itself just enough to avoid transforming at all.

8.7 Officials Hold All the Power

In any civilized democracy, power should ideally flow from the people, through elected representatives, and into institutions that serve the public with transparency and accountability. But in India's tax system, this flow is reversed. Power is hoarded at the top—by unelected, unaccountable officials who exercise sweeping authority over the lives, incomes, and freedoms of ordinary citizens. The tax machinery, though masked in the language of law and public service, is structured like a feudal empire. Its officers are not facilitators; they are gatekeepers and enforcers. And the deeper one peers into the functioning of this apparatus, the clearer it becomes that control—not justice or efficiency—is its ultimate purpose.

The average citizen has very little protection from arbitrary action by tax officials. The law gives them powers to conduct raids, freeze bank accounts, seize property, and demand documentation with minimal justification. While these powers are framed as tools to prevent evasion, their application often turns citizens into suspects. One clerical error, a delayed submission, or a mismatched invoice can trigger punitive measures that wreck livelihoods. These officials are judge, jury, and executioner in their domain. There is no immediate recourse for the individual. Appeals take years, cost money, and drain energy. The imbalance of power is so severe that most people prefer to comply—even when wrongly accused—rather than risk retaliation.

What worsens this reality is the near-total lack of transparency. Tax assessments are often arbitrary, based on vague interpretations of complex laws that even professionals struggle to decode. Communication from departments is frequently delayed or unclear, leaving citizens in a fog of confusion. Officials exploit this uncertainty. Many small business owners, self-employed professionals, and salaried individuals live in fear of that one phone call or notice that could turn their life upside down. It's not guilt—it's vulnerability. Systemic ambiguity gives officials room to intimidate and extract—sometimes legally, often coercively.

In a just system, checks and balances should prevent abuse. But in the Indian tax ecosystem, internal accountability mechanisms are weak or performative. Complaints against officers are rarely taken seriously. Disciplinary action is sluggish and rare. Promotions are more likely tied to revenue targets than ethical conduct. This creates a culture where harassment is not an exception—it's normalized. Officers who squeeze more out of citizens are rewarded. Those who show empathy risk being side-lined. The system doesn't promote service; it incentivizes aggression.

This power dynamic becomes even more dangerous when combined with political interference. Tax agencies have increasingly been used as instruments of intimidation against dissenting voices, NGOs, journalists, and opposition figures. Selective raids, freezing of accounts, and fabricated cases become tools to silence criticism. The message is clear: the tax system is not just an economic mechanism—it is a weapon. And the ones who control it can decide whose life gets dismantled and whose gets protected. This politicization erodes public trust and reinforces the idea that tax officials serve the state's interest, not the citizen's.

Even technology, which was supposed to democratize tax administration, has failed to dilute the grip of official power. E-filing portals, faceless assessments, and AI-based red flags have only made the system more impersonal—not more just. Behind every algorithm still sits an official who can trigger consequences without meaningful dialogue. Citizens now face an even colder wall—machines that enforce decisions made by invisible hands. There is no face, no conversation, no empathy—only authority.

The power imbalance also extends to how tax laws are applied unequally. Large corporations with elite lawyers can negotiate settlements, defer liabilities, or manipulate transfer pricing. But small traders, freelancers, and ordinary workers have no such leverage. They are visible, vulnerable, and voiceless. Officials know this and act accordingly. The more powerless you are, the easier it is for the system to extract from you. And in that asymmetry, the idea of justice collapses entirely.

A society cannot be called democratic when its people are constantly looking over their shoulders, not because they've done wrong, but because the system is structured to assume guilt. Power without restraint is tyranny, and the Indian tax administration, in its current form, functions like a tyrannical gatekeeper. It does not ask "how can I help you comply?" It demands "prove that you're not cheating," and until you do, you remain under suspicion.

To correct this imbalance, the structure itself must be reimagined. Citizens need independent grievance redressal forums, real-time transparency, simplified legal language, and above all, a redefinition of the official's role—from enforcer to guide. Until then, tax officials will continue to wield disproportionate, unchecked power over the very people they are meant to serve—not as protectors of public interest, but as custodians of a system built to command, control, and crush.

8.8 Modern Tax Slavery

In the past, slavery was defined by physical chains and overt domination. The enslaved were visibly oppressed, their bodies and labour extracted without consent or fair compensation. Today, the shackles of modern slavery are far more insidious. They are invisible, embedded into everyday life. The modern citizen is not forced into labour by a master with a whip but by a system that ties livelihood and well-being to an oppressive tax structure. The illusion of freedom is maintained, while the reality of captivity deepens.

In the modern tax system, citizens are coerced into lifelong compliance through a web of rules, penalties, and hidden costs that pervade nearly every aspect of their existence. From birth, they're entangled—directly or indirectly. Taxes aren't just a financial obligation; they become a way of life. Falling out of line—intentionally or otherwise—brings steep consequences. Late payments incur penalties. Errors trigger audits. Minor slips can lead to devastating outcomes. The system doesn't aim to serve citizens but to extract from them endlessly. It mimics historical subjugation, only more subtle and psychologically draining.

What makes modern tax slavery particularly dangerous is its disguise as civic duty. The system convinces citizens that taxation is for their own good—that paying is virtuous and patriotic. But in reality, it is a mechanism of exploitation. For most, taxes aren't a contribution to public welfare; they're a survival fee. Citizens have no choice but to pay, often without fully understanding their obligations or having any influence on how those funds are used. Their compliance is demanded, not earned.

Consider the all-encompassing nature of taxes in India. Whether it's goods, services, or personal income, tax infiltrates every transaction. It's not just the obvious ones like GST or income tax; there's a multitude of smaller, often unnoticed taxes hidden in daily expenses. Most citizens don't even realize the full extent of what they're paying. The state demands compliance, yet offers little transparency in return. The burden is constant, with minimal relief or accountability. The result is a system that quietly drains without visible benefit.

The psychological toll is perhaps the most brutal aspect. The pressure to comply, the fear of scrutiny, and the uncertainty around what qualifies as "correct" behaviour form a heavy mental load. Many citizens live with the looming threat of error—not because they intend to cheat the system, but because the system is incomprehensible. The awareness that much of the collected tax does not improve public services only deepens the despair. Education, healthcare, and infrastructure remain substandard despite growing tax revenues. The poor pay the most relative to what they receive, while the wealthy often escape with minimal sacrifice. This structural imbalance leaves citizens powerless over how their money is spent. They are forced to fund a bloated, inefficient machine that does little to serve their interests. The lack of transparency in how funds are allocated and the rampant misuse of public resources erode any remaining trust. Essential services remain starved of funds. Roads decay, public hospitals fail, and schools underperform, while the citizen keeps paying, receiving little in return.

The most tragic part is that those most harmed by this system—working-class individuals, small entrepreneurs, the marginalized—are often made to feel they are the problem. The idea of civic responsibility is twisted to imply that questioning the system equates to betrayal. This subtle manipulation deepens the psychological trap. It disarms resistance and encourages silent endurance. People begin to believe that this is just the way things are. Hope for change fades. The elite, who benefit most from the current structure, continue unaffected while the masses remain trapped in economic servitude.

The tax system enforces a form of economic slavery. It does not rely on violence but on control—psychological, financial, and bureaucratic. Taxes, once a civic duty, have become a tool of coercion. The system reinforces existing hierarchies and perpetuates inequality. And now, with the addition of digital surveillance, AI-based red flags, and faceless bureaucracy, the chains have become harder to detect and even harder to break.

It's a prison without walls. Every digital transaction, every monthly income, every bill paid is tracked, taxed, and fed into a system that watches more than it serves. Escape seems impossible. Even protest is muted, as citizens fear punishment more than they hope for justice. Compliance is safer than resistance, even when it means accepting injustice. The modern state, instead of being a protector, becomes an extractor—ensuring that the majority remain busy surviving, never thriving.

In essence, modern tax slavery is not about funding progress; it's about enforcing control. The mechanisms have changed, but the outcome is the same: a few hold the power, while the many works endlessly to sustain a structure that exploits them. This invisible captivity, draped in legality and patriotism, is perhaps the most effective form of subjugation ever created.

8.9 Work Day and Night, Stay in Same Place

The promise of progress, prosperity, and upward mobility is a constant refrain in modern societies. We are told that hard work and perseverance will lead to success, that diligence and sacrifice will eventually pay off. This narrative is deeply ingrained in our understanding of life and work. We are conditioned to believe that by working hard—day and night—we can rise above our circumstances, break free from the shackles of mediocrity, and achieve a better life. However, in the reality of the tax system, this promise is often a cruel illusion. No matter how much we work, how many hours we dedicate to our craft, or how hard we strive for success, many people find themselves trapped in the same cycle, barely able to break free. The system keeps them tethered to the same place, with little hope of true progress.

The modern tax system is one of the key mechanisms that keeps this illusion alive. It demands that citizens work tirelessly, often without respite, while offering very little in return. The majority of people, particularly those in the lower and middle classes, spend their entire lives paying taxes—an endless stream of deductions that take away from their earnings, while offering them little in terms of tangible benefits. For the common person, the result is a never-ending cycle of work and taxation, with no clear path forward. They are stuck, often forced into long hours of labour just to make ends meet, with the hope that their hard work will eventually translate into financial stability. But as they toil away, the tax system continues to drain their income, ensuring that any small step forward is followed by two steps back. This cycle is made even more brutal by the fact that, for many, the work they do is largely invisible. Whether it's a small business owner working tirelessly to stay afloat, a salaried employee struggling to make ends meet, or a labourer working long hours for a meagre wage, their efforts are often undervalued. The tax system, in its complexity and harsh enforcement, adds another layer of obscurity to their labour. No matter how much time and energy they dedicate to their work, the system does not acknowledge their efforts in a meaningful way. It simply extracts from them—constantly, relentlessly—leaving little room for financial growth or personal development.

The tax system reinforces this trap by imposing its demands on every facet of life. From income tax to GST to other indirect taxes, every transaction is a reminder that the state has a claim on one's earnings. For those in formal employment, the payroll tax and mandatory deductions further reduce their take-home income. For those running businesses, the pressure is even more intense, as they face a complex maze of rules and regulations that are constantly shifting. It doesn't matter if the business is thriving or struggling; the taxman demands his share, without regard for the individual's ability to pay. And for those who are employed or working in precarious jobs, the burden is often insurmountable.

As a result, despite the long hours worked and the apparent devotion to achieving a better life, many find themselves in the same place, year after year. They may be able to afford a modest lifestyle, but real financial freedom remains out of reach. The system is designed to prevent them from moving beyond their current position. The promise of upward mobility is a mirage, visible but always just beyond the horizon. The harder one works, the more the system extracts, and the further away true freedom becomes. This is not just a financial trap; it is a psychological one as well. The constant pressure to comply with ever-changing tax rules, the fear of audits, and the nagging anxiety that comes with the knowledge that a mistake could ruin everything, creates a sense of stagnation. The individual becomes consumed by the need to keep up, to ensure that every tax obligation is met, while forgetting about their personal aspirations and long-term goals. Their work, instead of being a means to an end, becomes an endless loop of survival. In this environment, success is not defined by achieving one's dreams, but by simply managing to stay afloat.

For the rich and powerful, the system works differently. They are not bound by the same rules. They can hire lawyers, accountants, and financial planners to navigate the complexities of tax laws. They can find ways to minimize their tax liabilities, often legally, but sometimes through loopholes and manipulations that the average citizen cannot access. They are not burdened by the constant struggle to make ends meet. Instead, they accumulate wealth with little concern for the taxes they pay—or more accurately, the taxes they don't pay. For them, the system is designed to ensure that they are not trapped in the same cycle of labour and tax that keeps the common person bound to their work.

This disparity highlights the true nature of the tax system. While the average citizen works day and night, trying to earn enough to survive, the wealthiest have the luxury of remaining free from the system's most oppressive demands. The tax laws, far from creating equality, serve to widen the gap between the rich and the poor. The common person is stuck in the same place, struggling to move forward, while the powerful continue to amass wealth, sheltered from the very system that was supposedly designed to create fairness and equity. The promise of progress is an illusion—a cruel trick played by the system to keep people working without ever truly escaping their circumstances.

In this environment, the cycle becomes self-perpetuating. The more one works, the more one pays, and the less room there is for true personal or financial growth. It is a system designed to maintain the status quo, to keep people locked in a perpetual state of labour, without ever allowing them to truly break free. The modern tax system, rather than being a tool of progress, is a mechanism that ensures the entrapment of the working class, keeping them in the same place, forever toiling away for the benefit of a few.

8.10 Lifetime Loot in the Name of Nation

The concept of taxation is often framed as a civic duty—a contribution to the well-being of the nation, a collective effort to build infrastructure, provide services, and ensure national security. However, the reality of how taxes are collected and distributed reveals a darker truth. Rather than being a fair and transparent system designed for the benefit of all citizens, modern taxation has become a tool for the relentless extraction of wealth from the masses, funneled into the hands of a few. The so-called "nation-building" that taxes are supposed to support is often an illusion, masking the fact that the majority of tax revenue is siphoned off, misused, or misdirected. Citizens work tirelessly for their entire lives, paying taxes that they believe are building their country, but in reality, they are financing a system that benefits the elite few.

From the moment an individual begins earning, they are locked into a cycle of payment that lasts a lifetime. Every salary increment, every new source of income, every financial success is met with the heavy hand of taxation, drawing money away from the individual, seemingly for the betterment of society. The tax system is portrayed as the price for living in a functioning country, for enjoying the benefits of roads, healthcare, education, and social security. But what the system fails to acknowledge is that the majority of these services are inadequate, underfunded, or mismanaged. The money that is collected through taxes does not equitably translate into the services promised. In fact, much of it disappears into bureaucratic black holes, wasted on inefficiency, corruption, and systemic mismanagement. The masses continue to pay, working harder to contribute, while seeing little in return for their efforts.

The rich, by contrast, are able to avoid the burdens that the average citizen faces. With their wealth, they can afford to hire financial experts, lawyers, and tax consultants who navigate the complexities of the system and exploit loopholes. These individuals are often able to reduce their tax liability, ensuring that they contribute a fraction of what they should be paying. Meanwhile, the average citizen, without such resources, is forced to comply with the tax demands—an ever-increasing portion of their income siphoned away. The inequality is stark, with the tax system functioning as a vehicle for the perpetuation of wealth for the few, while draining the life force of the many. This dynamic is particularly evident in the way taxes are levied on individuals who have little to no control over the vast majority of their earnings. A salaried worker has their taxes deducted at source, with little say in how much they contribute. Business owners face an overwhelming amount of red tape and regulation that often leaves them with little time or energy to focus on growing their business. Meanwhile, the elite—those with power and influence—are able to manipulate the system, ensuring they are not burdened by the same tax obligations that the common citizen faces. The disparity between the rich and the poor grows ever wider, with the tax system acting as the vehicle for the wealthy to consolidate their control over the nation's resources, while the masses are kept in a perpetual state of financial struggle.

In essence, the modern tax system has become a form of legalized theft—a lifetime of forced labour and financial sacrifice in the name of national service, with little to show for it in terms of tangible benefit. People are made to believe that their hard-earned money is being used for the greater good, but in reality, it is often being funneled into the coffers of the few, who already enjoy the privileges of wealth, power, and influence. The illusion of national unity and progress is nothing more than a smokescreen, behind which a system of exploitation is perpetuated. This cycle of lifetime financial extraction benefits only the powerful, creating an entrenched class system that prevents the upward mobility of the working masses. The state, instead of being a protector of its citizens, becomes an instrument of control and exploitation. The taxes that individuals pay throughout their lives become the means by which the rich and powerful maintain their dominance, while the rest of society remains stuck in a never-ending struggle for survival.

The false narrative that taxes are a necessary and patriotic duty is constantly reinforced by the state and its institutions, ensuring that citizens believe in their role as contributors to the greater good. But this narrative is a lie, designed to placate the masses and keep them docile in the face of an unjust system. In reality, taxes have become a tool of financial oppression, forcing citizens to work endlessly for a system that never truly rewards them. The promises of a better future—of nation-building, of progress, of prosperity—are nothing more than empty words, while the actual outcome is a lifetime of financial servitude.

As people continue to work day and night, contributing to a system that does little to serve them, the nation's true beneficiaries are those who never face the hardships that the common citizen endures. The rich grow wealthier, the powerful grow more powerful, and the cycle continues. The system is designed not to build a fair and just society, but to entrench inequality and ensure that the elite remain firmly in control, profiting from the labour of those who will never see the fruits of their efforts. The lifetime loot collected in the name of the nation is, in fact, the theft of individual potential, a system built to ensure that the poor remain poor, and the rich remain rich.

In the end, the truth behind the tax system is one of manipulation and exploitation. What was once presented as a collective effort for national prosperity has morphed into a mechanism designed to keep the majority in a constant state of struggle. The complexity of the rules, the constant changes, and the disproportionate burdens placed on ordinary people ensure that the vast majority remain trapped in a cycle of labour without true progress. The idea of upward mobility becomes an illusion, as no matter how hard one works, the system ensures they remain in the same place, with little chance of breaking free. The notion of nation-building masks a reality where taxes are used as a tool for the powerful to continue amassing wealth, while the common person is left bearing the brunt of the system. It is a modern form of enslavement, where the promise of a better life is overshadowed by an unrelenting burden, leaving individuals with nothing but empty promises and a lifetime of sacrifice.

Chapter 9
What Other Countries Do Right

Tax systems around the world vary greatly in terms of fairness, transparency, and efficiency. While many countries have complicated, often oppressive tax structures that leave their citizens feeling burdened and disillusioned, there are others that have crafted systems which are not only simple and straightforward but also built with the people in mind. In this chapter, we will explore countries that have designed tax policies that respect their citizens, foster fairness, and provide valuable lessons for others, including India. By examining these models, we can understand what works and how their systems serve their populations effectively. Ultimately, the goal is to highlight the stark differences and present actionable ideas for how India and other nations can learn from these successful examples to improve their own tax systems.

9.1 Countries That Treat Citizens Fairly

Some nations have managed to create tax systems that prioritize fairness and ensure their citizens are treated with respect. In these countries, the tax system is not a tool for oppression, but a means of contributing to the common good in a way that benefits everyone equitably. These nations recognize the importance of a transparent, simple, and fair system that does not disproportionately burden any one segment of society.

For instance, countries like Sweden, Norway, and Denmark have long been praised for their tax systems. These nations operate under the principle of progressive taxation, where the tax rate increases with income, ensuring that those who earn more contribute more. However, the difference in these countries lies in the fact that their tax systems are not just about extracting money, but about making sure that citizens see tangible returns on their contributions in the form of high-quality public services.

In Sweden, for example, taxes are collected at both the national and local levels, but the government has built a robust system where citizens benefit from universal healthcare, world-class education, and social welfare programs.

The high tax rates are balanced by the certainty that the money will be used to improve the quality of life for all citizens, making the system feel fair and just. People in these countries do not fear the tax authorities, but rather feel that their taxes contribute to the public good, and in return, they receive services that make their lives better.

What sets these countries apart is the transparency of their tax systems. Citizens understand how their taxes are being spent because the government is open about where the money goes. There is also an emphasis on simplicity and accessibility. Tax codes are designed to be as straightforward as possible, minimizing confusion and the potential for mistakes. This transparency fosters a sense of trust between the government and its citizens, which is crucial for maintaining compliance and public support. Furthermore, these countries invest in a strong social safety net, which not only supports individuals during times of need but also ensures that the benefits of a strong economy are felt by everyone, not just the wealthy. This reduces inequality and promotes a more cohesive society where citizens feel their contributions to the tax system are directly linked to the services they receive.

By contrast, many countries with more oppressive tax systems often lack this level of fairness and transparency. In places where tax policies are complex, punitive, and unclear, citizens feel alienated from the process and skeptical about the system's efficacy. In these environments, tax compliance becomes less about civic duty and more about fear of penalties and prosecution.

The key takeaway from these fair tax systems is the understanding that taxes are not merely a financial obligation but an investment in the collective well-being of the society. Citizens who feel their contributions are used effectively are more likely to comply willingly, knowing that they are part of a system that treats them fairly and equitably. This is the model that other nations should strive for, where taxation serves as a bridge between citizens and the government, promoting a sense of unity and mutual benefit.

9.2 Simple Flat Tax Systems

While progressive tax systems can offer significant benefits, they often come with complexity that can confuse or overwhelm citizens. In contrast, some countries have adopted simpler flat tax systems, which impose a uniform tax rate on all income levels. This simplicity removes the layers of bureaucracy and intricate regulations that can create barriers for taxpayers and lead to inefficiencies. With a flat tax, citizens can more easily understand their obligations, and the government can reduce administrative costs associated with tax collection.

One of the most notable examples of a successful flat tax system is found in Estonia. This small Baltic nation has been praised for its straightforward and transparent approach to taxation. Estonia implemented a flat tax rate of 20% on both personal and corporate income, which has helped streamline tax compliance while simultaneously boosting the nation's economic performance. The flat tax model makes it easier for individuals and businesses to calculate how much they owe, reducing the need for complex tax filings or costly tax preparation services. Furthermore, it eliminates the disincentives that often accompany progressive tax rates, where higher income levels are taxed at progressively higher rates, which can discourage savings, investment, and economic growth.

In countries like Estonia, the simplicity of the flat tax system allows for better transparency, making it clear to citizens exactly what their obligations are. There are fewer loopholes, and the system is difficult to manipulate, which helps curb tax evasion. The lack of a convoluted set of rules also enables the government to focus more on ensuring that the tax revenue is spent efficiently, rather than constantly engaging in complex tax audits and compliance enforcement.

Other countries, such as Russia and some nations in Eastern Europe, have also adopted flat tax systems with varying degrees of success. In many of these cases, the flat tax has been credited with driving economic growth and improving compliance rates. By maintaining a simple, predictable tax structure, these countries have created an environment that encourages entrepreneurial activity and attracts foreign investment. Investors and business owners are often deterred by complicated tax codes that require navigating through a maze of deductions, credits, and exemptions. In contrast, the predictability of a flat tax system simplifies decision-making and makes it easier for businesses to plan long-term.

Moreover, flat tax systems tend to encourage fairness in taxation. In a progressive system, there is often a sense of inequality, as individuals in higher income brackets are required to pay increasingly higher tax rates. In contrast, a flat tax treats everyone the same, regardless of their income level. This universality can promote a sense of equality, as all citizens contribute the same percentage of their income toward national development.

While a flat tax system may not be suitable for every country, especially those with large income disparities, it offers important lessons in simplicity, fairness, and transparency. It shows that tax systems need not be complicated to be effective. By removing unnecessary layers of complexity, governments can ensure that citizens and businesses alike are treated equitably, while reducing the chances of corruption or inefficiency. In nations like India, where the tax code is notoriously complex and difficult to navigate, exploring the possibility of a flat tax system could simplify the entire process and foster a greater sense of trust between the government and its citizens.

9.3 Nations With No Tax and Free Services

While most countries rely on taxes to fund government services, a few have experimented with systems where taxes are either minimal or non-existent, yet citizens still receive essential public services free of charge. These nations represent an interesting alternative model that challenges the traditional reliance on taxation for the financing of government functions. By finding other means of revenue generation or restructuring government priorities, these countries have managed to provide high-quality public services without burdening their citizens with the complex tax systems many other nations face.

One of the most well-known examples of a country that has successfully implemented a low or no-tax system is the United Arab Emirates (UAE). In this oil-rich nation, there is no personal income tax, and the government generates a significant portion of its revenue from the sale of oil and natural gas. Despite the lack of personal income tax, the UAE offers a range of free or heavily subsidized public services, such as healthcare and education, to its citizens. The government has made strategic investments in its natural resources, allowing it to fund public services and infrastructure projects without the need to impose heavy taxes on its population.

This model of relying on alternative revenue sources, such as natural resources or sovereign wealth funds, is not unique to the UAE. Other countries with abundant natural resources, such as Qatar and Kuwait, follow similar strategies. By using their resource wealth to fund government functions, these nations are able to provide their citizens with high-quality public services without the need for a complicated or burdensome tax system. For example, in these countries, healthcare services are typically free or highly subsidized for citizens, and education is provided at no cost.

Another example is the principality of Monaco, a small city-state on the French Riviera. Monaco is famous for its tax policies, which are notably lenient compared to most other countries. The government does not impose personal income taxes, and it also has low business taxes. Monaco's revenue primarily comes from tourism, real estate, and the highly lucrative gambling industry, particularly through the famous Casino de Monte-Carlo. The wealth generated by these industries allows the government to offer free public services, such as healthcare, education, and even public transportation, to its citizens and residents.

The concept of no-tax systems is not limited to wealthy, resource-rich nations. Some nations with smaller populations, such as certain Pacific Island nations, also utilize similar models. For example, the island nation of Nauru, once wealthy from phosphate mining, has relied on mining revenue to fund public services and infrastructure projects without imposing a personal income tax on its citizens. However, these models come with challenges. Relying on natural resources or other forms of wealth can be volatile, especially when markets fluctuate or resources are depleted.

Despite the challenges, these nations provide an alternative approach to public service funding. The key lesson they offer is that it is possible to provide free public services without burdening citizens with complex and onerous tax systems. These nations demonstrate that revenue for government services does not always have to come from the traditional model of income tax. By focusing on sustainable sources of revenue, whether through natural resources, tourism, or other industries, governments can provide essential services without the need for extensive taxation, ensuring that the cost burden on citizens is minimized.

For countries like India, where the tax system is often criticized for its complexity and burden on the average person, exploring such alternative models could offer valuable insights. While it may not be feasible for India to completely eliminate taxes, finding ways to ease the tax burden by diversifying revenue sources and offering more efficient public services could go a long way in improving the overall experience for taxpayers. If governments can adopt policies that allow for the delivery of essential services without excessive taxation, they may build a more harmonious relationship with their citizens, leading to greater satisfaction and improved compliance.

9.4 Taxpayers Respected, Not Feared

In many countries, taxpayers are treated with a sense of suspicion and fear, often viewing their relationship with the government as one of adversarial compliance. This fear stems from the threat of audits, penalties, and a complex web of laws that make it difficult for individuals to navigate the tax system without the constant concern of making a mistake. However, there are nations where the relationship between the government and its citizens is based on respect rather than fear, creating an environment where taxpayers feel valued and trusted.

One of the key features of these systems is a recognition that taxes are the collective contribution of citizens to the well-being of society, not a punishment or a burden. In countries like Finland and the Netherlands, tax authorities are designed to be more approachable, ensuring that the process is straightforward and transparent. In these countries, taxpayers are not seen as potential criminals, but as active participants in the national growth and development. The tax office is viewed more as a service-oriented institution than an enforcement agency.

In Finland, for example, the tax system is known for its simplicity and efficiency. The Finnish tax administration system allows individuals to file their taxes easily, with many citizens receiving pre-filled tax returns, reducing the time and effort required for compliance. Additionally, Finland's public services are top-notch, and citizens can see how their tax money is used to fund essential services such as healthcare, education, and infrastructure. This transparency builds trust, and because citizens see the value of their contributions, they are more likely to comply voluntarily, viewing taxes as a fair and necessary part of living in a functioning society.

In the Netherlands, the tax office takes a proactive approach to ensure that taxpayers feel supported throughout the tax process. The government provides clear information, accessible online tools, and responsive customer service to help individuals understand their tax obligations. Rather than relying on fear tactics, the Dutch system encourages voluntary compliance by making the process as smooth and easy as possible. The government also takes steps to ensure that the tax burden is shared equitably, with progressive rates that reflect the individual's ability to pay. As a result, taxpayers feel that the system works for them, not against them, and that the tax authorities are there to help rather than penalize them.

What sets these countries apart is the culture of mutual respect between the government and its citizens. In nations like these, taxpayers do not fear the tax authorities; instead, they trust that the system is working fairly and effectively. This positive relationship results in higher compliance rates and a greater sense of civic duty, as people understand that their contributions go toward improving the quality of life for everyone in the country.

In contrast, countries with punitive tax systems create a climate of distrust, where taxpayers are constantly worried about making mistakes or facing penalties. This leads to anxiety and reluctance to pay taxes, further complicating the situation and decreasing overall compliance. In many cases, these countries also waste resources on costly enforcement measures, such as audits, investigations, and legal proceedings, all of which could be avoided if the system were built on mutual respect rather than fear.

For India, where the tax system is often criticized for its complexity and the suspicion surrounding its enforcement, adopting elements of these respectful approaches could improve public confidence and ensure better tax compliance. By shifting the focus from enforcement to service and support, the government could foster a relationship with citizens based on trust and cooperation. This would not only simplify the tax system but also reduce the need for harsh penalties and punitive measures. When taxpayers are treated with respect and feel confident that the system is fair, they are more likely to willingly participate in the system, contributing to the overall strength and success of the nation.

9.5 Government Services That Actually Work

In many countries, citizens' taxes are seen as a direct investment into the nation's welfare, yet far too often, the services provided in exchange for these taxes fail to meet expectations. Bureaucracy, inefficiency, and corruption can diminish the effectiveness of public services, leaving citizens feeling as though their contributions have gone to waste. However, there are nations where government services are not only functional but excel in quality, providing real, tangible benefits to their citizens. These countries demonstrate that when tax revenue is used efficiently and effectively, it can lead to the creation of public services that work as intended, improving the overall quality of life for everyone. One of the most impressive examples of well-functioning government services is found in Scandinavian countries like Denmark, Sweden, and Norway. These nations are known for their high levels of public service efficiency and the wide-ranging benefits provided to their citizens. In these countries, taxes are viewed as an investment in the collective good, and the government ensures that the services funded by tax revenue are accessible, of high quality, and serve the needs of the population.

In Denmark, for example, the healthcare system is universally available and is regarded as one of the best in the world. Medical services are free at the point of delivery, ensuring that every citizen, regardless of income, has access to essential healthcare. The education system is similarly well-funded, with free education provided from primary school through university. The quality of these services is consistently high, due in part to the efficient allocation of resources and the government's strong commitment to ensuring that public services are responsive to citizens' needs.

Sweden is another country where government services are recognized for their efficiency. The Swedish social welfare system, which provides universal healthcare, parental leave, and pension benefits, is one of the most comprehensive in the world. These services are funded through taxes, but citizens receive excellent value in return. The system is designed to ensure that everyone, regardless of their background, has access to the services they need to thrive. As a result, Sweden has some of the highest rankings for quality of life and citizen satisfaction globally. The trust that Swedish citizens have in their government's ability to deliver services is reflected in the high tax rates, as citizens know that their contributions are being used effectively.

Norway is another prime example of government services that actually work. The country's extensive public services include free healthcare, free education, and a strong social safety net. Norway's government also manages a sovereign wealth fund, the Government Pension Fund Global, which invests the country's oil revenue to ensure future generations benefit from the nation's resources. The transparency of how tax revenue is spent and the public's ability to hold their government accountable have made Norwegian public services a model of efficiency and reliability.

In addition to the Nordic countries, nations like Singapore also provide high-quality government services funded by taxes. Singapore's government has a reputation for being exceptionally efficient and transparent. The country's healthcare system, for example, is based on a combination of mandatory savings accounts and government subsidies, ensuring that citizens have access to care without placing a heavy burden on taxpayers. The educational system is rigorous and results-oriented, and the public transport network is widely regarded as one of the best in the world. Singapore's focus on efficiency and innovation has allowed it to provide world-class services while maintaining a sustainable fiscal policy.

The key to the success of these countries' government services lies in their efficient use of tax revenue. These nations have established systems where public services are directly linked to the tax contributions of their citizens. Unlike in countries where bureaucracy, corruption, and inefficiency waste taxpayer money, these governments have designed transparent and accountable systems that deliver tangible results. This efficiency not only enhances the quality of life for citizens but also fosters trust in the government, which in turn leads to higher levels of tax compliance and civic engagement.

For India, the takeaway from these examples is clear: efficient government services are essential to gaining public trust and ensuring that taxpayers feel their contributions are being put to good use. India's tax system is often criticized for its inefficiency, and many government services are seen as underfunded or poorly managed. By focusing on improving the quality and efficiency of public services, India could make a significant improvement in its citizens' trust in the system. Ensuring that tax revenue is spent wisely and that services are accessible, reliable, and of high quality would go a long way in reshaping how taxpayers view their relationship with the government and may even inspire greater participation in the tax system.

9.6 Where India Stands in Global Rankings

India, with its massive population and complex socio-economic structure, faces unique challenges when it comes to governance, taxation, and public service delivery. While the country has made significant strides in recent years, it lags behind many other nations in key areas such as the quality of government services, tax efficiency, and citizen satisfaction. Global rankings provide a snapshot of how India compares to other countries across various domains, highlighting both the strengths and areas that need improvement.

When it comes to global rankings on tax systems, India often finds itself near the bottom of the list, particularly in areas like ease of paying taxes, transparency, and overall efficiency. The World Bank's "Paying Taxes" report, which ranks countries based on the ease with which businesses and individuals can comply with tax regulations, consistently places India in the middle to lower tiers. This ranking reflects the complexity of the Indian tax system, which is notorious for its multiple layers, frequent changes, and the burden it places on taxpayers. The introduction of the Goods and Services Tax (GST) was a step toward simplifying the system, but the complexities involved in its implementation have led to confusion and frustration among taxpayers.

India also ranks poorly in the area of government services, particularly in sectors such as healthcare, education, and infrastructure. While the country has made impressive progress in some areas—such as increasing access to primary education and reducing poverty—many public services are still underfunded and inefficient. For instance, despite being one of the world's largest economies, India struggles to provide universal access to quality healthcare. According to the World Health Organization (WHO), India's public health spending remains low compared to other nations, and the country faces significant challenges in ensuring equitable access to healthcare for all citizens, especially in rural areas.

In global education rankings, India also has room for improvement. While the country boasts a large number of prestigious educational institutions, such as the Indian Institutes of Technology (IITs), the majority of schools in India face significant challenges in terms of infrastructure, teacher quality, and student outcomes. The disparities between urban and rural areas are particularly pronounced, with rural schools often lacking basic facilities and resources. This gap has a direct impact on the overall quality of education and the future prospects of India's younger generation.

Infrastructure is another area where India lags behind many developed nations. While the country has made strides in developing its transportation networks, including roads, airports, and railways, India still faces significant challenges in terms of urban infrastructure. Cities are overcrowded, public transport systems are inadequate, and sanitation services are often subpar, particularly in smaller towns and rural areas. These infrastructure issues hamper the country's overall development and contribute to the inefficiencies of government services.

India's performance on the Corruption Perceptions Index (CPI), published by Transparency International, also highlights the challenges the country faces in terms of governance. While India has made progress in tackling corruption in recent years, it still struggles with pervasive corruption across various levels of government. This corruption erodes trust in public institutions and undermines the effectiveness of government programs, particularly in sectors like welfare distribution, public procurement, and law enforcement.

In terms of overall quality of life, India ranks relatively low on the Human Development Index (HDI), which measures factors such as life expectancy, education, and income. While the country has seen improvements in life expectancy and poverty reduction, challenges remain in providing adequate healthcare, education, and social services to its large and diverse population. The disparities between different states, and between urban and rural areas, are stark, with some regions facing far greater challenges in terms of development and access to services.

Despite these challenges, India has areas of strength that contribute positively to its global standing. The country is home to a rapidly growing economy, a dynamic entrepreneurial ecosystem, and a vibrant culture of innovation. Additionally, India's digital transformation in recent years, particularly in areas like financial inclusion and e-governance, has been noteworthy. The government's push for initiatives like Digital India has led to significant strides in improving access to government services, especially in rural areas. However, these successes are often overshadowed by the deeper structural issues within the country's governance and public service systems.

For India to improve its standing in global rankings, a comprehensive overhaul of its tax and public service systems is necessary. Simplifying the tax code, improving transparency, and reducing the burden on taxpayers would go a long way in improving the overall business environment. Additionally, greater investment in public services like healthcare, education, and infrastructure is essential to ensure that all citizens have access to the resources they need to thrive. Tackling corruption and improving the efficiency of government operations would also help rebuild public trust in the system and ensure that tax revenue is being used effectively.

India's position in global rankings serves as both a reflection of the progress made and a reminder of the significant challenges that lie ahead. By focusing on governance reform, improving service delivery, and addressing inequalities, India has the potential to move up in these rankings and offer its citizens a better quality of life.

9.7 Easy Filing, No Harassment

One of the most significant factors that influence a taxpayer's experience is the ease with which they can file their taxes. In many countries, the process is streamlined, digitalized, and made simple enough for citizens to complete on their own, without the need for cumbersome paperwork or bureaucratic hurdles. In contrast, the tax filing process in India remains complicated, opaque, and riddled with inefficiencies. The constant fear of making mistakes, facing audits, or getting entangled in legal issues creates a climate of uncertainty and distrust. But in countries where tax filing is straightforward, citizens can file their taxes with confidence, knowing that the system is transparent, user-friendly, and fair.

Countries that excel in this area prioritize user-friendly interfaces and make tax filing accessible to all. For example, nations like Estonia, New Zealand, and the United Kingdom have designed tax systems that allow individuals and businesses to file their returns online with minimal effort. In Estonia, the government has created a fully digital tax filing system where most citizens can file their returns with just a few clicks. Thanks to advanced e-government initiatives, the system is efficient and automated, making it easy for taxpayers to track their financial records and submit their taxes.

In New Zealand, the tax system operates on a similar principle of simplicity. The Inland Revenue Department (IRD) allows taxpayers to file their returns online using an intuitive system. New Zealand also boasts an impressive level of transparency, ensuring that taxpayers are informed about how their tax money is spent and the results it yields. These systems are designed to reduce unnecessary paperwork, eliminate the need for intermediaries, and allow citizens to comply with their tax obligations without stress.

The United Kingdom has also made significant strides in making the tax filing process simple and accessible. Her Majesty's Revenue and Customs (HMRC) has introduced an online portal that allows both individuals and businesses to file their taxes easily. The system is integrated with real-time data, meaning that taxpayers don't have to worry about manual calculations or tracking every expense. The online filing system is designed with simplicity in mind, ensuring that even individuals with minimal tax knowledge can navigate it.

Perhaps one of the most notable benefits of these systems is the elimination of harassment. In countries where tax filing is easy and transparent, there is minimal fear of audits, penalties, or unnecessary scrutiny. Citizens are confident that the system will treat them fairly, and in return, they are more willing to comply with their tax obligations. The clear communication of tax rules and deadlines, as well as the availability of help for taxpayers who need it, ensures that the filing process is free from intimidation.

India's tax system, on the other hand, still relies heavily on manual paperwork, multiple forms, and complicated procedures that can be overwhelming for the average taxpayer. While there has been progress with the introduction of online filing, the system remains plagued by technical issues, frequent updates, and a lack of clarity. The constant changes to tax laws and forms create confusion and lead to delays in the filing process. Furthermore, many taxpayers still face difficulties in accessing proper support or guidance, making it difficult for them to navigate the system without encountering roadblocks. Even minor errors can result in penalties or the threat of an audit, creating an atmosphere of fear that discourages compliance.

India's tax system also lacks the level of integration seen in more developed countries. The lack of a seamless connection between government departments, banks, and tax agencies means that taxpayers often have to juggle multiple portals and platforms to complete their filings. This fragmentation adds to the complexity of the process and increases the likelihood of errors. Furthermore, the lack of real-time data integration means that individuals have to manually track and calculate their earnings, deductions, and liabilities, which is both time-consuming and prone to mistakes.

Moreover, the fear of harassment by tax authorities looms large in India. Many citizens are wary of making even minor mistakes for fear of facing punitive actions or lengthy investigations. The system, which sometimes appears to focus more on generating revenue than providing support, has created an environment in which taxpayers are often treated as potential offenders. This undermines trust in the government and discourages citizens from willingly participating in the tax system.

The solution to these challenges lies in reforming the way India handles tax filing. Learning from the best practices of countries like Estonia, New Zealand, and the UK, India can simplify its filing system, reduce paperwork, and create a more transparent and accessible process for taxpayers. An online system that integrates all aspects of tax filing—from reporting income and expenses to paying taxes—would significantly ease the burden on taxpayers. By incorporating real-time data, creating clear communication channels, and offering easy access to support, India can build a tax system that is both efficient and citizen-friendly. India must work to shift the perception that tax authorities are adversaries. Instead, tax agencies should focus on offering assistance and guidance to taxpayers, helping them comply with regulations without fear of repercussions. When the process is straightforward, and taxpayers feel respected rather than harassed, compliance rates improve, and the system functions more effectively.

An easy, transparent, and non-intimidating tax filing system would not only reduce frustration for Indian citizens but also foster greater trust in the government. When taxpayers see that the system works for them, they are more likely to contribute willingly, helping to create a cycle of fairness and cooperation that benefits everyone.

9.8 What India Must Learn

To make substantial progress in its tax system and overall governance, India must look to the countries that have successfully implemented systems that prioritize ease, fairness, and efficiency. While India is undoubtedly a complex and diverse country with its unique challenges, the experiences of other nations offer valuable lessons that can help reshape the future of taxation and public service delivery. What India must learn is not just about adopting new technologies or systems but about cultivating a fundamental shift in how governance is approached—where citizens are treated as partners rather than subjects, and where the systems are designed with their welfare in mind.

The first lesson India can learn is the importance of simplification. Countries with successful tax systems have managed to make filing taxes a straightforward, transparent process, free of unnecessary complexity. In countries like Estonia and New Zealand, tax filing is a seamless process where most of the work is automated, and citizens are required to input minimal data. The government has already gathered much of the necessary information through integration with banks, employers, and other agencies, which greatly reduces the burden on individuals. In contrast, India's tax system remains an intricate web of forms, instructions, and complicated procedures. Simplifying the entire tax filing process would not only reduce errors but also foster a sense of ease and transparency among the citizens.

Another lesson lies in creating a culture of trust and respect between the government and the people. In nations where the tax system works efficiently, citizens feel that their tax money is used responsibly. There is transparency in how funds are allocated, and people can see tangible benefits in the form of well-functioning public services, robust infrastructure, and a general sense of fairness. For India, building trust would require a multi-pronged approach, including regular updates on how tax revenues are being spent, along with visible improvements in sectors like education, healthcare, and infrastructure. When citizens see that their contributions are directly benefiting their communities, they are more likely to comply willingly.

India must also learn the importance of accessibility in governance. A key aspect of the tax systems in countries that rank highly is how accessible the system is to all citizens, regardless of their education, income, or technological familiarity. The system should be easy to navigate, with clear guidelines and real-time help available at every stage. This means investing in user-friendly interfaces and providing support to individuals who may face difficulties. A helpline, easily accessible tutorials, or community outreach programs could help bridge the digital divide and ensure that everyone, from the rural poor to urban professionals, can navigate the tax system with ease.

Equally important is the lesson that India must create a system that values its citizens' time and minimizes unnecessary bureaucracy. In countries with efficient tax systems, filing taxes takes only a few minutes, and compliance is encouraged, not enforced with punitive measures. The focus is on making the process as convenient as possible. In India, the cumbersome process often leads to delays, penalties, and a perception that tax authorities are working against the people. To rectify this, the government must streamline tax processes, eliminate redundant steps, and make the filing process faster and more efficient.

Moreover, India can learn from countries that have a clear focus on digitalization. Many nations have adopted fully digital tax filing systems that allow individuals to submit their returns with minimal physical paperwork. In India, while there has been progress with digital filings, the system is still fragmented and not fully integrated. The push for e-governance must continue, and the government should focus on making tax filings and public services available to all, not just those who are digitally literate or have access to advanced technology. In countries like Estonia, digital systems are not just about filing taxes but about creating a complete digital experience where citizens can interact with all government services in one place. This includes everything from healthcare to business registration, making life more convenient and efficient for everyone.

India must also learn from the example of nations that have fostered a sense of community involvement in the tax process. For example, in some Nordic countries, citizens are not only encouraged to pay taxes but are actively involved in decisions regarding how those taxes are spent. The government's role is seen as a facilitator, creating policies and programs based on the collective input of the people. This level of engagement helps build a sense of ownership and responsibility, where taxpayers feel that their contributions are shaping the future of their nation. In India, however, the disconnect between the government and the public often creates an adversarial relationship, making it difficult for citizens to feel that they have any meaningful input into the process. Creating more channels for public participation, feedback, and debate could go a long way toward improving governance.

Finally, India must learn the importance of educating its citizens about taxes and public services. In many developed countries, there is an emphasis on educating the public about the tax system, how it works, and how it benefits everyone. This includes clear information about where tax money goes and how it contributes to the well-being of society. In India, there is a lack of basic financial literacy, which leads to confusion and skepticism about taxes. Public education campaigns about the purpose of taxes and their benefits could help foster a more informed and cooperative citizenry.

The lessons that India must learn are not simply about implementing new technologies or policies, but about fostering a cultural shift towards transparency, trust, and efficiency. The country has the potential to build a tax system that is fair, accessible, and effective—one that respects its citizens and serves their needs. By looking at the successes of other nations, India can take the necessary steps to overhaul its own system and build a future where citizens are empowered, government services are streamlined, and the tax system works for everyone.

India's path to an improved tax system requires not just the adoption of better practices but a complete transformation in its approach to governance. By learning from the experiences of countries that have successfully simplified their tax processes, prioritized transparency, and cultivated a sense of trust between citizens and the government, India can begin to create a system that works for all. It will require a commitment to making the tax process accessible, fair, and efficient, while also fostering public education and engagement. The goal should be to build a system where compliance is driven by respect and understanding, not fear and confusion, and where the government is seen as a partner in national progress rather than an adversary. By embracing these lessons, India can pave the way for a more equitable future, where its citizens are empowered to contribute to the nation's growth without the burden of a complicated and oppressive system hanging over them.

Chapter 10
The Way Ahead – Reform or Break Down

The need for reform in India's tax system has never been more pressing. With growing public disillusionment, an over-complicated bureaucracy, and increasing compliance burdens on citizens, India stands at a crossroads. The question is no longer about whether reform is necessary, but about how far the system is willing to go to change the lives of its people. Reform is the only way forward, but if the country fails to act swiftly, it risks the collapse of an already fragile system that undermines the very citizens it is meant to serve. This chapter will explore the critical areas where change is required and what steps need to be taken for India to move toward a tax system that is fair, efficient, and equitable for all. The way ahead is clear—India must either reform or face the consequences of continued breakdown.

10.1 Make Income Tax Simple

One of the most urgent changes India must implement is simplifying the income tax system. Currently, the income tax structure is a labyrinth of exemptions, deductions, and complex calculations that leave most taxpayers confused and overwhelmed. For the common citizen, understanding how much tax they owe is often an arduous task that requires professional help, adding to the costs and frustration. The complexity of the system also increases the chances of errors, which can result in penalties, audits, or even legal consequences.

Countries that have simplified their tax codes, such as New Zealand and Singapore, have shown that it is not only possible but highly beneficial to reduce the complexity of income tax systems. A simplified tax system makes compliance easier, reduces the burden on taxpayers, and, most importantly, ensures that more citizens will comply willingly, as they will better understand their obligations. For India, simplification could mean fewer exemptions and deductions, a flat tax rate, or an automated filing system that pre-fills most of the information for taxpayers.

Reducing the tax code's complexity would also benefit the government.

With a simpler system, the government would find it easier to collect taxes, reduce errors in filings, and eliminate the need for excessive audits and investigations. A streamlined approach would also significantly reduce the administrative cost of tax collection, freeing up resources that could be better spent elsewhere—like improving essential services. In countries where tax systems are simpler, citizens are more likely to feel that the government is working for their benefit, creating a climate of trust and mutual respect.

Making income tax simpler doesn't mean reducing tax rates or cutting government revenue. It means eliminating the unnecessary red tape, removing loopholes that allow for tax evasion, and making the process transparent and easy to follow. Instead of taxpayers spending days, weeks, or months navigating through complicated forms and rules, they should be able to file their taxes in a matter of hours—at most. The tax filing process should be intuitive, using technology to pre-fill most of the data and provide a clear breakdown of how much is owed, which should be as straightforward as possible. Ultimately, a simplified income tax system would encourage more people to file their taxes honestly and on time, reduce government reliance on coercion and punitive measures, and increase the sense of fairness within the system. In doing so, it would create a tax culture that prioritizes efficiency and transparency—core elements that are sorely needed in India's current system.

10.2 Remove GST from Essentials

One of the most pressing issues within India's taxation system is the Goods and Services Tax (GST), particularly its application to essential goods and services. While GST is designed to streamline the tax process and create a uniform tax structure across the country, its imposition on basic essentials such as food, healthcare, and education places an unnecessary burden on the common citizen. For many families, the added GST costs on everyday items push them further into poverty, increasing their financial strain and reducing their ability to meet basic needs.

The rationale behind applying GST to essentials needs to be reassessed. Basic goods like rice, vegetables, milk, medicines, and educational services are vital for every household, and taxing them disproportionately affects the lower and middle-income segments of the population. Unlike luxury items, which individuals purchase when they have surplus income, these essentials are non-negotiable and necessary for survival. Taxing them makes life harder for those who are already struggling to make ends meet, and it undermines the very purpose of a tax system, which should be designed to serve the public, not drain their already limited resources.

Countries around the world that have progressive tax systems often apply lower or no taxes to essential goods. In the United States, for example, many states have exemptions for food and medicine, understanding that these are critical to maintaining public well-being. Similarly, in the European Union, several member states provide exemptions or reduced VAT rates for essential products to ensure that citizens are not burdened with excessive taxes on their basic needs. India can take inspiration from these examples and consider removing GST from essentials entirely, or at the very least reduce the rate to make them more affordable for everyone.

The removal of GST from essentials would not only ease the financial pressure on families but also help reduce the inequality that exists in India's current tax structure. By making basic goods and services more accessible and affordable, the government would not only improve the standard of living for millions of people but also foster goodwill and trust between citizens and the state. This move would also be a step toward more inclusive governance, where the needs of the most vulnerable sections of society are prioritized.

Moreover, removing GST on essentials would help bridge the growing disparity between the rich and the poor. While the wealthy can afford to pay taxes on luxury goods and services, the poor cannot afford to be taxed on the necessities that sustain them. By eliminating this additional burden on the less fortunate, the government would promote fairness and equity, ensuring that taxation does not exacerbate existing social and economic divides.

In addition to the immediate financial relief it would offer, removing GST from essentials would also send a strong message about the government's commitment to prioritizing the welfare of its citizens. It would indicate a tax policy that places human dignity and basic needs at its core, rather than treating citizens as mere revenue sources. The long-term benefits of such a move would be substantial, both in terms of public health and the nation's overall economic well-being.

10.3 Give Free Services for Basic Needs

One of the most effective ways for the government to ease the burden on its citizens is by providing free services for basic needs such as healthcare, education, and sanitation. These are the foundational pillars of a healthy, prosperous society, yet they remain out of reach for many due to high costs and insufficient public support. While many developed nations offer free or heavily subsidized services in these essential sectors, India has yet to fully embrace this approach. By providing these basic services free of charge, India could ensure that no citizen is left behind, regardless of their financial standing.

Healthcare is an area where the provision of free services could dramatically improve the quality of life for millions of Indians. In a country where a significant portion of the population lives under the poverty line, medical expenses can quickly become overwhelming. For the poor, even the cost of a simple consultation or medicine can lead to catastrophic financial strain. By making healthcare free at the point of delivery, the government would ensure that no one has to choose between their health and their financial well-being. This would also reduce the dependence on private healthcare providers, which often charge exorbitant rates, making essential services accessible to all. Such a shift would not only improve public health but also contribute to greater economic productivity by reducing preventable diseases and improving the overall well-being of the population.

Similarly, education is another critical area where free services are essential. While there are numerous government schools in India, the quality of education remains inconsistent, with many institutions underfunded and overcrowded. Free education, from primary to tertiary levels, would ensure that every child, regardless of their background, has the opportunity to access quality learning. This would be a long-term investment in the nation's future, as an educated population is more likely to contribute to economic growth, innovation, and societal progress. Providing free education would also reduce the economic strain on families, especially in rural areas, where parents often struggle to afford school fees, uniforms, and books. It would empower individuals to break the cycle of poverty and build better lives for themselves and their families.

Sanitation, another crucial aspect of public welfare, must also be prioritized. Access to clean water, proper sewage systems, and waste management are essential for preventing disease and maintaining public health. In many parts of India, poor sanitation remains a major issue, leading to outbreaks of preventable diseases such as cholera and dysentery. Providing free, reliable sanitation services would not only improve health outcomes but also create cleaner, more livable environments for millions of people, especially in rural and underserved urban areas. Ensuring access to clean water and sanitation is not only a matter of public health but also a basic human right.

Providing free services for basic needs would also foster a sense of social justice. It would signal that the government values its citizens' well-being above all else, recognizing that access to healthcare, education, and sanitation is essential for a dignified life. By investing in these sectors, the government would be making a direct contribution to reducing inequality, helping to close the gap between the rich and the poor.

The financial feasibility of such a move should not be underestimated. While the government would need to allocate substantial funds to support free services, the long-term benefits would far outweigh the costs. A healthier, better-educated, and more productive population would contribute significantly to the nation's economy. Additionally, the savings in healthcare and other sectors resulting from a healthier population could offset much of the investment required. In the end, providing free services for basic needs would be an investment in India's future—one that would yield benefits for both individuals and the nation as a whole.

10.4 Show Citizens Where Their Tax Goes

One of the major issues in India's current tax system is the lack of transparency in how the tax collected from citizens is used. For most taxpayers, there is little to no understanding of how their hard-earned money is spent once it leaves their pockets. This lack of visibility leads to widespread mistrust in the government, as people feel their taxes are either wasted or used inefficiently. To build a system based on trust and accountability, it is essential that the government shows its citizens exactly where their tax money goes.

Transparency in tax usage is not a novel concept. Many developed nations already have systems in place that allow their citizens to track how their taxes are being spent. For example, some countries provide annual breakdowns or even real-time access to budgets and expenditures, allowing citizens to see how funds are allocated to areas such as infrastructure, healthcare, education, and defence. By adopting a similar approach, India could rebuild trust in its tax system and reduce the perception of corruption and mismanagement.

One of the simplest ways to achieve this would be to create a publicly accessible digital platform where taxpayers can see how their money is allocated and spent. The platform could provide a clear, detailed breakdown of the government's budget, showing the percentage of funds going to various sectors, and offering citizens insight into ongoing projects and their progress. This would also allow the government to highlight areas where tax revenue is being used effectively, thereby fostering a sense of civic pride and encouraging more people to comply with tax regulations.

The government could also introduce an annual tax receipt, where citizens can see exactly how much tax they paid in a given year and how it was distributed across different sectors. For example, if a taxpayer paid a certain amount in income tax, the receipt could show how much of that money was allocated to healthcare, education, roads, defence, and other services. This would provide a tangible connection between the tax system and the services citizens receive in return, making the process more transparent and equitable.

Another step toward increased transparency would be to publish detailed audits and reports on government spending. These reports should be easy to understand and available in the public domain, ensuring that citizens can hold the government accountable for how their taxes are being spent. If there are inefficiencies or wasteful expenditures, these audits would serve as an opportunity for public scrutiny and prompt corrective action.

By showing citizens exactly where their tax money goes, the government would not only foster trust but also ensure that the taxpayers feel a sense of ownership and involvement in the decision-making process. People are more likely to accept and comply with taxes if they feel that their contributions are being used to improve their lives and their country. This transparency would also reduce the likelihood of tax evasion and corruption, as citizens would be able to hold both the government and businesses accountable for any misuse of public funds.

In addition to improving trust, demonstrating how taxes are used could also inspire a greater sense of civic responsibility. When citizens see that their contributions lead to tangible improvements in infrastructure, education, healthcare, and other public services, they will likely feel more connected to their country and more willing to engage in the democratic process. This could also lead to a stronger, more cohesive society, where people are motivated to contribute to the nation's growth and well-being.

Ultimately, by showing citizens exactly how their taxes are spent, the government would take a major step toward a fairer, more accountable tax system. Transparency will not only foster trust but also make the entire process of taxation more equitable, ensuring that everyone—from the poorest to the wealthiest—feels they are getting value in return for their contributions to the nation.

10.5 Protect Those Who Pay Honestly

One of the most pressing issues in India's tax system is the widespread fear and mistrust among honest taxpayers. Many individuals who pay their taxes diligently often feel that they are punished for their integrity, while others evade taxes without consequence. The system's complexity and the frequent harassment by tax authorities only deepen the frustration for those who comply. To create a more equitable and functioning system, it is essential for the government to protect and support honest taxpayers, ensuring they are not penalized for fulfilling their civic duties.

The first step in this direction is providing legal safeguards for taxpayers against arbitrary or unjust treatment by tax authorities. In many cases, honest taxpayers find themselves entangled in bureaucratic red tape or subjected to intrusive audits, simply because they are seen as easy targets for the authorities. Rather than focusing on those who have failed to pay taxes, the system often unfairly burdens those who follow the rules. By establishing clear guidelines that protect honest taxpayers from unwarranted scrutiny, harassment, and delays, the government can ensure that those who comply with the system are treated fairly and with respect.

In addition to legal protection, it is essential that the tax system be streamlined and simplified. Taxpayers who fulfil their obligations should not have to spend excessive time and energy navigating a convoluted system. Currently, the complexities of the income tax filing process, frequent changes to tax laws, and numerous compliance requirements make it difficult for even well-meaning taxpayers to remain in full compliance. To protect honest individuals from inadvertently falling into non-compliance, the government needs to simplify the filing process and ensure that it is user-friendly. This could include the development of better online portals, clear instructions, and personalized guidance, making it easier for people to meet their tax obligations without unnecessary stress.

Equally important is ensuring that taxpayers who consistently pay their taxes on time and in full are rewarded for their commitment. In many countries, tax-paying citizens receive benefits or incentives, such as reduced rates for future filings, rebates, or special privileges for public services. Such recognition would encourage more individuals to comply with the tax system and demonstrate that their efforts are appreciated. For example, those who have a history of paying taxes without evasion could be granted access to a "fast-track" service for tax-related queries, reducing waiting times and ensuring that their concerns are addressed promptly. These kinds of incentives would create a more positive environment for taxpayers, reinforcing the idea that honesty and integrity are valued.

Moreover, the government should create platforms for taxpayers to voice their concerns and grievances without fear of retaliation. In many instances, honest taxpayers who encounter issues with the tax system feel powerless, as they are often treated with suspicion or met with bureaucratic roadblocks. Establishing independent, transparent grievance redressal mechanisms would allow citizens to challenge unfair treatment or incorrect assessments, giving them a sense of justice and recourse. Additionally, strengthening institutions that oversee tax practices, such as the Tax Ombudsman or a specialized tax tribunal, would help ensure that those who pay their taxes are not subjected to unjust treatment or exploitation.

It is also critical to build public awareness and support for those who adhere to the tax system. In a culture where tax evasion is often seen as a norm, promoting the value of paying taxes honestly can encourage social recognition for compliance. Public campaigns could highlight the importance of tax payments and the role they play in national development, providing a moral and ethical incentive for citizens to stay compliant. This approach would not only protect honest taxpayers but also foster a more civic-minded society where individuals take pride in contributing to the country's welfare.

Additionally, creating systems that track and publicly recognize the contributions of taxpayers would help build a culture of accountability and trust. A transparent system, where those who contribute to the public good are celebrated, would go a long way in countering the cynicism and disillusionment that often surround the tax system. This could involve public acknowledgment of consistent taxpayers through certificates, awards, or simply featuring them in national campaigns as role models of civic responsibility.

Finally, protecting those who pay honestly means ensuring that the tax burden is shared equitably. It is essential that the system be progressive, with those who earn more contributing a fairer share. At the same time, those who consistently pay their taxes should be protected from the burden of an unfair, regressive tax system. By enforcing rules that prevent the wealthy from exploiting loopholes while offering legal protections for honest taxpayers, the government can create a more just system for all.

By protecting and valuing honest taxpayers, the government would send a powerful message: the citizens who support the nation's progress and contribute to its welfare are the bedrock of the system. It is their unwavering commitment that will drive India's future prosperity, and their efforts deserve to be recognized, respected, and safeguarded.

10.6 Stop Favouring Rich Corporates

One of the most glaring and persistent failures of India's tax system is its overt favouritism towards large corporates and high-net-worth individuals. While the average middle-class taxpayer is squeezed through complex compliance, overregulation, and indirect taxation on daily essentials, corporate giants continue to receive tax breaks, exemptions, bailouts, and policy benefits that further concentrate wealth at the top. This preferential treatment has created a system where those with power and resources can bend rules or avoid obligations, while the majority bear the true cost of nationhood. If any genuine reform is to happen, it must begin with dismantling this deeply embedded corporate favouritism that erodes public trust and institutional fairness.

A primary mechanism through which corporates benefit is the strategic use of legal tax loopholes. While common citizens pay taxes on every rupee earned and every product purchased, many large companies exploit provisions, exemptions, or offshore structures to reduce their effective tax rate drastically. Despite earning profits running into thousands of crores, some corporations pay taxes lower than a salaried employee. These discrepancies are often legal—but that legality is crafted by policymakers who are lobbied, influenced, and in some cases, directly benefiting from corporate relationships. It creates a system where laws are not designed for equality but tailored to protect the interests of the rich under the guise of economic growth.

Government incentives for corporates, especially in the form of tax holidays, SEZ benefits, or production-linked incentives (PLI), are often justified as necessary for job creation or economic expansion. But the reality remains that these schemes are rarely audited for outcomes, and the actual number of quality jobs or tangible public benefit is often far below the projections. On the other hand, these incentives come at the cost of public spending—reducing the funds available for education, healthcare, and infrastructure for ordinary citizens. When a government waives massive corporate loans or defers tax dues for conglomerates, it is indirectly making honest taxpayers cover the shortfall through indirect taxes like GST or reduced public services.

The undue influence of corporate lobbies in shaping tax policy also undermines democracy. Policies that should be designed through public debate and citizen representation are instead often written with inputs from corporate consultancies and pressure groups. Laws like retrospective taxation, capital gains exemptions, and complex depreciation benefits are rarely designed for ordinary business owners or taxpayers. They are engineered to serve large players who can afford teams of tax lawyers and accountants. The absence of transparency in how such decisions are made only deepens the suspicion that the tax system serves the powerful first, and the people last.

Another angle of concern is how tax enforcement disproportionately targets small businesses and individuals while letting corporate offenders go free. While income tax officials aggressively pursue salaried class audits and GST inspectors raid local shops, the biggest defaulters—many of whom owe hundreds of crores—often escape with minor settlements, prolonged litigation, or political cover. This selective enforcement not only defeats the purpose of justice but actively penalizes smaller players who lack influence or resources to defend themselves. The result is a climate of fear among the middle and lower economic classes, and a climate of impunity for the elite.

This pattern of corporate favouritism becomes especially visible in budget allocations and tax policy announcements. Each year, tax relief for corporates is celebrated as a pro-growth measure, while welfare or subsidies for the poor are portrayed as burdensome. This narrative shift reshapes public opinion, making people believe that the country's prosperity depends on the success of billionaires, not the well-being of its working citizens. However, the true engine of national development is not found in boardrooms but in the homes of those who pay their taxes, run local businesses, teach in schools, or work in essential services without any exemptions.

For reform to be meaningful, India must establish a fair and accountable framework for corporate taxation. Companies should pay based on actual profits and market share, with no access to disproportionate exemptions. Laws must be rewritten to eliminate unnecessary complexity and close loopholes that allow profit shifting and base erosion. Moreover, the names of top corporate defaulters should be made public, and enforcement must be swift and impartial. Whistle-blower protections should be strengthened to uncover corrupt practices in tax settlements involving big business. Only when the system is seen as impartial and firm can citizens begin to trust it.

Also, the idea that corporates should always be protected for the sake of "ease of doing business" needs re-evaluation. A business-friendly environment must not come at the expense of equity and justice. It is possible to create a climate that supports entrepreneurship and innovation while also demanding fairness and social responsibility from big players. Instead of tax cuts for the rich, governments should invest in skill development, micro-enterprise growth, and infrastructure that empowers the broader economy.

Until the day honest middle-class taxpayers are treated with the same respect and privilege as large corporates, there can be no true equity in the tax system. The ongoing favour shown to the powerful is not a strategy for national growth—it is a betrayal of public trust. Reform must not be about cosmetic adjustments or new slogans, but about rewriting the system to work for those who carry the real burden of the nation's economic engine. Ending corporate favouritism is not a radical idea—it is a long overdue correction that will determine whether India becomes a just republic or continues as a two-tiered society divided by privilege and exploitation.

10.7 Let People Be Part of Policy Decisions

One of the most glaring flaws in the Indian tax system—and in governance as a whole—is the almost complete absence of citizen participation in policy formulation. While democracy promises representation, the actual process of shaping tax policies, setting rates, deciding exemptions, and crafting fiscal laws remains shrouded in bureaucratic and political corridors, far removed from the common citizen. Tax decisions, which affect every working individual and every household in the country, are routinely made without public consultation, without debate among affected groups, and without transparent feedback mechanisms. This centralization of policy-making has created a power vacuum where a few elite stakeholders decide for the many—often to the benefit of the few and the detriment of the masses.

People are forced to follow tax rules that they never approved, barely understand, and cannot influence. In a country with a population as diverse and complex as India's, it is dangerous and undemocratic to allow a handful of bureaucrats, consultants, and lobby groups to dictate the financial obligations of over a billion people. This top-down model fosters resentment, confusion, and alienation. The citizen becomes a passive subject—expected only to pay, comply, and remain silent—while all major decisions are made behind closed doors. This disconnection between citizens and tax authorities results in an unequal relationship where distrust replaces cooperation, and compliance is often driven more by fear than civic duty.

In many advanced democracies, tax reform proposals are subject to public consultation periods, during which citizens, advocacy groups, and small business representatives can submit suggestions, voice concerns, and influence final outcomes. Policy drafts are made publicly available, discussed in forums, and debated in media, ensuring that taxation remains a truly public affair. The Indian system, in contrast, releases final policies suddenly—through budget speeches or gazette notifications—without seeking input from the very people it impacts most. This not only weakens accountability but also results in poor-quality laws that are disconnected from ground realities.

The lack of citizen involvement also means that tax policies are seldom tailored to local and regional economic conditions. A uniform policy, when blindly applied across states with vastly different cost structures, employment patterns, and income levels, often creates unintended hardships. For instance, GST rules framed without adequate feedback from traders in rural markets end up hurting small enterprises. Income tax limits are rarely adjusted to reflect real inflation or cost of living. Taxation of digital freelancers, gig workers, or micro-entrepreneurs is still handled with outdated templates, all because their voices never reach the decision-making table. Real reform is impossible without first opening the gates of participation.

When citizens are invited into the process, policy outcomes become more equitable, rational, and widely accepted. If the salaried class could vote on whether standard deduction limits are adequate or if income slabs should be adjusted, the system would be more realistic. If working mothers, pensioners, and small vendors could explain their challenges directly to policymakers, fiscal policy would be shaped with more empathy and accuracy. True democracy is not about voting once every five years—it is about continuous dialogue between the governed and those who govern, especially when it comes to money collected from the people and spent in their name.

Technology offers unprecedented opportunities to democratize policy-making. Online platforms can be used to collect structured feedback, conduct public hearings, and share draft policies in multiple languages. Apps, portals, and social media tools can be leveraged to gather citizen input across income groups, regions, and occupations. Citizens should have the right to petition tax changes, demand clarity, and hold officials accountable through structured platforms backed by law. These participatory mechanisms don't need to be radical—they simply need to be institutionalized with intent and sincerity.

Citizen participation also fosters tax morality. When people feel heard, when they are part of shaping the system, they are more willing to comply voluntarily. Tax evasion decreases not through surveillance but through engagement. If a taxpayer knows that their voice helped improve a tax refund process or change an unjust penalty clause, they begin to see themselves not as victims of the system but as co-owners of the system. Trust replaces suspicion, and governance evolves from a power game into a shared responsibility. This shift is essential if India wants to build a truly inclusive, modern fiscal framework.

Of course, the entrenched elites and bureaucratic machinery may resist this opening of gates. They fear losing control, facing dissent, or exposing their inefficiencies. But that fear cannot be allowed to dictate the structure of a democracy. The financial architecture of a nation must reflect the will, wisdom, and worries of its citizens. And that is only possible when tax policy-making becomes a participatory process—not a bureaucratic diktat.

Ultimately, letting people be part of policy decisions is not just about fairness—it is about survival. A system built without input from its users will collapse under its own weight. The more the government hides behind jargon, secrecy, and executive orders, the more alienated and resistant the people will become. But when citizens are invited into the temple of policy-making, they bring with them insight, accountability, and the moral force that no bureaucracy can replicate. True reform begins when every citizen is not just a taxpayer but a stakeholder in the future of the system they sustain.

10.8 Restore Dignity to the Indian Taxpayer

The most silent crisis in India's taxation system is not just about the rates, the loopholes, or the bureaucratic excess—it is the erosion of dignity that every honest taxpayer suffers silently. To restore the soul of a democratic and economically just society, the dignity of the taxpayer must be made a foundational principle. Today, the system treats taxpayers not as the primary stakeholders in the nation's development, but as suspects who must be monitored, coerced, and constantly reminded of their obligations while receiving little in return. This imbalance in power, respect, and recognition has created a toxic culture where compliance is driven by fear and not by pride, and this must change if India hopes to build a sustainable and just economic order.

For every rupee collected in taxes, there is a person behind it—a worker, a business owner, a mother running a household, a youth starting a career, a pensioner who continues to contribute. Yet, in the way the system is designed and implemented, there is no reflection of this human reality. Notices arrive without empathy, portals glitch during deadlines, refunds are delayed without apology, and queries are handled like criminal interrogations. The taxpayer is treated like a commodity—expected to pay, file, and keep quiet. The basic respect that should be afforded to someone contributing to the nation's progress is completely absent from policy, process, and tone. There is no national campaign celebrating honest taxpayers, no institutional commitment to ensuring their experience is smooth and dignified, and certainly no moral acknowledgment of their sacrifices.

India's cultural history places a strong value on duty, or dharma, and paying one's fair share should be seen in that sacred light. But what kind of dharma asks for sacrifice without recognition? What kind of social contract rewards silence and punishes participation? In many developed countries, the act of paying taxes is treated as a form of civic pride, supported by visible public services and reinforced by respectful institutional interaction. In contrast, Indian taxpayers are made to feel like they're fulfilling a burden they should be ashamed of complaining about. This oppressive cultural messaging turns taxpayers into silent sufferers instead of empowered citizens.

Even worse is the double standard. While the common taxpayer is subjected to rigid scrutiny, delays, and penalties, large corporations and politically connected entities often enjoy favourable treatment, extended deadlines, waivers, and secret settlements. This creates a moral chasm where the system not only fails to honour its honest participants but actively demotivates them by showcasing how the powerful play by different rules. Dignity erodes when rules are not applied fairly. It erodes when small mistakes are criminalized for one class while large evasions are forgiven for another. It erodes when a teacher paying GST on tutoring services is harassed while billionaire defaulters dine with policymakers.

Restoring dignity requires a top-down change in the language, practices, and philosophy of tax administration. Start with basic human courtesy—make systems user-friendly, remove jargon, and offer explanations without arrogance. Officials must be trained not just in technical protocol but in human interaction. Taxpayers should be treated as collaborators in nation-building, not as adversaries of the state. Communication from tax departments should be respectful, transparent, and written in a tone that builds trust. Refunds must be processed promptly, grievances resolved efficiently, and mistakes forgiven without hostility when made in good faith.

Public narratives must also shift. Why does India not have an annual "Taxpayer Appreciation Week"? Why are there no honours or awards for exemplary compliance by citizens and small enterprises? Why is there no public-facing dashboard showing how taxpayer money improves lives, schools, and infrastructure? These aren't gimmicks—they are moral acknowledgments that help people feel seen, valued, and respected. Just as the soldier is saluted for defending borders, the taxpayer deserves a salute for funding every function of the republic. Without their unglamorous, daily sacrifices, there would be no nation to defend.

Technology should be a dignity enabler, not a new form of oppression. Automated systems must be designed for clarity, not intimidation. When artificial intelligence flags inconsistencies, human officers should first inquire respectfully before jumping to conclusions. Algorithms should assist, not accuse. Portals should make lives easier, not add to frustration. Each touchpoint must reflect a belief that the citizen is fundamentally honest, and the state is here to serve, not dominate.

Perhaps most crucially, a culture of accountability must exist within the system itself. When tax officials make mistakes, delay refunds, or misuse power, they must face disciplinary action and public transparency. Dignity for the taxpayer cannot exist if the officials overseeing them are not held to the same ethical standards. For too long, the Indian taxpayer has been expected to bow in submission while those collecting taxes remain unanswerable. This power asymmetry must end if dignity is to be restored. India's economic future depends not just on raising revenues, but on building a just relationship between the state and its citizens. That relationship must be built on mutual respect. And respect begins with dignity. Until every taxpayer is treated as a vital pillar of the nation, not a replaceable unit of revenue, no reform will ever be complete. Restoring dignity is not a technical fix—it is a moral imperative. It is time India rises to it.

For a nation to truly evolve, it must begin by looking inward and acknowledging the silent cries of its people—the very hands that build it, fund it, and sustain it. A fair and just tax system is not simply about arithmetic; it is about trust, accountability, and mutual respect. When citizens are reduced to cogs in an unforgiving economic machine, the soul of the republic fades. Reform is not an option—it is a necessity. Every suggestion outlined is not just a demand for relief but a call for reinvention. The system must stop being a fortress of intimidation and become a bridge of cooperation, where the government does not stand above the people, but walks beside them. This book is a mirror held up to a deeply flawed reality—a reflection not just of policy gaps, but of moral failure. It does not ask for charity or pity; it demands justice, clarity, and above all, dignity. If India is to emerge not just as an economic power but as a civilized, conscious society, it must treat every contributing citizen with reverence, not suspicion. The way forward is not paved by slogans and fear, but by honest dialogue and courageous restructuring. Let this not remain another voice lost in the noise—let it be a trigger for the silent revolution every Indian taxpayer has long deserved.

Glossary

1. Income Tax Act, 1961 The primary statute governing income tax in India. It outlines rules for tax computation, deductions, exemptions, penalties, and appeals.
2. Goods and Services Tax (GST) A unified indirect tax on the supply of goods and services across India, subsuming multiple previous taxes like VAT, excise duty, and service tax.
3. PAN (Permanent Account Number) A unique 10-character alphanumeric code assigned by the Income Tax Department to track tax-related transactions.
4. TDS (Tax Deducted at Source) A mechanism where tax is deducted from certain payments (e.g., salary, rent, interest) at the time of payment and deposited with the government.
5. Advance Tax Tax paid during the financial year on estimated income, applicable when tax liability exceeds Rs. 10,000 annually.
6. Self-Assessment Tax Tax paid by the taxpayer on remaining dues after accounting for TDS and advance tax before filing returns.
7. Income Tax Return (ITR) A form submitted annually to report income and taxes paid. Different ITR forms cater to various categories of taxpayers.
8. Section 80C A provision allowing deductions up to Rs. 1.5 lakh for specified savings and investments such as PPF, LIC premiums, ELSS, and tuition fees.
9. Section 80D Allows deduction for premiums paid toward medical insurance for self and family.
10. Capital Gains Tax Tax on profit from the sale of capital assets. Short-term and long-term rates apply based on the holding period.
11. Exempt Income Types of income excluded from total taxable income, such as agricultural income or certain government allowances.
12. Standard Deduction A flat deduction allowed to salaried individuals to reduce taxable income.
13. GSTIN (Goods and Services Tax Identification Number) A 15-digit registration number under GST allotted to businesses.
14. Composition Scheme (GST) A scheme under GST for small businesses allowing payment of tax at a reduced rate with minimal compliance requirements.
15. Input Tax Credit (ITC) A credit for the tax paid on purchases, which can be used to offset tax liability on sales.

16. Excise Duty A tax on manufactured goods within India. Now largely subsumed by GST except for a few items like fuel and liquor.
17. Customs Duty Tax on goods imported into or exported from India, comprising basic duty and additional levies.
18. Professional Tax A state-level tax imposed on professionals, trades, and employment.
19. Wealth Tax (Abolished) A tax formerly levied on the net wealth of individuals and companies, abolished from FY 2015–16.
20. Tax Audit (Section 44AB) Mandatory audit of accounts for taxpayers whose turnover exceeds prescribed limits.
21. HRA (House Rent Allowance) A salary component partly exempt from tax for those paying rent.
22. Assessment Year (AY) The year following the financial year in which income is assessed and taxed.
23. Financial Year (FY) The 12-month period (April 1 to March 31) in which income is earned.
24. Section 234A/B/C Sections imposing interest for delays or shortfalls in filing returns or paying advance tax.
25. Surcharge An extra charge on income tax payable by high-income individuals and entities.
26. Cess A levy collected for specific purposes, like health and education, over and above regular taxes.
27. Black Money Undisclosed income or wealth not reported to tax authorities, often held in cash or assets.
28. Benami Transactions Deals where property is held by one person but paid for by another, to conceal the true owner's identity.
29. Tax Evasion Illegal non-payment or underpayment of taxes, often through misreporting income or expenses.
30. Tax Avoidance The legal use of tax laws to reduce one's tax burden by exploiting loopholes.
31. Faceless Assessment A system of tax scrutiny without physical interaction between taxpayer and tax officer, ensuring transparency.
32. Double Taxation Avoidance Agreement (DTAA) Treaties between India and other countries to avoid taxing the same income twice.
33. GST Council A constitutional body that governs and recommends policies and rates related to GST.
34. Indirect Tax A tax collected by intermediaries from consumers, such as GST and customs duties.
35. Direct Tax A tax directly paid by individuals or entities on their income

or wealth, like income tax or corporate tax.

36. AIS (Annual Information Statement) A comprehensive report provided by the Income Tax Department detailing a taxpayer's financial transactions from various sources for a particular financial year.
37. Form 16 A certificate issued by employers showing TDS deducted on salary and details of salary income paid to the employee.
38. Form 26AS A consolidated annual tax credit statement that shows details of tax deducted, collected, and deposited with the government on behalf of the taxpayer.
39. Section 44ADA A presumptive taxation scheme for professionals with gross receipts up to Rs. 50 lakh, allowing 50% income to be declared as profit without maintaining detailed accounts.
40. Section 24(b) Provides deduction up to Rs. 2 lakh on interest paid on home loan for a self-occupied property.
41. Section 10(13A) Covers exemption for House Rent Allowance (HRA) received by salaried individuals, subject to specified conditions and limits.
42. Section 80G Allows deduction for donations made to certain relief funds and charitable institutions.
43. Section 80E Provides deduction on interest paid on education loans for higher education.
44. Section 80TTA Allows deduction up to Rs. 10,000 on interest earned from savings accounts.
45. Section 87A Provides a rebate to individual taxpayers with total income up to a prescribed limit, reducing tax liability.
46. DIN (Document Identification Number) A unique number allotted to every communication by the Income Tax Department to improve transparency.
47. E-verification The process of electronically validating income tax returns using Aadhaar OTP, net banking, or other methods.
48. Refund Excess tax paid over actual liability that is returned to the taxpayer by the department.
49. Notice under Section 143(1) An intimation sent by the IT Department after preliminary processing of returns showing accepted income, deductions, and tax computation.
50. Rectification Request Filed by a taxpayer if there's a mistake in an already processed return or intimation from the department.

Bibliography

1. Bahl, Roy, and Wallace, Sally. Fiscal Decentralization and Revenue Assignment: A Comparative Study. The World Bank, 2007.

2. Bird, Richard M., and Zolt, Eric M. Tax Policy in Emerging Countries. UCLA Law Review, Vol. 59, 2012.

3. Chelliah, Raja J. Towards Sustainable Growth: Essays in Fiscal and Financial Sector Reforms in India. Oxford University Press, 1996.

4. Government of India. Economic Survey of India 2022-23. Ministry of Finance, Department of Economic Affairs, New Delhi.

5. Government of India. Report of the Task Force on Direct Taxes. Ministry of Finance, 2019.

6. Kelkar, Vijay L. India's Fiscal Deficit and its Implications. NIPFP Working Paper No. 3, 2003.

7. Musgrave, Richard A., and Musgrave, Peggy B. Public Finance in Theory and Practice. McGraw-Hill Education, 1989.

8. Oxfam India. Inequality Kills: India Supplement 2022. Oxfam Briefing Paper, January 2022.

9. Piketty, Thomas, and Chancel, Lucas. Indian Income Inequality, 1922–2015: From British Raj to Billionaire Raj? WID.world Working Paper Series, 2017.

10. Rao, M. Govinda. Reforming India's Fiscal System: Some Reflections. National Institute of Public Finance and Policy, 2005.

11. Rao, M. Govinda, and Tulasidhar, V.B. Fiscal Decentralization in India: Theory and Practice. NIPFP, 2005.

12. Sen, Amartya. Development as Freedom. Oxford University Press, 1999.

13. Slemrod Joel, and Bakija Jon. Taxing Ourselves: A Citizen's Guide to the Debate over Taxes. MIT Press, 2008.

14. Subramanian, Arvind. Of Counsel: The Challenges of the Modi-Jaitley Economy. Penguin Books, 2018.

15. The Constitution of India. Government of India.

16. World Bank. Doing Business Report. World Bank Group, Annual Editions.

17. World Inequality Lab. World Inequality Report 2022.

18. Income Tax Department, Government of India. Annual Report 2023–24. https://incometaxindia.gov.in

19. Press Information Bureau (PIB). Press Releases on Taxation and Fiscal Policy. Government of India.
20. Reserve Bank of India. Handbook of Statistics on Indian Economy. RBI Annual Publications.

www.ingramcontent.com/pod-product-compliance
Ingram Content Group UK Ltd.
Pitfield, Milton Keynes, MK11 3LW, UK
UKHW041318190726
13845UKWH00025B/353

9 789334 302332